JERUSALEM AND ALBION

JERUSALEM AND ALBION

The Hebraic Factor in
Seventeenth-Century Literature

by

HAROLD FISCH

LONDON

ROUTLEDGE & KEGAN PAUL

First published 1964
by Routledge & Kegan Paul Ltd
Broadway House, 68-74 Carter Lane
London, E.C.4

Printed in Great Britain
by T. & A. Constable Ltd
Hopetoun Street, Edinburgh

© *Harold Fisch 1964*

LC 64-57139

FOR
GEOFFREY BULLOUGH

CONTENTS

PREFACE

IN THE early stages of this work, I enjoyed the encouragement as well as the admonitions of many friends. In particular I should mention Professor G. Wilson Knight, Professor Bonamy Dobrée, Professor Kenneth Muir, and Mr. Peter Mann, all of whom I knew as colleagues at Leeds University where I taught until 1957. More recently it was my good fortune to be advised on many important matters by Professor Charles I. Glicksberg of Brooklyn College, New York, who spent a year with us in Israel as a Fulbright visitor from 1958-9. To two colleagues of my own Department at Bar-Ilan University I owe a special debt of gratitude for reading the entire typescript, bringing to bear on it an insight born of mental kinship: they are Dr. Murray Roston and Dr. Marcel Mendelson. Finally, it would be difficult for me to estimate the debt I owe to Professor Geoffrey Bullough, now of King's College, London, to whom this volume is dedicated in much affection and esteem. It was he who, as far back as 1940, laid before me, as before so many others, the baroque splendours and rococo delights of seventeenth-century letters.

The journey from Sheffield, Oxford, and Leeds, to Ramat-Gan has been indeed a journey from Albion to Jerusalem. It has helped me to confirm for myself the truth of Blake's assumption that Albion is never wholly divorced from his spiritual partner, and shows traces of Jerusalem even when he most vigorously repudiates all that Jerusalem stands for. That is really what this book tries to show. In the course of writing it, I have also, alas, become conscious of the fact that, for her part too, Jerusalem has far to go to achieve wholeness and integrity. Blake would no doubt have expressed this by saying that Jerusalem has as much need of Albion as Albion has of Jerusalem. But that is the subject of another book.

HAROLD FISCH

Bar-Ilan University,
Ramat-Gan, Israel.
January, 1964

ix

INTRODUCTION

Instead of Albion's lovely mountains and the curtains of Jerusalem
I see a Cave, a Rock, a Tree deadly and poisonous, unimaginative.

Jerusalem has departed from Albion

WILLIAM BLAKE, *Jerusalem.*

WHATEVER may be the precise critical value of the term 'dissociation of sensibility' introduced by Mr. T. S. Eliot in his Essay on the Metaphysical Poets in 1921,[1] it has certainly had the merit of generating a great deal of inquiry into seventeenth-century origins:[2]

> In the seventeenth century a dissociation of sensibility set in, from which we have never recovered. . . . The language went on and in some respects improved. . . . But while the language became more refined, the feeling became more crude. . . .

The loss of poetic unity revealed by cruder feelings and a simpler texture of style is the outward manifestation, so Mr. Eliot hints, of an inward impoverishment of soul, a metaphysical split. In the final analysis, he declares, 'it is something which happened to the mind of England between the time of Donne . . . and the time of Tennyson'. The worst offenders in the story of the separation of thought and feeling are Dryden and Milton.

Now, while few students of the seventeenth century would

---

[1] Reprinted in *Selected Essays* (New York, 1932).

[2] Mention may be made (from the extensive literature on the subject) of S. L. Bethell, *The Cultural Revolution of the Seventeenth Century* (London, 1951), *passim*; Basil Willey, *The Seventeenth Century Background* (London, 1946), pp. 87 f., with emphasis on the significance of Descartes's dualistic thinking; Cleanth Brooks, *Modern Poetry and the Tradition* (London, 1948), pp. 41-3. There is disagreement as to Eliot's philosophical sources. F. W. Bateson holds that the idea is to be traced to Rémy de Gourmont (*Problème du Style*), whilst E. Thompson with more probability has made out a case for Eliot's debt to F. H. Bradley's *Essays on Truth and Reality* (see *Essays in Criticism*, Oxford, July, 1951, and April, 1952). See also Hugh Kenner, *The Invisible Poet: T. S. Eliot* (London, 1960), pp. 45 f.

I

disagree that it was an age in which old thought-forms were breaking down, and new, more functional and practical ways of writing and thinking were being devised, and that such change proceeded side by side with a certain loss of poetic vision, not everyone at this time of day endorses Mr. Eliot's account of the 'dissociation of sensibility' as a fair analysis.

For one thing one has the feeling that behind Mr. Eliot's (as also Mr. Bethell's) critical conclusions there is a sort of unexpressed lament for the passing of medieval scholasticism. The lights of the Middle Ages had all too clearly waned in the seventeenth century; hence the rather excessive degree of adulation given to Donne as perhaps the last representative of the 'undissociated' sensibility, and hence too a frigid reserve towards Milton who is said to have 'triumphed with a dazzling disregard of the soul'. Milton was, even in his precocious college days, a rebel against traditionalism in religion and science, and contemptuous in particular of the scholastic method. But is there not something perverse in thinking of the author of *Paradise Lost* as having 'triumphed with a dazzling disregard of the soul'? If we are going to divide the writers of the century into dissociated goats and undissociated sheep, then let us be prepared to see that Donne with his obsessive conflicts is not indubitably amongst the sheep, and Milton with his capacity for inward reconciliation, for 'calm of mind all passion spent', is not indubitably amongst the goats. The position is surely a great deal more contradictory than that.

In a cleverly argued thesis directed against the neo-scholastic critics, as she terms them, namely, T. S. Eliot, T. E. Hulme, and Basil Willey, Miss Kathleen Nott has tried to redefine the 'dissociation of sensibility'.[1] She admits that something of the sort, a split between intellect and emotion, did happen in the seventeenth century, but she questions whether the cause of it is to be found, as the neo-scholastic writers had thought, in the new science and the new humanism which, in the seventeenth century, came to overthrow the inherited orthodoxy of the Middle Ages. Her view is that the enemies of poetry were the dogmatists (amongst whom she includes Locke, Hobbes, and the Puritans), whilst the true empirical scientists dealt, like the poets themselves, with concrete matters of experience. 'What

[1] *The Emperor's Clothes* (Bloomington, 1958).

2

neo-scholastic critics dislike in the "Renaissance" spirit, which gave us humanism and science, is precisely that which gives us the most complete poetry.'[1]

Certainly, the positive and energizing factors introduced into literature at the time of the Renaissance deserve to be given their full weight in any judgements on this subject and it is useful to be reminded that the finest (and presumably most unified) poetry of the Elizabethans owed more than a little to this new spirit of the time. On the other hand, it is difficult to accept the distinction that Miss Nott makes between the true empirical scientists (who were good for poetry) and the scientific dogmatists and theorists (who were bad for poetry). Where are the new scientists who did not dogmatize and generalize about their experiments? Surely, we must be aware that this distinction does not hold good for any major scientific writer. Galileo, Kepler, Robert Boyle, and Newton were all committed to various kinds of religious hypotheses and spent a great deal of their time in writing philosophical essays. Indeed the most decided empirics of the new age were the alchemists and iatro-chemists, and they were involved in metaphysical theory and speculation of the most esoteric order.

One cannot help feeling that the word 'dogmatism' is used by Miss Nott in too synoptic, too uncritical, and one must add, too dogmatic a fashion. She combines in one list the medieval scholastic tradition, the scientific dogmatism of Hobbes (the most outstanding rebel against the Aristotelian tradition), the Puritans (who overthrew the medieval *Summae Theologiae* and replaced them by an individual experience of God), and indeed all theology whatever. One of the things Miss Nott has not weighed (presumably because it was alien to her taste) is the impact of the Scriptures as a *first-hand* imaginative experience. She talks a great deal about religious dogma as the enemy of poetry, but she fails to see that for Tyndale, the Scottish covenanters, for Milton and Herbert, the reading of Scripture was not a matter of accepting dogmas; it was a matter of being exposed to a direct, even blinding spiritual illumination. Surely no student of the seventeenth century, even if not drawn to the Bible himself, can doubt the empirical evidence of this. The tremendous effect which the Bible had upon men, the awe, the

[1] *Ibid.*, p. 194.

terror, and ecstasy which it undoubtedly inspired, should be sufficient to convince the sceptic that the men of the Reformation were concerned with real and mighty facts of experience. The Bible may indeed have given rise to dogmas (dogmas of the most various and contradictory kinds), but in itself it was not a collection of dogmas; it was an experiential factor no less than the new empirical sciences and the new humanism of the Renaissance. Calvin indeed is the source of a major system of dogmatics which had a powerful influence on seventeenth-century England, but behind and beneath his dogma is this 'experimental' awareness of the power of Scripture 'carrying its own evidence and authority along with it'. It constrains the spirit and the imagination:

> we feel a divine energy living and breathing in it—an energy by which we are drawn and animated to obey it, willingly indeed, and knowingly, but more vividly and effectually than could be done by human will or knowledge.[1]

The light of God, itself too dazzling for mortal eyes, was reflected in the 'mirror'[2] of Scripture; thus, from Scripture the knowledge of God could as certainly be obtained as the knowledge of physical laws from the world of Nature. The men of the seventeenth century were, in fact, conscious of three realities: God, Man, and Nature; and it will not do to think of the second and third as matters of experience or imagined experience, and the first as a matter of mere 'belief' and dogma. Moreover, the Scripture, as well as being the Word of God, was literature. It enlightened the eyes, but it also nourished the literary imagination; of this too the men of the seventeenth century were aware. Thus, for a literary student seeking out the causes of poetic integration and disintegration in that century, one would have thought that the contact with Scripture as a literary-empirical factor was by no means to be ignored.

The biblical poet Milton, in particular, has proved an offence and a stumbling-block to most of the critics who have devoted themselves to the problem of dissociation. Eliot, in 1918, had spoken of 'the Chinese Wall of Milton'; Miss Nott, too,

---

[1] Calvin, *Institutes of the Christian Religion* (trans. H. Beveridge, Edinburgh, 1845), Bk. I, ch. 7, sect. v.

[2] Cf. *ibid.*, Bk. III, Ch. 2, sect. vi.

4

find the explanation for those literary changes—changes in the form and texture of writing—which are held to be the outer manifestation of the alleged metaphysical split.

Some critics have, it is true, widened the field of inquiry by introducing the prose-writers,[1] but instead of summarizing the work of any more of Eliot's successors, one could at this point more profitably go back to two of his predecessors whose contribution to this subject has not been fully acknowledged to date. In his still memorable essay on 'The Study of Poetry' (1880), Matthew Arnold takes as his standard of poetical excellence the poetry of the Elizabethans and 'the continuation and close of this poetry in Milton'. Here, he claims, is a 'real estimate'. Shakespeare and Milton are, for him, the poetical classics. He then asks, What happens in the succeeding age? 'Are Dryden and Pope poetical classics?' And he answers that they are rather the 'classics of our prose'. Merely elegant poetry has taken the place of the imaginative grandeurs, the passionate sublimities of Milton. Some quite drastic change has occurred. Here Arnold performs a useful service by switching the attention to prose itself. True, Arnold may not have had quite the same literary criteria in mind as Eliot had when he spoke of a 'dissociation of sensibility'. He did not desiderate that ability of the metaphysical poets to 'feel their thoughts as immediately as the odour of a rose'. Arnold spoke more simply of a 'touch of frost to the imaginative life of the soul'—and this, he said, was best revealed by observing the new post-Restoration trend towards plain prose—plain prose for sermons, for literary essays, for journalism, for everything.[2] Nor does he maintain that this was all loss. He is near enough to the classical standard of taste and decorum to place a high value on the new prose, and he is disposed to regard it as an advance on the 'obsolete and inconvenient' prose of Milton and the Elizabethans; but in spite of all

[1] For instance, S. L. Bethell, *op. cit.*; L. C. Knights, 'Bacon and the Dissociation of Sensibility', *Scrutiny* (Cambridge, 1943), usefully and properly puts Bacon in a central position in the dissociation story: cf. also by the same author, *Drama and Society in the Age of Jonson* (London, 1937), Appendix A.

[2] Twentieth-century critics have discussed this phenomenon in detail, for example, Joan Bennett, 'An Aspect of the Evolution of Seventeenth Century Prose', *R.E.S.*, XVII (Oxford, 1941), 281-97. For further bibliography, see Chapter II, *infra*.

its many virtues, virtues of regularity, uniformity, precision, and balance, Arnold is emphatic that the 'almost exclusive attention to these qualities involves some repression and silencing of poetry'.

Now, why, according to Arnold, did prose cease to be poetical? What was the nature of the change which caused it to lose its imaginative, and emotional qualities, and to divide in this absolute way from poetry? It is interesting to note that Arnold does not say anything here about poetry having been endangered by the new Science and the new Humanism; nor does he speak exactly of the cramping effect of religious dogmatism. What he does say in the following passage is rather different from this:

> But after the Restoration the time had come when our nation felt the imperious need of a fit prose. So, too, the time had likewise come when our nation felt the imperious need of freeing itself from the absorbing preoccupation which religion in the Puritan age had exercised. It was impossible that this freedom should be brought about without some negative excess, without some neglect and impairment of the religious life of the soul; and the spiritual history of the eighteenth century shows us that the freedom was not achieved without them.[1]

Now, here is a broadly-based account of what happened in the seventeenth century, and still highly suggestive in spite of its generalizations and its traces of partiality. Arnold is our first great critic of Puritanism, and the sentences quoted above may be regarded as a footnote to his discussion of Puritanism in such works as *Culture and Anarchy*, and *Literature and Dogma*. Clearly, there is an important sense in which, for Arnold, Puritanism is the enemy of literary culture. But Puritanism is no such simple matter as that, and the imaginative frost which descended upon English prose and poetry was brought about, he tells us, not by Puritanism itself, but by the recoil from Puritanism in the Restoration period. It was an aspect of the desire of people to free themselves from the preoccupation with religion in the Puritan Age. Puritanism is thus, for all its faults and restrictions, not an entirely negative force in the history of the Imagination.

[1] *Essays in Criticism*, Second Series, ed. S. R. Littlewood (London, 1951), p. 23.

This ambiguous character of Puritanism suggested in Arnold's treatment of the relation between literature and religion in the seventeenth century will have to be considered further.

All this is only a hint, however, and no one would pretend that Arnold had written the story of English Literature upheld by the insights of intellectual history. But one predecessor of Arnold, not usually thought of as an intellectual historian nor even as a literary historian, did much to link these spheres together, and he too was concerned, more even than either Eliot or Arnold, to reveal and explore the physiology (or should we perhaps say, the pathology?) of dissociation. That writer was William Blake. Blake, we should remind ourselves, was engaged, indeed obsessed, with the problem of spiritual disunification, and in particular, such disunification as occurred in the England of the seventeenth century, for his chief *dramatis personae* were Milton, Bacon, Locke, and Newton. Blake was neither philosopher nor critic; he judged rather by the imaginative vibrations of the work before him, and it was the presence or absence of these which he used as his key to the evaluation of particular ideologies. His hatred of Puritanism and Baconian scientism was precisely owing to what he felt to be the threat which they posed to the life of the Imagination; at the same time, his sense of their ominousness and importance led him to relate these local manifestations to a primordial metaphysical disaster, a kind of pre-cosmic fall. In his attempt to give the situation its full cosmic value he invented (or if we are devout Blakeians, we would say, he discovered) a mythological framework which does something towards defining the real forces of association and dissociation underlying the phenomena.

In the quotations from *Jerusalem* prefixed to this Chapter, Blake lays hold of the metaphysical split which that poem celebrates in terms of a mythical divorce of Jerusalem from Albion. In the 'spectral' Albion when attached and united to its 'emanation' in Jerusalem, he finds the lineaments of an unbroken and wholesomely imaginative world: only when Jerusalem has departed from Albion do we see 'a Cave, a Rock, a Tree deadly and poisonous, unimaginative'. What, we may ask, is the exact meaning for Blake of 'Jerusalem'? Does it bear more than a fanciful relation to the situation of English Literature in the seventeenth century, and secondly, does it retain anything of its correct Hebraic signification? The answer to both questions is, I think, a qualified affirmative. Etymologically, 'Jerusalem' denotes the City of Peace, and for Blake likewise it came to mean the undivided unity of flesh and spirit, reason and imagination, fact and symbol, corresponding to an outer realm from which the glory of God (and the terrors of God) have not been banished. He variously characterized this State as Eden, or Beulah (from *Isaiah* lxii), but the principal symbol he employed was 'Jerusalem'. When she is restored to Albion all things are renewed and all things are made one. And was there any intimation of the achievement in seventeenth-century literature of such a state of union and spiritual fulfilment? The careful student of Blake will supply a number of names here, names such as, Robert Fludd, the eccentric author of *Mosaicall Philosophy* (1638), Thomas Vaughan, the alchemist, Traherne, and Milton. All these, and especially the last-mentioned writer, exercised a significant influence on Blake, and encouraged him in his various poetical, theosophical, and kabbalistic leanings.[1] What they had in common was a vital store of Hebraic intuitions and images, and a certain resistance to the frigidities and intellectual abstractions of Greek culture. As for Milton's Puritanism, Blake has the same suspicion of Puritan narrowness as Arnold later on, and he represents Milton as having to undergo a purging treatment before he can be regenerated in the world of eternity and before his spirit can become reincarnated in Blake himself; but the vital inspiration of Milton which causes him to stand as the supreme model for inspired poetry is to be related to that

---

[1] Blake got to know the Kabbalah through various intermediate and highly unreliable sources, such as the *Kabbala Denudata* of Knorr von Rosenroth, published at the end of the seventeenth century, or the esoteric doctrines of the Rosicrucians (see for this side of Blake, D. Saurat, *Blake and Modern Thought*, London, 1929, pp. 104 f.). Nevertheless, he evidently did acquire some important insights. Albion, his chief actor, is rather like the primordial man, or *Adam Kadmon*, of the Kabbalah, a mystical anthropos who includes in his limbs the whole universe both of time and eternity, (cf. G. Scholem, *Major Trends in Jewish Mysticism*, revised ed., New York, 1946, pp. 215 f.). His Jerusalem, on the other hand, resembles the *Shekhinah*, or mystical divine Immanence, a feminine principle. Blake's emphasis on the sexual inner life of the mythological Divine Spectres and Emanations is also, in a way, kabbalistic, (cf. Scholem, *op. cit.*, pp. 227 f.).

intense preoccupation with the Bible in an Age of Faith such as the seventeenth century. It was that which Blake himself sought to restore, and it was that which gave historical content and meaning to the concept of Jerusalem as applied to English Literature and History in the seventeenth century.

But of course looking back as he did from the latter end of the eighteenth century Blake was more conscious of splitting up, of what Arnold termed the 'touch of frost to the imaginative life of the soul'. He was indeed haunted by the idea of separation, the splitting up of primal unities to produce autonomous forces, which, because they are, so to speak, hypostatized, and divorced from the organic wholeness of existence, necessarily become sources of evil power. Blake was one of the first to draw our attention to this spiritual law and relate it to the current situation in Science, Religion, and Poetry: Albion, he maintained, had now come under the influence of Urizen, symbol of will, intellect, Puritan morality, and the laws of Locke.

> I see the Four-fold Man, The Humanity in deadly sleep
> And its fallen Emanation, The Spectre & its cruel Shadow.
> I see the Past, Present & Future existing all at once
> Before me. O Divine Spirit, sustain me on thy wings,
> That I may awake Albion from his long & cold repose;
> For Bacon & Newton, sheath'd in dismal steel, their terrors hang
> Like iron scourges over Albion: Reasonings like vast Serpents
> Infold around my limbs, bruising my minute articulations.
>
> I turn my eyes to the Schools and Universities of Europe
> And there behold the Loom of Locke, whose Woof rages dire,
> Wash'd by the Water-wheels of Newton: black the cloth
> In heavy wreathes folds over every Nation: cruel Works
> Of many Wheels I view, wheel without wheel, with cogs tyrannic
> Moving by compulsion each other, not as those in Eden, which,
> Wheel within Wheel, in freedom revolve in harmony and peace.
>
> *(Jerusalem* 15)

The dynamic energies which Albion discovers within himself, instead of being traced back to their spiritual source in Jerusalem, are suffered to express themselves in forms, and in pursuit of aims, alien to Jerusalem.

The rectifying of this state of affairs, according to Blake, is a task of such magnitude and difficulty that it demands an apocalyptic transformation of all things on heaven and earth

—including the very form of human nature and instinct. This is the significance of the building of Golgonooza as described in *Jerusalem* and *Milton*. It is the City of Art and Poetry, and, though it is in a sense to be brought into existence through Blake's own poetry, it is essentially not of this world. We may say that for Blake salvation is achieved through mythology, just as the Fall itself is metahistorical rather than historical. He backs away from the known and normal processes of history, and from the known and normal facts of human nature. To that extent, we may add also that he parts company with Hebraic origins. For Hebraism is indeed a doctrine of salvation, but of salvation which we may behold as a condition of our existence in this world. It claims to provide an account of the relationship between Man, God, and Nature in its permanent, historical character.[1] From the Hebraic point of view, Jerusalem is not a mythical ideal but rather one capable of resurrection in history through the exercise of our human faculties. In this respect, the men of the seventeenth century whom Blake admired, and the many more Hebraic writers whom he had not encountered, were more realistic than he was. Even the extravagant thought of Robert Fludd and Thomas Vaughan has an earth-bound character, a practical dimension that Blake's lacks. If it is true that Jerusalem and Albion were joined in marriage (of however brief duration) in the seventeenth century, then the union was consummated not only in poetry and philosophical prose, but also in the world of politics, of practical science, and practical divinity. This is the difference between the Hebraism of Blake and that of his forbears in the seventeenth century.[2]

[1] Modern historiographers and students of Hebraism have given full weight to the Hebraic concern with history as the proper arena of divine action. E. Voegelin speaks of the 'Israelite discovery of history as a form of existence' (*Order and History*, Louisiana, 1956, I, 126); cf. also, Karl Loewith, *Meaning in History* (Chicago, 1949), Introduction; Paul Tillich, *Biblical Religion and the Search for Ultimate Reality* (Chicago, 1955), p. 40. The works of Mircea Eliade and of Martin Buber are also relevant here.

[2] Hebrew learning in the seventeenth century is a subject that deserves more attention than it has received so far. Except for monographs and articles on particular authors to be referred to in the appropriate Chapters below (notably the work of Denis Saurat and H. F. Fletcher on Milton, Marjorie Nicolson on More, L. C. Martin on Henry Vaughan, and Basil Willey's handling of the Cambridge Platonists in his *Seventeenth Century*

Introduction

But properly speaking we are not concerned here with Blake at all, but rather with the spiritual and intellectual conflicts of the seventeenth century, which Blake did something to illuminate by importing therein the vocabulary of Hebraism. It will not be thought ungracious perhaps if the present author, as a latter-day inhabitant of Jerusalem, but native of Albion, makes the grave oracles of Blake his own point of departure, yet at the same time redeems the terms for his own use, and sets out to study the seventeenth-century situation in accordance with his own sense of the meaning of 'Jerusalem' and 'Albion'.

Background) literary scholars have rarely shown cognizance of it. From the direction of Hebrew scholarship proper there is also a scanty harvest. The fullest essay to date is by the late Professor Leon Roth, 'Hebraists and Non-Hebraists of the Seventeenth Century,' *The Journal of Semitic Studies*, VI (Manchester, 1961), pp. 204-21. There is a briefer essay by J. L. Teicher, 'Maimonides and England', *Transactions of the Jewish Historical Society*, XVI (London), pp. 98-100. On Kabbalism, some background is provided by J. L. Blau, *The Christian Interpretation of the Cabala in the Renaissance* (New York, 1944), and for guidance on the whole issue of Hebraic learning and influence in the West, the appropriate chapters of *The Legacy of Israel*, ed. I. Abrahams (Oxford, 1927) are still helpful. Additional items are listed by Cecil Roth, *Magna Bibliotheca Anglo-Judaica* (London, 1937), pp. 157-71.

The seventeenth century was after all the great age of oriental scholarship in England, boasting such luminaries as Edward Pococke, John Lightfoot, and John Selden, and such a literary monument as Walton's Polyglot Bible. The King James Bible itself, in addition to its many other still-active merits, was, and still is, a remarkable example of Hebrew learning in England. A useful pilot-study of this aspect is provided in D. Daiches, *The King James Version of the English Bible* (Chicago, 1941), pp. 148-218.

One would have thought that the whole subject of Hebrew learning in the seventeenth century would have attracted the attention of a suitably qualified bibliographer who might have paved the way for a detailed evaluative study. The present work is not concerned with Hebrew learning as such, but rather with the 'Hebraic factor' as a deeper and more pervasive influence, often manifesting itself in authors (such as Bacon and Hobbes) who had no access to the original sources and perhaps only a slight acquaintance with the Latin renderings of the post-Biblical Jewish classics. That there is such a factor and that it is, or should be, of serious concern to students of Western Literature was made clear in the striking opening Chapter of Erich Auerbach's *Mimesis* (Berne, 1946).

PART ONE

The Background of Style

I

THE BONUS RHETOR

WHEN WE consider the history of prose style in England, from the sixteenth century onward, we are struck by the fact that the pattern is not one of progressive decline from the high ground of the Elizabethans to the humble plain of the Restoration. If there was a Golden Age of English prose it came later, not precisely at the 'Shakespearian moment' but in the mid-seventeenth century, in Thomas Browne, Jeremy Taylor, Milton, and Traherne.[1] The prose writers of the Elizabethan period proper were, by fairly general consent, of lower standing.

What we often find in the Elizabethan Age, in prose, is a magistral style good enough for grand oratorical statement, but rarely elastic enough for subtler expositional purposes. This oratorical mode, or *genus grande*, is the typical mode of the 'High Renaissance' as found in England in Hooker, Lyly, Ascham, and Wilson, and it goes back to the formal system of ordonnance beloved of the writers of the Italian Renaissance. The fashion, though susceptible of many varieties, may be described as 'Ciceronian', Cicero being regarded as the chief classical model for imitation; on the theoretical side, authority for it was found chiefly in Aristotle's *Rhetoric*.

Now there was in England a 'pure' Ciceronianism, elaborate but at the same time, clear and transparent, and there was also a more heavily decorated and affected Ciceronianism distilled from medieval patterns of eloquence. Of the former, Ascham in praise of Cicero may be taken as fair example. The structure of the Latin period is evident:

> But where Tullie doth set vp his saile of eloquence, in some broad deep Argument, caried with full tyde and Winde, of his witte and learnyng, all other may rather stand and looke after him, than

[1] Cf. C. S. Lewis, *English Literature in the Sixteenth Century* (Oxford, 1954), p. 536.

19

hope to ouertake him, what course so euer he hold, either in faire or foule.[1]

In the second type of prose expression, represented chiefly in England by John Lyly, the 'Euphuist' and his imitators, the author seems prepared to sell all for a balanced, alliterating phrase and for the jingle of the isocolon; above all, wit—that supreme talent of authorship—is known by the skill in 'amplifying', by every rhetorical means, the tritest thought or image.[2] Shakespeare in his early plays is not above these mannerisms,[3] though later he came to satirize them in the character of Osric. Such self-conscious styles flowered exotically in Spain in the writings of Antonio de Guevara: in England it is perhaps true to say that they were never thoroughly naturalized, and the vogue, though considerable, was short-lived.

The mention of Lyly and Guevara reminds us that 'wit' is not merely a matter of style: it also includes a certain high-minded attitude, a nobility (or at least an affected nobility) of character.[4] In the Ciceronianism of the Renaissance, Ethic and Rhetoric are still substantially one. In Guevara's *Familiar Epistles* (as rendered by an Elizabethan translator in 1577) we find him addressing us on the responsibilities that go with birth and breeding, and doing so with the help of all the dainty tricks of amplification:

> That which maketh the knight to be a perfect gentleman, is to be measured in his wordes, liberal in giuing, sober in diet, honest in liuing, tender in pardoning, and valiant in fighting. Notwithstanding anyone be noble in bloud, and mightie in possessions, yet if he be in his talke a babbler, in eating a glutton, in conditions ambitious, in conversation malicious, in getting couetous, in trauels impacient, and in fighting a cowarde: of such we shall rather say to haue more abilitie for a carle, than for a knight.[5]

---

[1] *The Scholemaster* (1570), reprinted, London, 1870, p. 151.
[2] See M. W. Croll and H. Clemons, ed., *Euphues* (London, 1916) Introduction.
[3] Cf. *King John*, Act IV, scene iii, lines 40-50.
[4] Cf. A. C. Clark, 'Ciceronianism', in *English Literature and the Classics*, ed. G. S. Gordon (Oxford, 1912), pp. 118-19.
[5] *The Familiar Epistles of Sir Anthonie of Gueuara*, translated by Edward Hellowes (London, 1574).

Similarly, Lyly's *Euphues* (1579) was a kind of courtesy-book, aimed no less than Spenser's *Faerie Queene* to 'fashion a gentleman or noble person in vertuous and noble discipline'.

The rhetorical ideal of the late sixteenth century, indeed, is that of the *bonus rhetor*, the author of sweet and copious eloquence who is thereby fitted to be the instrument of all good causes. This easy symbiosis of Rhetoric and Ethic is the common assumption of the manuals of Rhetoric, and indicates, we may say, a certain child-like faith in the innate possibilities of human nature, a faith which we may perhaps envy from the standpoint of our sadder experience. The moral and aesthetic principles naturally flow together, belonging as in Plato (for the standpoint here is essentially Greek) to the same ideal world of Truth, Beauty and Goodness. Richard Rainolde maintained that 'nothing can bee more excellently giuen of nature than Eloquence, by the which the floryshing state of commonweales doe consiste: kingdomes uniuersally are gouerened, the state of euery one priuatlie is maintained'. Here is a very large claim indeed for eloquence, but we must remember that true eloquence is *ipso facto* eloquent truth, and the true orator is he who can 'copiouslie dilate any matter or sentence' so as to animate princes and rulers 'to godlie affairs and business'.[1] The notion had been most clearly defined in the well-known saying of Quintilian, 'orator est vir bonus dicendi peritus'.

The training of the child in eloquence—perhaps the main aim of the classical education given at the time—was thus essentially ethical training. It was aimed at fitting him to be a good and worthy man, especially a good and worthy man holding a high position of responsibility. This qualification is necessary, for the conception is markedly aristocratic. Indeed, the whole Elizabethan notion of 'wit' is governed by an aristocratic sense of inborn moral qualities made effective through a training in the arts of expression. The *naturally* good is perfected by *nurture*, and this nurture is really only effective with the naturally good, sc., the gentleman born. We are here at a very great distance from the lower bourgeois conception of the Puritans according to which the vision of goodness is as

---

[1] R. Rainolde, *A Booke called the Foundacion of Rhetorike* (London, 1563), facsimile reproduction (New York, 1945), *fol.* i, a-b.

likely to be vouchsafed to the unlettered and the ignorant as to the well-bred. Nashe complained of preaching sectaries who 'leape from the coblers stal to their pulpits'.

We are nowadays inclined to side with the humanists (like Nashe) in their war against the Puritans. The Puritans believed, indeed, that the arts of elocution were taught by the Devil; but we should consider very carefully whether it is more logical to hold with Nashe, Spenser, and the above-quoted Rainolde and Guevara that there is some pre-ordained harmony between sweetness of expression, noble birth, and the virtuous life! Is it more reasonable to hold that eloquence comes from God than that it comes from the Devil? Or is the former view not just as likely to lead us astray as the latter?

Sir Philip Sidney was sure that 'wit' was the mark of the Divine Image in which man was created, almost the equivalent of what the Puritans would call Grace. Of the true poet he says,

> he goeth hand in hand with nature, not enclosed within the narrow warrant of her gifts, but freely ranging only within the zodiac of his own wit.[1]

'Our erected wit', he tells us, 'maketh us know what perfection is, and yet our infected will keepeth us from reaching it.' Here is a glowing and serene confidence in the saving virtue of the gifts of nature, entirely typical of the Hellenistic-Christian synthesis of the century of Erasmus and Hooker. The world is saved by the *logos* which is at once Word and Idea, Beauty and Goodness. This faith in Rhetoric is still found later on in Milton who condemns the unfortunate Bishop Hall (with whom he had incidentally much more in common than he realized[2]) by an extraordinary syllogism: (*a*) a bad man cannot write well, (*b*) a bishop is a bad man, (*c*) therefore a bishop (and specifically Bishop Hall) cannot write well. But Milton was also on the other side: Puritan that he was, he makes Satan ('his words replete with guile') his prime example of the orator. The danger lurking in the arts of language are all too obviously acknowledged in the picture of the infernal leader compared to

---

[1] *An Apology for Poetry* (1595).

[2] Cf. Audrey Chew, 'Joseph Hall and John Milton', *E.L.H.*, XVII (1950), 274-95.

>   some oratore renouned
>   In Athens or free Rome,

who wins all too easy entrance into the heart of Eve.

The principle of the Renaissance and that of the Reformation do not always live peacefully together in Milton; in the *Areopagitica* for instance, he himself adopts the pose and gesture of some 'orator renouned in Athens or free Rome'. But then this is only one contradiction in the complex of contradictions that we shall later have to note in Milton's attempt to find some new reconciliation between the demands of the Greek and Hebrew genius. In the meantime we may note in Milton's suspicion of Rhetoric—one of the clouds which were in the seventeenth century to darken the sunny landscape of Renaissance humanism.

II

REALISM AND REVOLT

THE ATTACK on the High Renaissance conception of eloquence with its easy symbiosis of Rhetoric and Ethic came swiftly and sharply in the early seventeenth century, and it came on three fronts—Science, Theology, and Anthropology. To start with the scientific writers, we find Bacon announcing a new inductive method aimed at overthrowing the old scholasticism. His announcement might almost be regarded as a reply to Sidney's definition of Wit quoted in the previous Chapter. Wit is for Bacon no divine principle enabling us to construct a world more perfect than that given by Nature.

> I, on the contrary—he states—dwelling purely and constantly among the facts of nature, withdraw from them no further than may suffice to let the rays and images of natural objects meet in a point, as they do in the sense of vision; whence it follows that the strength and excellency of the wit has but little to do in the matter.[1]

Here we meet a new conception of eloquence, or rather of discourse that might eschew eloquence altogether for its own urgent, pragmatic purposes. There is a contradiction in the passage of course: he says that dealing with the facts of nature, he has no use for wit, yet he speaks of achieving a distance from the mere *res naturae* in order that the rays might meet in a point, in order, that is, to achieve a unified or harmonized vision. And this suggests the presence of a focusing and creative eye, of a faculty akin perhaps to what Coleridge called the 'primary Imagination'.[2] Indeed Bacon's whole system is riddled with the contradiction between the empirical quest, the attempt to rest the mind on the concrete and particular phenomena of the world, on the one hand, and the quest for

[1] *The Great Instauration* (1620). From the Preface. See *Works*, ed. Spedding, Ellis, and Heath (London, 1857-59), IV, 19.
[2] The relevance of Coleridge's view of the Imagination for scientific discourse and the scientific view of reality has been well urged by D. G. James: see *Scepticism and Poetry* (London, 1937), pp. 30-43.

axioms, that is, for inclusive insights, on the other. The Elizabethans would have regarded the latter as the work of 'Wit',
and Shelley, who spoke of Bacon as a poet, would no doubt have
agreed. But Bacon would have resisted such an inference: like
Jerome, he looked upon poetry as a deceiving idol, and like
Plato, or like any thoroughgoing Puritan of his day, he maintained of poetry that 'it filleth the imagination; and yet it is but
with the shadow of a lie'.

Bacon's own ideal in writing was the plain style without
affectation or flourish.[1] But even so, he was too good a psychologist to ignore the existence of the imagination as a psychological phenomenon. The problem was to contain it, to confine
it permanently within its limits. It was with this object that he
devoted a whole section of the Second Book of *The Advancement
of Learning* to Rhetoric, treating it as an accessory science in the
great work of what he calls 'the tradition of knowledge'. In a
well-regulated composition, he thought, it could be subordinated to Reason. 'The duty and office of Rhetoric', he declared
in a famous sentence, 'is to apply Reason to Imagination for
the better moving of the will.' And a little later on, he makes
his point even more explicitly: 'The end of Rhetoric is to fill the
imagination to second reason, and not to oppress it.'[2] By this
means Bacon had succeeded in removing from his path a
dangerous source of error, prior to moving on to *The Great
Instauration* and the task therein proposed of classifying the
whole universe on rational and empirical lines. By turning
Rhetoric into an instrumental art he was really denying the
connexion hitherto recognized between Rhetoric and Ethic;
He was denying to Rhetoric any ideal content or purpose.[3]

[1] See Rawley's Life of Bacon in *Works, ed. cit.*, I, 11.

[2] *Ibid.*, III, 409.

[3] In theory, Bacon does not emasculate Rhetoric or divide it from its
traditional partners, Ethic and Logic. He regards it as standing between
them and 'participating of both' so maintaining the traditional point of
view, cf. K. R. Wallace, *Francis Bacon on Communication and Rhetoric* (Chapel
Hill, 1943), pp. 35, 211 f. But Mr. Wallace somewhat overstates the case
for Bacon's conservatism. Bacon, like a good lawyer, astutely uses the terms
and formulae of ancient authorities but the fact is that the terms have been
forced out of their traditional moulds. In Bacon's system, Ethic is, like
Rhetoric itself, made subservient to the demands of the practical Reason.
See *Works*, IV, 455-6.

This policy, derived from the teaching of the sixteenth-century anti-Aristotelian philosopher, Ramus (and his partner Talaeus)[1] had an enormous attraction also for the Puritans; both for them and for Bacon it came to underpin their bourgeois insistence on the importance of the matter in hand, as distinct from the savour and charm of style: it came to support their sense of the priority of Matter over Manner, Doctrine over Style, Reason over Imagination. It lies somewhere at the heart of the 'dissociation of sensibility'.

The drift of Bacon's theory of communication is clearly revolutionary, even if his terminology sometimes suggests a conservative, Aristotelian approach. He goes even further than Ramus, as a matter of fact, for Ramus merely urged the separation of spheres, whilst Bacon holds that the strict inquiry into Nature demanded by his new method would not require Rhetoric at all. It would not 'supply matter for disputations or ornaments for discourse', and he goes on:

> It does not lie in the way. It cannot be caught up in passage. It does not flatter the understanding by conformity with precon-ceived notions. Nor will it come down to the apprehension of the vulgar except by its utilities and effects.[2]

A new unrhetorical mode of communication must be found; in fact his whole philosophical position (with its stress on empirical evidence) involves a basic criticism of rhetorical

[1] On Bacon's debt to Ramus, see *Works*, I, 91 (Ellis's Introduction to the *Novum Organum*); III, 205. Cf. also, J. B. Mullinger, *University of Cambridge* (1884), II, 405. Bacon himself wrote slightingly of Ramus and his use of epitomies (*Works*, III, 530), but this should not blind us to his consistent use of the general features of Ramism such as the grand axioms of truth and wisdom for which he expresses admiration in the *De Augmentis*. The influence of Ramus, especially as felt in Cambridge in Bacon's time and after, was an example of the new anti-scholastic intellectual currents which were to gain in power during the seventeenth century. Milton wrote a digest of Ramus's Logic later on. His example was felt in France in the Port-Royal also (see Sainte-Beuve, Port-Royal, Book IV, ch. 2 and 3). In Bacon's case, the influence of Ramus's technique is clear in the use of dichotomies—the seemingly endless bifurcation and selection of subject matter which we note for instance in *The Advancement of Learning*. In general, Ramus taught Bacon the primacy of Logic over Rhetoric and the possibility of treating the latter as an instrumental art.

[2] *Works*, IV, 42.

discourse as such; and rhetorical invention is not properly invention at all, since, unlike scientific invention which discovers new knowledge, its object is only to 'recover or resummon that which we already know'.[1]

Bacon's influence was clearly felt in the growth of a scientific plain-style in the seventeenth century and the recurring attempt, first adumbrated in *The Advancement of Learning*, to give words the status of mathematical symbols.[2] It was felt later both by Pascal and Hobbes that linguistic reform might proceed on the model of that truest of all sciences, Geometry. Thus the descriptive or mathematical modes came to attract the attention of philosophers working outside the field of natural philosophy proper, even though it was amongst the men of science that it found its most practical application. Bacon himself tried to approximate it in *Sylva Sylvarum*, and we find the men of the Royal Society later on 'bringing all things as near the mathematical plainness as they can; and preferring the Language of Artizans, Countrymen, and Merchants, before that of Wits, or Scholars'.[3] Nathaniel Fairfax, one of the new scientific *virtuosi*, expressed the common view in 1674 when he said, 'When I look at things, I can afford to overlook words.'[4]

This, however, was only one spearhead of attack upon the Renaissance ideal of eloquence. On another front, that of the philosophical essay and epistle, an equally strong anti-Ciceronian movement was developing. Here the new writers adopted, not indeed the scientific style of report, which would not have suited their purpose, but the Senecan style newly recovered by the stoical philosophers. Naturally the new trends overlapped, especially when we consider that Bacon was a principal contributor to the Senecan essay-style also. But it is nevertheless worth keeping these separate in so far as they were differentiated from one another both as to their aims and subject-matter.

[1] *Ibid*. III, 389.   [2] *Ibid*. III, 396-7.
[3] T. Sprat, *The History of the Royal Society* (ed. of 1734), p. 113. Cf. H. Fisch and H. W. Jones, 'Bacon's Influence on Sprat's *History of the Royal Society*', *M.L.Q.*, XII (1951), 399-406.
[4] *A Treatise of the Bulk and Selvedge of the World*, Preface to the Reader, ed. A. K. Croston (Liverpool, 1949), p. 36. On the scientific movement for plain prose, see R. F. Jones, 'Science and English Prose Style' and 'Science and Language in England of the Mid-Seventeenth Century', in *The Seventeenth Century* (Stanford, 1951).

The scientific style was designed to express the new sense of the outer world and of man's relation to it; whilst the loose athletic style of the new anthropologists and essayists was designed to express a secular, stoical psychology and a realistic, disenchanted view of man.

A great deal of attention has been paid to the Senecan movement in prose by historians of literature in recent years[1] and the informality, the rational secular note of the new writers such as Montaigne, and Lipsius on the Continent, and Burton, Bacon, Cornwallis, and many others in England, have been adequately explored. It is only necessary here to locate this movement in the general pattern of reaction against the aureate mode of the 'High Renaissance' and indicate its ideological implications. Bacon is our man once more. He was almost as much concerned with Human Philosophy as with Natural Philosophy, devoting himself to the former in his collections of Essays which appeared with revisions and additions from the year 1597 to 1625. As in his treatment of Natural Philosophy, so here he refused to be misled by idealistic prejudices. The aim of this style likewise was to reflect exactly the processes of consciousness: it was introspective, leading away from large, emotional statements to something more exact, scrupulous, abbreviated, energetic, and complacently sententious. It is Brutus speaking in the market-place and summing-up his ideas in a series of apparently impregnable aphorisms—the 'Attic' style for which he was noted and which Shakespeare had captured so well:[2]

> As Caesar loved me; I weep for him; as he was fortunate, I rejoice at it; as he was valiant, I honour him; but as he was ambitious, I slew him. There is tears for his love; joy for his fortune; honour for his valour; and death for his ambition.

[1] Cf. D. C. Allen, 'Style and Certitude', *E.L.H.*, XV, 175 f.; M. W. Croll, 'The Baroque Style in Prose', *Studies in English Philology* (University of Minnesota, 1929), and elsewhere in many articles; G. Williamson, 'Senecan Style in the Seventeenth Century', *P.Q.*, XV (1938), and his longer study, *The Senecan Amble* (London, 1951). For a brief summary, see G. Highet, *The Classical Tradition* (Oxford, 1949), ch. 18, on 'Baroque Prose'.

[2] Plutarch in his Life of Brutus speaks of his 'brief, compendious manner'. See J. A. K. Thomson, *The Classical Background of English Literature* (London 1948), p. 185.

Realism and Revolt

After this scientific account of Brutus's motives for murder, we may turn to Bacon; the accent, the stylistic pattern, and the balance are the same:

> Studies serve for delight, for ornament, and for ability. Their chief use for delight, is in privateness and retiring; for ornament, is in discourse; and for ability, is in the judgment and disposition of business. . . . To spend too much time in studies is sloth; to use them too much for ornament, is affectation; to make judgment wholly by their rules, is the humour of a scholar.

There is no room here in this utilitarian summary of the benefits of learning, for that more glowing phraseology in which he concludes his treatment of the same topic in *The Advancement of Learning* saying that knowledge and learning ought to be a 'rich storehouse for the Glory of God and the relief of man's estate'.

In general, it would be true to say that the moral essayists employing the 'hopping' Senecan style were limited to a kind of analytical survey of human nature which inhibited emotional expression and especially that emphatic language of the heart which belongs to relationships of love whether human or divine. Bacon's Essay 'Of Love' lacks all romantic vibration. The movement of the mind is essentially axial—turning upon itself—rather than orbital, having reference to some reality outside the subjective consciousness. The Senecan style belongs to the sphere of what Buber would call the I/It (or perhaps the I/Myself) rather than the I/Thou. But it has the incomparable advantage of exactness in the registering of consciousness. It portrays not rounded and digested thoughts, but a mind thinking, moving spirally towards a conclusion.

It thus represents a clear parallel to the scientific style of report, whilst having a different model, namely, the stoic paradox or aphorism,[1] and a different subject-matter, namely Man, the heart of Man, and human life. But like the scientific style devoted to the description of, and inquiry into, the works of Nature, its tendency is to overthrow the traditional Ciceronian Rhetoric of the schools.

In condemning the oratorical style, Bacon in a brilliant

[1] The primitive style of bare dialectic practised by the ancient stoics, which is of course much refined and smoothed out in Seneca, is discussed by E. V. Arnold, *Roman Stoicism* (Cambridge, 1911), pp. 148-51.

phrase summed up its danger as being that of authorizing 'a contract of error between the deliverer and the receiver'. No better motto than this could be found to introduce the third anti-rhetorical tendency of the period, namely, that of many of the Puritan writers and preachers.[1] The Puritan objection to gorgeous rhetoric was sounded earlier in the sixteenth century, but we may take as our first example the angry criticism of 'Certain English Protestants' writing in 1599 against Hooker's recently published *Laws of Eclesiastical Polity*, that great master-piece of Ciceronian oratory and Christian humanism. In their letter, they call Hooker to account for his various heresies, not the least amongst which was his addiction to a rich, classical type of oratory of the kind which the Devil used to deceive the mother of the human race!

> And as by a faire shew of *wishing well*, our first parents were fowlie deceaued; so is there a cunning framed method, by excellencie of wordes and intising speeches of man's wisdome, to beguile and bewitch the verie Church of God.

The linguistic policy of the Puritans owed much to the precept and example of St. Paul whose first letter to the Corinthians is echoed in the above-quoted passage. The texts from the Apostle which have most bearing on the Puritan preference for the plain style and which were always quoted in the seventeenth century in connexion with the movement for plain preaching, are as follows:

> And I, brethren, when I came to you, came not with the excellency of speech or wisdom, declaring with you the testimony of God.

> And my speech and my preaching was not with enticing words of man's wisdom, but in demonstration of the Spirit and power.
> (1 *Corinthians* ii, 1, 4)

> Seeing that we have such hope we use great plainness of speech.
> (2 *Corinthians* iii, 12)

[1] For a more extensive treatment, see H. Fisch, 'The Puritans and the Reform of Prose Style', *E.L.H.*, 1952, XIX, 229-48. Also, W. F. Mitchell, *English Pulpit Oratory from Andrewes to Tillotson* (London, 1932), pp. 99, 100, 258 f.; Perry Miller, *The New England Mind*, vol. 1 (New York, 1939), Ch. 12.

The last quotation occurs in a context in which Paul seems to be engaged in a polemic against the 'literary' character of the Old Testament as compared with the more 'psychical', inward nature of the new ministry, the latter written 'not on tables of stone but in fleshly tables of the heart', 'not of the letter but of the spirit'.

The austere style of the Puritans thus had (like the exact style of the scientists, and the strenuous style of the Senecan essayists) its own special object. It was designed to express their theology of Grace and absolute divine transcendence. The Puritan preachers in their search for a plainer, more direct mode of exhortation swept away the old Ciceronian schemes of oratory which had served the preachers of the gospel for hundreds of years, and replaced them by a new, more direct utterance articulated according to the formula of Doctrine, Reason, and Use. Similes and allegories are omitted in the interests of a higher truth. This is what we find in Chaderton, Baxter, and the host of plain preachers throughout the seventeenth century. It is perhaps difficult for us to understand how severely bare and unadorned a composition written according to these principles might be. Most of it never found its way into print, for the simple reason that the Puritan 'prophets' were essentially extemporary preachers obeying the motions of the spirit, and perhaps our best impression is derived from parodies. Eachard, for instance, later on imagines a Puritan plain preacher haranguing his audience with nothing more than a copy of the Bible in his hand by way of ornament:

> This is the Book, this is the Book: Here it is, here it is; no word like this word, no book like this Book, no writing like this writing, no reading like reading here, no searching like searching here, no considering like considering here . . . etc.[1]

The insensitivity to the symbolic or sensuous qualities of things and to the symbolic values of words may be viewed as a kind of implied polemic against graven images and the Catholic view of the sacraments, but it also served the Puritans as a means of attack upon (or rather a defence against) the poetic ambiguity of the Scriptures themselves. In a Puritan paraphrase of Ramus's

---

[1] J. Eachard, *Some Observations upon the Answer to an Enquiry into the Grounds and Occasions of the Contempt of the Clergy* (1671), ed. of 1705, p. 108.

Dialectica, the twenty-third Psalm is handled as follows. Its imaginative colour and depth are lost, and the whole is reduced to a sterile argument:

> *Though I walke through the valley of the shadow of death, I will feare no evill.*
>
> A man so walking may justly feare: but the Prophet saith he would not feare; Therefore in him to walke in the shadow of death, and to feare disagree as divers things.[1]

This is an example of Ramus's famous disjunctive syllogism. It is hardly necessary to stress the bareness of this new technique of exposition. The Psalm instead of being treated as sublime poetry, is being regarded as the exemplification of a logical argument. The expositor in the above-cited passage looks upon the Psalmist as a logician who embellishes an argument by means of appropriate imagery; and consequently he treats the sentence under discussion as a proposition rhetorically expressed rather than, what in fact it was, a living experience. The literary unit of the Old Testament is, after all, not the parable but the poetic image. When the prophet Hosea declares that God will be 'like the dew to Israel' (xiv, 5), behind that image lies a host of concrete associations; there is the 'speech distilled as dew' of *Deut.* xxxii, 2, and there is the actual physical manifestation of the dew as a seasonal blessing marking the divine favour towards a farming community (*Genesis*, xxvii, 28; *Zech.* viii, 12; *Deut.* xxxiii, 13). In Hosea's image indeed the saving activity of God in the realm of history and his blessings in the sphere of Nature are brought together. Now such a rich ambiguity belongs to the inner soul of Old Testament poetry. It is destroyed as soon as the imagery is looked upon as merely functional. To say of the twenty-third Psalm, as yet another Ramist expositor does, that it is an example of a continued trope 'called an Allegorie' wherein the 'care of God towards his Churche, is set foorth by the words proper to a Shephearde',[2] is to lose not merely the literary complexity and richness of the Psalm but also the direct and immediate awareness of the divine reality springing out of a shepherd's experience, for this is the

---

[1] Anthony Wotton, *The Art of Logick* (London, 1626), p. 49.

[2] Dudley Fenner, *The Artes of Logike and Rethorike . . . openings of certaine partes of Scripture, according to the same* (1584), sig, D1ᵛ.

awareness on which the image is based and this is the reality which it is intended to explore.

The non-organic, non-ambiguous simplicity counselled by the Puritans in their sermons and works of divinity is of a piece with the other anti-poetical tendencies in the prose of the period, many of them likewise brought about (or at least encouraged) by the Ramist disjunction of style and subject. But it should be pointed out that though for the Ramists Logic always preceded Rhetoric, there might well be room for Rhetoric as well, *after* Logic had done its work. The object of Rhetoric would be to clothe the constructs of the Intellect in decorative form. Here, we have I think one of the roots of dissociation in the history or prose. It has been well said by one investigator that, 'composition performed under such principles lacked the unity of conception and execution which is necessary to the highest art'.[1] Ramus 'filled the world with logic-choppers'.

As a result of this dissociative principle, there would either be a horizontal separation of Logic and Rhetoric in any particular piece of writing, or else two different kinds of composition proceeding side by side, one excessively logical, the other excessively rhetorical. Thus, Rhetoric was by no means abandoned. Indeed, from a practical point of view, the Puritans were in no position to abandon it. They were after all propagandists, preaching a doctrine of salvation. It was all very well for Baxter to emphasize the supreme virtue of plainness,

> All our teaching must be as Plain and Evident as we can make it. For this doth most suit to a Teacher's Ends. He that would be understood, must speak to the capacity of his Hearers, and make it his Business to make himself understood—[2]

but the hortatory and didactic purpose made clear in those very words of Baxter would obviously dictate, from time to time, a mode of exposition different from that used in Wotton's handling of the twenty-third Psalm previously quoted. The contradiction here lies at the heart of Puritanism itself. This dual approach to imaginative discourse indirectly reveals in fact all the paradoxes of Puritanism, a religion compounded

[1] P. A. Duhamel, 'The Logic and Rhetoric of Peter Ramus', *M.P.*, XLVI (1949), 163-71.
[2] *The Practical Works of Richard Baxter* (London, 1707), IV, 358.

of Old Testament activism and New Testament quietism; a faith which rests on the belief in inexorable Grace and the unavailingness of human effort, and on the other hand, an energetically propagandist movement urging men to follow this road or that for the salvation of their souls.

Thus it came about that there was on the one hand a genuinely plain type of Puritan sermon which reminds us (with allowance made for its different object and its different emotional context) of the simplicity of Descartes or the Baconian scientists, and on the other hand there was, as has been said, 'the highly emotional preaching which, from time to time, can advance *pari passu* with the pursuit of plainness'.[1] There was the attempt to flatten meaning into didactic form so as to make possible clear and immediate comprehension, and there was also a kind of unrestrained impetuosity, a maximal use of tautology, exclamation, and rhetorical question combined with an untiring use of Biblical quotation and echo, metaphor and simile, as in such a work as Baxter's own very popular *A Call to the Unconverted* (1657). In a way the Puritans are, in this, like St. Paul himself. For though in the second Letter to the Corinthians he expresses his distrust of the 'vail of Moses' as that which obscures the light of Grace, and aims to achieve rather a pure transparency of utterance, whereby somehow the language of the old Adam with its earthly savour would be purged away, he is nevertheless himself a preacher liable to employ the devices of Rhetoric and the enticing words of man's wisdom. More than that he is a poet 'able to speak with tongues more than you all', and in the thirteenth Chapter of the first Letter to the Corinthians, he makes eloquent use of the poetic manner of the Old Testament and its parallelistic cadences. It is part of the character of the man that the recognition of these poetic gifts in himself should have led him elsewhere to intensify his effort at imaginative self-denial and self-restraint. The two opposed aims are never really reconciled.

Many of the Puritan writers and preachers were no doubt ignorant, unlettered, and lacking in all literary and imaginative gifts, but there were some who, like Paul himself, had to reckon with strong rhetorical impulses in themselves. And for them

[1] W. J. Ong, 'Peter Ramus and the Naming of Methodism', *J.H.I.*, XIV (1953), 244-5.

too such impulses might be satisfied by drawing upon the poetic resources of the Old Testament.

It is this that gave rise to the 'babylonish dialect' satirized in Butler's *Hudibras* which continued to characterize a certain type of 'low-church' preacher down to the nineteenth century. Richard Flecknoe in 1653 remarked on the entry of 'the Scripture Style amongst the common *Rabble*, who are our *Rabbies* now, and *Gypsies* cant it in the Hebrew phrase'. Examples of the use of this style in the mid-seventeenth century could be multiplied from the writings of Lilburne and Winstanley on the left, and from Bastwick and Prynne over on the right wing of Puritanism, and from Samuel Rutherford among the Scots Presbyterians.[1] One example from Winstanley's *The New Law of Righteousness* (1649) will suffice at this point:

> He will throw down the mountaines of the flesh, fill up the low valleys of the spirit, he will make rough ways smooth, and crooked ways strait, he will make the earth fruitfull, and the winds and the weathers seasonable; he will throw all the powers of the earth at your feet, and himself will be your governour and teacher, and your habitations on earth shall be in peace . . .[2]

All this is of a piece with the Puritan appropriation of the vocabulary of election as provided in the Old Testament; (for the theme of election was common to all the sects however much they might vary in point of Calvinist orthodoxy). The Diggers, to whom Winstanley adhered, represented themselves as Jacob and the landowning class as Esau, a covenant formulation which provided them with a kind of strategic command of all Old Testament history, and enabled them to borrow its Rhetoric on a sort of analogical credit basis.

Perhaps the most interesting example of this use of the power and authority of the Old Testament at the literary level is provided by Bunyan's writings. But I would hesitate to take Bunyan as an example of true Hebraic prose; he will readily quote in one of his Sermons 'He inviteth thee to a banquet of wine, yea, to come into his wine-cellar, and his banner over thee shall be love.' But this is for Bunyan *pure* allegory: the

---

[1] Cf. W. F. Mitchell, *op. cit.*, pp. 262-4.
[2] *The Works of Gerard Winstanley*, ed. G. H. Sabine (New York, 1941), p. 153.

sensuous and imaginative implications of the original are being not only ignored, but even resisted. For there is no suggestion in Bunyan of recommending the earthly delights of love and wine. Bunyan is, as Plato might have said, at three removes from the reality of the Old Testament with its this-worldly orientation. In *Holy War* he makes free use, as trope, of Old Testament imagery drawn from the sphere of real physical conflict. He lets us hear the 'noise of the soldiers and shoutings of the captains' (see *Job* xxxix); but *Holy War* is scarcely concerned with the real Old Testament dimension of historical action; its subject is a metaphysical and psychological struggle. It represents the thorough interiorization of the Hebraic world in the interests of a more evangelical summons to piety.[1] The systematic use of Old Testament poetry as mere trope or allegory comes for the Puritans in fact as a further reinforcement of Calvinistic inwardness. They know little of what J. C. Powys has called 'the human wisdom, the human sensuality, the human anger, the human justice, the human magnanimity, the human triumph, of this old shameless literature of the Old Testament'.[2] On the contrary, their aim, even when they are quoting from the Old Testament is to urge us on in the unremitting 'Pauline' struggle against the World, the Flesh and the Devil.

For this reason, the Puritans as a whole and as such will not be taken in this study as the examples of Hebraism in prose or in doctrine. Naturally the revival of Hebraism and the new understanding of it achieved in the seventeenth century owed much to them, but it also owed much to the swift and sharp reactions against them which we shall have occasion to note. Puritan prose as such in its essential character is to be classed rather with the Baconian and scientific ideal of expression in the seventeenth century different though its mode and subject-

[1] Bunyan exemplifies all the paradoxes of the Puritan attitude to literary expression. To offset his colourful use of Biblical poetry in citation or echo, we note his attachment to the cult of plainness attested in words of burning conviction: '*God* did not play in convincing of me; the *Devil* did not play in tempting of me; neither did I play when I sunk as in a bottomless pit, when *the pangs of Hell caught hold upon me*: wherefore I may not play in my relating of them, but be plain and simple and lay down the thing as it was. (Preface to *Grace Abounding*, 1666.)

[2] *Enjoyment of Literature* (New York, 1938).

matter might be from theirs. It is an example of true, modern prose, that is prose which has cut itself away, disunited itself, from poetry. That is the real significance of the new pragmatic, non-imaginative forms of expression cultivated by the Scientists, the Senecans, and the Puritans. Words are dangerous, therefore they must be avoided or else (as in the allegorical, tropological style of the Puritans) thoroughly sterilized and purged of their sensuous possibilities before use. For Bacon, words 'do shoot back upon the understanding of the wisest and mightily entangle and pervert the judgement'; they also threaten us with that symbolic and imaginative experience of Nature, Man, and God, which must be ignored or abolished before his method can be made to prevail. With the Puritan, poetry is suspected because it embarrasses him by carrying to him the savour of our fallen nature (or, perhaps poetry might whisper, of our unfallen nature). However that might be, it is that treacherous guest in the house who is always ready to open the door to the World, the Flesh, and the Devil, and though his house has many mansions, the Puritan cannot convince himself that it has room for guests like these.

III

HEBRAIC PROSE

WE MAY turn to a group of prose writers whose work, by fairly general agreement, constitutes the high-water mark of English prose in the seventeenth century, and perhaps in any century. The great age of English prose is that which embraces Milton, Thomas Browne, Traherne, and the great Anglican sermon-writers, such as Jeremy Taylor, John Donne, and Joseph Hall. These are writers who are all capable of a rich strain of eloquence, of aureate imagery, and of sound effects similar to the *figurae verborum* of the Ciceronian orators of the sixteenth century. But one would be quite wrong to think of them either collectively or singly as representing a continuation of the Ciceronian manner of the High Renaissance, whether one has in view the purer Ciceronianism of Hooker or the more artificial mode of the Euphuists. Even of Taylor, the most decoratively poetical of these mid-seventeenth-century prose writers, it has been justly remarked that, 'The figurative and poetical element is not large in proportion to the bulk of relatively plain writing.'[1] Theirs was a rhetoric not stiff or mannered in the fashion recommended in the old rhetoric books with their formal schemes for the oration, but flexible, personal, and energetic. All the writers to be dealt with here and they include some of the greatest in the history of English prose, had in fact gone through the purging experience of Puritanism, or of Stoicism, or of the new Scientism, or of all three. Thus, their styles, though undoubtedly grand, can only be fully appreciated by reference to the reactions against the magistral style described in the previous Chapter. They have always the abbreviated, athletic, anti-Ciceronian manner in reserve.

Above all, the men with whom we are here concerned are men of the new age: they are not sixteenth-century humanists

[1] D. Bush, *English Literature in the Earlier Seventeenth Century* (Oxford, 1945), p. 317.

in love with the charm of antiquity or the theology of Thomas Aquinas. Both in ideology and in expression they share the sterner approach of the age of Bacon, the new realism of Hamlet. But they do not write like Bacon either: Browne's writings on the same scientific or psychological topics as Bacon's have a vividness and power which give wide play to Imagination as well as Reason. These writers are capable of analysis, but also of a resonant emotional utterance. This flexibility and this organic richness of sensibility which permit of verbal playfulness and dread seriousness at the same time are marks of what one may justly call a 'unified sensibility'. Such a sensibility, achieved briefly and vividly in a group of poets and prose writers in the middle of the seventeenth century, was not a residue of the Middle Ages, but a product rather of the post-Renaissance and the post-Reformation world as that world temporarily sought a balance and reconciliation of old and new.

We may take Milton as our first example: the first, most obvious thing to say about his prose style is that he does not write like the general run of Puritans:

> I cannot better liken the state and person of a King then to that mighty Nazarite *Samson*; who being disciplin'd from his birth in the precepts and the practice of Temperance and Sobriety, without the strong drink of injurious and excessive desires, grows up to a noble strength and perfection with those his illustrious and sunny locks the laws waving and curling about his god like shoulders.[1]

Milton's eloquence was greatly welcomed by the Puritans because they could make use of it as a match for the eloquence of the Bishops and writers of the anti-Puritan party, but at the same time a Baxter or a Perkins must have been embarrassed by the unpuritan glow of the sentence quoted. *The Reason of Church Government*, the work from which the passage is taken, is probably as near to being a statement of the presbyterian position as Milton ever got, but the kind of enthusiasm which breathes from the passage is nevertheless a strangely non-evangelical enthusaism. Samson, representing Goodness united with Power, the King uniting the religious and political order

---

[1] Milton, *Works* (Columbia Edition, New York, 1931), III, Part 1, 276.

(Milton was later to change his mind about this)—these are symbols which whilst not exactly foreign to presbyterianism, do not form a major theme, a major source of excitement in the writings of presbyterian theologians comparable to their doctrine of Grace or Imputed Righteousness. Here Milton's imagination is geared to a concept of Law, of this-worldly righteousness, and it releases itself accordingly in a glowing pictorial image of controlled physical energy, and in a phraseology resonant with the suggestion of physical beauty, virility, and strength. This is, in fact, Milton giving rein in prose to his poetical impulses—Milton writing in the grand manner. But he also had the capacity for plainness—though not exactly Puritan plainness. He held up as his model 'the Scriptures protesting their own plainnes, and perspicuity',[1] and presented in a vernacular form so as to be understood by all sorts and conditions of men. This is the firm ground of his Reformation piety.

This plainness of Milton's writing can be illustrated even from so formal and 'classical' a piece of oratory as his *Areopagitica* where he often achieves an angry directness and a colloquial thrust unlike anything in the parallel orations of his humanist predecessors:

> When every acute reader upon the first sight of a pedantick licence, will be ready with these like words to ding the book a coits distance from him, I hate a pupil teacher, I endure not an instructer that comes to me under the wardship of an overseeing fist.[2]

The rhythm of Milton's prose is often that of the Bible, and more particularly of the poetic portions of the Hebrew Bible with their parallelistic movement. There is no ostentatious echoing—but it is there nevertheless in such a sentence as the following:

> We boast our light; but if we look not wisely on the Sun itself, it smites us into darknes. Who can discern those planets that are oft *Combust*, and those stars of brightest magnitude that rise and set with the Sun, untill the opposite motion of their orbs bring them

[1] Milton, *Works*, 'Of Reformation in England', p. 32.
[2] *Ibid.*, IV, 325-6.

to such a place in the firmament, where they may be seen evning or morning.[1]

or else:

Lords and Commons of England, consider what Nation it is wherof ye are, and whereof ye are the governours.[2]

Again in the handling of certain images in this work, notably the image of Light ('we boast our light', and 'the full midday beam', etc., cf. *Isaiah* lx) or of truth as a fountain (cf. *Jeremiah* ii, 13, xvii, 13, etc.) we see the influence of the Hebrew Scriptures. But above all, the moral passion and the tone of prophetical rebuke which give to the *Areopagitica* its special *sublimity* of character betray the influence of Amos rather than Demosthenes. The specific prose style of these mid-seventeenth-century writers, the style that we are here seeking to isolate is, in fact, in a special degree Hebraic, and not merely in an external sense as involving a certain colouring of Biblical rhythms and vocabulary, but in a more inward sense also, for this style is inseparable from Hebraic earnestness and sublimity. Longinus long ago, and Coleridge more recently, have taught us that sublimity is a mark of the Hebrew genius, and sublimity is that quality which so often distinguishes these 'Hebraic' prose writers of the mid-seventeenth century from the earlier Ciceronians.

The style of Jeremy Taylor is typically 'golden' and has a certain self-conscious mannerism not unlike that of the Ciceronians of the previous century, but it is again necessary to point out a greater degree of earnestness—an insistence on the importance of the matter in hand, the moral business, which is Hebraic rather than Greek. Taylor enjoys building up a golden image such as 'thus have I seen a river deep and smooth' or 'so have I seen a lark rising from his bed of grass', but the groundwork of his style both in his sermons and in his more sober practical works of casuistry is an expositional rhetoric in which there is no excessive use of schemes and tropes, but rather an earnest pursuit of the idea aided by a marked use of the Hebrew parallelism and a general inclination towards 'doubling' for emphasis:

When the flesh-pots reek, and the uncovered dishes send forth a

[1] *Ibid.*, p. 338.   [2] *Ibid.*, p. 339.

nidor and hungry smells, that cloud hides the face, and puts out the eye of reason.[1]

or else:

> This descending to the grave is the lot of all men, 'neither doth God respect the person of any man', the rich is not protected for favour, nor the poor for pity, the old man is not reverenced for age, nor the infant regarded for his tenderness; youth and beauty, learning and prudence, wit and strength lie down equally in the dishonours of the grave.[2]

The parallelism is a device to be distinguished from mere amplification: to define it rhetorically, one could say that it is a figure of emphasis rather than exornation. The prophets used it for calling attention to the portentousness, the weight of their message:

> Behold a king shall reign in righteousness, and princes shall rule in judgement.
> And a man shall be as an hiding place from the wind, and a covert from the tempest; as rivers of water in a dry place, as the shadow of a great rock in a weary land.
> And the eyes of them that see shall not be dim, and the ears of them that hear shall hearken.
>
> (*Isaiah* xxxii, 1-3)

Something of this urgent rhythm is carried over into the writings of those English divines of the seventeenth century who were most alert to the rhetorical character of the Hebrew Bible. Thomas Adams, 'the prose Shakespeare of Puritan theologians' has a decidedly non-Puritan love of words and an Elizabethan copiousness of phrase, but the pulse-beat of the parallelism preserves the note of single-minded intensity, of gravity, and solemnity:

> When you see an oppressor raising a great house from the ruins of many less, depopulating a country to make up one family, building his parlours with extortion and cementing his walls with the mortar of blood, you say, There is a foul Minotaur in a fair Labyrinth.[3]

---

[1] From his Sermon, 'The House of Feasting', in *Works*, (London, 1837), I, 702.

[2] Funeral Sermon for the Countess of Carbery (1650).

[3] *Works*, ed. J. Angus (*Nichol's Puritan Divines*, Edinburgh, 1862), II, 459.

Hebraic Prose

Among the Divines of the non-Puritan party, the Biblical style is perhaps most clearly revealed in the sermons of Donne. The latest editors of Donne's sermons whilst drawing attention to the Senecan element in his style have done well to insist also on the central importance of the Biblical parallelism as a feature in his developed pulpit-manner.[1] I suspect that the parallelistic mode of asseveration was of special value to Donne in that it afforded him the possibility of combining in one type of discourse the advantages of Rhetoric and Dialectic. The traditional sermon was supposed to provide both these elements, and this was usually achieved by a division of the sermon into separate parts, logical and exegetical analysis coming at the beginning, and rhetorical adornment, towards the end.[2] Donne's mode of composition was less discerptive than this; he aimed at being extremely dialectical and extremely vehement at one and the same time. The 'strain of passionate ratiocination'[3] which, we are told, marks his metaphysical poetry is no less evident in his prose. In the prose the key to this union of thought and feeling may be found in the parallelistic mode which enabled him to combine logical emphasis and rhetorical amplitude. For parallelism is a specific device of non-dissociated discourse. In *Job* it is used for argument and debate, but also for elegy and lyric.

Moreover, Donne was fully conscious of the special value for his purpose of the Rhetoric of the Scriptures. He tells us in Sermon LV that for him, 'there are not in all the world so eloquent Books as the Scriptures' and that they are furnished 'with height of metaphors and other figures'. The Holy Ghost,

---

[1] The *Sermons of John Donne*, ed. G. R. Potter and E. M. Simpson (California University Press, 1953), Introduction to vol. I, pp. 88 f. 'His sermons are saturated with the language of Hebrew poetry, and also with its parallelism and antithesis.'

[2] The 'parts' of the Sermon resemble the 'parts' of the Oration as taught in the sixteenth-century rhetoric manuals of Thomas Wilson and others. In Bartholomew Keckermann, *Rhetoricae Ecclesiasticae* (Hanover, 1606), the two elements of the sermon are said to be 'textus tractatio' and 'tractorum exornatio' (p. 33). The detailed partition of the Sermon is as follows: '1. Praecognitio textus. 2. Partitio et propositio. 3. Explicatio verborum. 4. Amplificatio. 5. Applicatio' (p. 41).

[3] H. J. C. Grierson, *Metaphysical Lyrics and Poems of the Seventeenth Century* (Oxford, 1921), Introduction, p. xxxv.

43

he says elsewhere, in a penetrating observation, is 'a vehement, and an abundant author, but yet not luxuriant'. (Sermon LXXIX.) These should be hints sufficient to enable us to find in the Scriptures the key to certain leading features of his own prose style. He may turn sometimes to the spiral movement of Senecan prose for the analytical portions of his sermons, and to formal Ciceronianism for occasional 'sonorous harmonies of sound' but the more urgent pulse beat of the parallelism carries the main emotional emphasis and the central argument.

To put it very simply, one could say that the advantage of the Biblical style for Donne, Taylor, Milton and many others was that it enabled the prose writer to preserve in his prose medium something of the depth and energy of poetry. Is *Ecclesiastes* prose or verse? It would be hard to say. The first two Chapters are, I suppose, prose, but prose which has taken on an extra suggestiveness and emotional stress. At the same time, the patterning has the minimum of formality. The parallelism gives us the energy of poetry without its formal discipline. The idea rather than the form is supreme. Indeed, the formal distinction between prose and poetry determined by the practical object of the former as against the aesthetic values of the latter are foreign to the Hebrew spirit. If we were to consider the type of moral philosophy (signified by the Hebrew term *Hokhmah*) which the book seeks to inculcate we would notice likewise that it takes in rational expediency, but also wonder, awe, and devotion. This itself tends to demand an appropriately rich and flexible style which shall have the extra weight of poetical expression in reserve. Koheleth has something of the irony and disillusionment of the Stoic-Cynic diatribes, as well as something of their dialectical manner,[1] but unlike the Stoics (and unlike Bacon) the Jewish sage can drop his irony and detachment and give rein to a more personal and emotional impulse. The self-sufficiency of the Stoic philosopher is finally lacking:

> Be not rash with thy mouth, and let not thine heart be hasty to utter any thing before God: for God is in heaven, and thou upon earth: therefore let thy words be few. (v. 2.)

[1] Cf. R. Gordis, *Koheleth—The Man and his World* (New York, 1955), pp. 52-3.

And then one remembers the grave elegiac poetry of the last Chapter on the approach of old age and death, compared to the onset of the wet season in the Land of Israel:

> Remember now thy Creator in the days of thy youth, while the evil days come not, nor the years draw nigh, when thou shalt say, I have no pleasure in them. While the sun, or the light, or the moon, or the stars, be not darkened, nor the clouds return after the rain.

Without the formalities of verse, this is surely deeply imagined poetry; but it is flexible enough to alternate with a kind of dry prose, detached, ironical, even humorous, as when the Preacher, after having 'set in order many proverbs', wryly warns his disciples that 'of making many books there is no end; and much study is a weariness of the flesh'.

This particular Hebrew model, that of the Wisdom Books, inspired as a matter of fact a great many English prose writers of the early and mid-seventeenth century and helped them to achieve a warmer, more morally impassioned type of essay-style than that available on the models of Seneca and Tacitus. There is, for instance, Sir Walter Ralegh, whose book of moral guidance, addressed to his son (*Instructions to his Son*, 1632) has to my knowledge never been considered from this point of view. He cautions his son against drunkenness in a style which is neither Ciceronian, nor Senecan, but that of the Wisdom Literature of the Bible:

> Take heed therefore that such a careless canker pass not thy youth, nor such a beastly infection thy old age.[1]

Or else he advises his son to avoid duelling.

> To shun therefore the private fight, be well advised in thy Words and Behaviour, for Honour and Shame is in the Talk and the Tongue of Man causeth him to fall.

Sometimes the parallelism is less obtrusive, as in the opening paragraph of the treatise, but it forms the basis of the style of the work which is punctuated by frequent quotations from the Wisdom Books, *Proverbs* and *Ecclesiastes*. Joseph Hall had also in his treatise *Salomons Divine Arts* (1609) tried to build up a

---

[1] *Works*, ed. Birch (London, 1751), II, 342.

system of 'Human Philosophy' based upon extensive direct quotation (without supplementary comment) from the Wisdom Books.

Thomas Fuller followed Montaigne and Bacon in the loose moral essay genre in his *Holy and Profane State* (1642) but differed from them in introducing the tone and rhythm of the English Bible and together with that something of its attitude of wonder and reverence. But the most colourful practitioner of the Hebrew style in England at this period was not strictly a divine or a moral essayist (although he occasionally undertook to speak in both these capacities) but rather a scientist. That writer is Thomas Browne. Browne, like Milton and Donne, read the Bible as an eloquent achievement of holy rhetoric. And this led him to adopt a style which, whilst admittedly original, even idiosyncratic, had behind it the antithetical and balanced rhythms of the Hebrew Bible. Thus from the *Hydriotaphia*,

> But who knows the fate of his bones, or how often he is to be buried?
> who hath the Oracle of his ashes, or whether they are to be scattered?[1]

Examples could be multiplied from many of Browne's works, especially the *Religio Medici*, but the more imaginatively adorned *Hydriotaphia* gives us his stylistic features in their most ample deployment. It has wit and antithesis, as well as passages of emotional expansiveness.

The *Hydriotaphia* (1658) is intended as an anthropological account of ancient burial customs supported by expert evidence (based on observation and experiment) about bodily putrefaction. As a follower of Bacon, Browne shows us the scientific style of report adopted, and then broken through, as the writer catches a glimpse of some truth, denied to, or at any rate excluded by, the Baconian world-view. He insisted in the manner of Bacon that 'strict and definitive expressions'[2] must be the basis of a correct style for philosophy, and indeed in his tone of detachment, his use of technical terms, and his direct-

---

[1] *The Works of Sir Thomas Browne*, ed. Charles Sayle (Edinburgh, 1927), from the 'Epistle Dedicatory' prefixed to *Hydriotaphia*; III, 89.
[2] *Pseudodoxia Epidemica*, Book I, ch. 9. *Works*, I, 179.

ness of syntax, he is often seen pursuing the Baconian task honestly and competently:

> A full spread *Cariola* shews a well-shaped horse behinde, handsome formed sculls, give some analogy of flesh resemblance. A critical view of bones makes a good distinction of sexes. Even colour is not beyond conjecture, since it is hard to be deceived in the distinction of *Negro's* sculls.[1]

But soon we find the tone of detachment drops: the writer is held fascinated by the paradox of Man's physical decay and the gloriousness of his self-assertion even in death:

> But man is a Noble Animal, splendid in ashes, and pompous in the grave, solemnizing Nativities and Deaths with equal lustre, nor omitting Ceremonies of bravery, in the infamy of his nature.
> Life is a pure flame, and we live by an invisible Sun within us. . . .[2]

There is even a touch here of Ciceronian eloquence (the repeated use of the *cursus* is noteworthy), but the sun and light imagery is Biblical. Elsewhere we have the same type of imagery, of which Browne was particularly fond, in an undoubtedly Biblical context:

> Light that makes things seen, makes some things invisible, were it not for darknesse and the shadow of the earth, the noblest part of the Creation had remained unseen, and the Stars in heaven as invisible as on the fourth day, when they were created above the Horizon, with the Sun, or there was not an eye to behold them. The grandest mystery of Religion is expressed by adumbration, and in the noblest of Jewish Types, we find the Cherubims shadowing the Mercy-seat: Life it self is but the shadow of death, and souls departed but the shadows of the living: All things fall under this name. The Sunne it self is but the dark *simulachrum*, and light but the shadow of God.[3]

The sinewiness, the occasional brevity, the use of antithesis, and the telling simplicity of much of this passage show well the influence of the Senecan movement. But there is an emotional emphasis about it, especially at the end which suggests that the illumination sought is more profound and inclusive, and at the same time, more obscure, than that pursued by the Senecan

[1] *Ibid.*, III, 125. [2] *Ibid.*, III, 142.
[3] *The Garden of Cyrus*, ch. 4. *Works*, III, 199-200.

essayists. In the last sent ence, the Biblical parallelism is evident, just as the imagery throughout is Biblical.

Amongst the Anglican bishops of the *via media*, special mention should be made of Joseph Hall, a considerable literary figure whose style, originally formed in the Elizabethan Age, had been chastened through the influence of such men as Laurence Chaderton whilst he was a student at that most famous of Puritan seminaries, Emmanuel College in Cambridge. In addition to these Puritan austerities, he had also, like so many of the younger philosophical writers at the beginning of the seventeenth century, taken a deep imprint from the short-breathed, antithetical style of Seneca's Epistles and Moral Essays. He was known in his own day as the Christian Seneca, and in fact it was he who introduced the Senecan epistle as a new genre in English, adapting the contents to Christian needs.

But as a matter of fact, Hall in his fully developed style was neither a Senecan practitioner of the neat moral theorem, nor a Puritan logic-chopper. In his Essay, 'Heaven upon Earth'—an imitation both in style and contents of Seneca's 'De Tranquillitate Animi'—he dismisses the Pagan precepts for tranquillity with the words, 'Not Athens must teach this lesson, but Jerusalem', and at the same time he leaves behind the Senecan clipped dialectic and goes over to a more ample style in the middle sections of his treatise.[1]

But Hall's most successful employment of 'holy Rhetoric' is not in his Essays or Epistles, but rather in that special devotional form which he helped to naturalize in England and which later enjoyed a remarkable vogue not only amongst theologians but amongst religiously minded men of letters generally. That special *genre* is the Meditation.[2] His two Centuries of Meditations published in 1605, were merely the first of a series of publications of this kind which continued to appear from his pen until a few years before his death, and his long line of followers and imitators testifies to a wide and instant popularity. In devising a pattern which should relate his observations

---

[1] For fuller treatment, see H. Fisch, 'The Limits of Hall's Senecanism', *Proceedings of the Leeds Philosophical Society* (Leeds, 1950), VI, Part vii, 453-63.

[2] For fuller treatment, see H. Fisch, 'Bishop Hall's Meditations', *R.E.S.* (Oxford, 1949), XXV, 210-21.

of human life and external nature to Divine Truth as far as he was able to apprehend it, he went back, like Augustine before him, to the Hebrew Scriptures, and especially the Book of *Psalms*. Nor did he use its style and imagery simply as an apparatus of Rhetoric: he tried to grasp its spirit, its attitude, and its organic form.

The practice of meditating on the Book of Creatures or on episodes from daily life had been developed by a number of continental writers as a normal literary-religious activity, and it has a certain basis in the Counter-Reformation spirituality outlined in the *Exercises* of Ignatius Loyola;[1] but, for the Protestant, the immediate inspiration, especially for the brief or ejaculatory Meditation, was undoubtedly the Book of Psalms itself. This is also the case with Robert Bellarmin, whose influential treatise, *The Mind's Ascent to God by a Ladder of Created Things* refers to the Psalmist as the primary model for the soul in meditation.[2] And there can be no doubt that a *literary* use was made of this Biblical model after the manner of the current practice of literary 'Imitation' applied to the ancient orators

---

[1] The immediate sources of the Meditation-genre have been traced by Louis Martz, in a valuable study, *The Poetry of Meditation* (Yale, 1954). He perhaps overstresses the importance of the continental examples and authorities, such as Loyola, Bellarmin, and St. François de Sales. Undoubtedly they exercised a great influence on the Anglican divines, but in the case of Hall, Professor Martz is pursuing a false trail in laying stress on the *Rosetum* of Joannes Mauburnus, itself based on the earlier *Scala Meditationis* of Johan Wessel of Gansfort. This is indeed the rhetorical pattern alluded to by Hall in his treatise, *The Art of Divine Meditation* (1606), but it is a pattern for the *long* meditation, and he makes it clear that there is no such artificial pattern for the shorter or ejaculatory Meditation. It is the short Meditation which he himself chiefly practised both then and later and which became the chief literary genre associated with his name. Of this type of writing he tells us, '*there may be much use, no rule* . . . In this kind, was that meditation of the divine Psalmist; which upon the view of the glorious frame of the heavens, was led to wonder at the merciful respect God hath to so poor a creature as man. . . .' (*Art of Divine Meditation*, ch. 3). The reference here to the eighth Psalm points to Hall's true literary model. Professor Martz indeed gives proper weight elsewhere in his book to the Psalms as literary and imaginative inspiration, 'In the Psalms lay the prime models for the soul in meditation: here, above all places, lay a precedent for . . . the poetry of meditation' (p. 279).
[2] Robert Bellarmin, *The Mind's Ascent to God by a Ladder of Created Things* (1615), trans. Morialis (ed., London, 1925), p. 92.

and poets of Greece and Rome. The Meditation-structure of the Psalms as well as their typical style and imagery was imitated. The great names associated with the Meditation-genre in England are Hall, Traherne, Jeremy Taylor, and Robert Boyle. Thomas Browne's *Religio Medici* and *Hydriotaphia* may be said also, in a certain sense, to belong to this genre.

What is the essential literary structure implied by the term 'Meditation'? Briefly, it may be said that the Meditation-writer develops a habit of extending through symbolism and moral commentary, the imaginative reference of the matter in hand. There is a progression from observed or related phenomenon (called by the continental theorists the *compositio loci*) through moral analysis, to a direct act of faith or devotion in which the meditating subject addresses God in thanksgiving or prayer (colloquy).[1] One could start from anywhere (even funeral urns), but one came back to the still centre. A good example of Hall's early method is to be found in the second Century of his *Centuries of Meditation*, on the theme (broadly speaking) of false security:

> We pittie the folly of the Larke, which (while it playeth with the fether, and stoopeth to the glasse) is caught in the fowlers net. . . .

The application, or *apodosis*, brings in echoes from the *Psalter*

> O Lord, keep thou mine eyes from beholding vanitie. And though mine eyes see it, let not my heart stoope to it, but loath it afarre off. And if I stoope at any time, and be taken, set thou my soule at libertie: that I may say, My soule is escaped, even as a bird out of the snare of the Fowler; the snare is broken, and I am delivered.[2]

This, it should be noted, is not merely a moral comment on a Biblical text: it is also a comment on the habits of the lark. Such a Meditation has a strongly personal element as well as an individual contact with external reality. There is a real movement of the mind from the outer to the inner experience, or more strictly, from what Buber would call, the sphere of the I/It to the sphere of the I/Thou, and this is reflected in the formal

[1] Cf. Martz, *op. cit.*, p. 34.
[2] *Meditations and Vowes* (1605), Century II, No. 25. *Works* (London, 1634), p. 21.

arrangement of *protasis* and *apodosis*. In the Meditation, Hall had found a pattern whereby he could bring the secular into the sphere of religion. 'I should hate all secular diversions,' he wrote towards the end of his life, 'if they should take thee for a moment quite out of my sight; if I did not find that I may still refer them to thee and enjoy thee in them.'[1]

There can be no doubt that here, in the Meditation, the devotional writers had found an authentically Hebrew imaginative structure. The Psalms are not marked by a formal design anything like so rigid as that applied by the Meditation-writers in their schematic use of the Rule of Three: composition, analysis, and colloquy; but there is in *Psalms* viii, xix, xciii, and many others, a similar though freer movement from the visual phenomenon to the argued moral thesis, and from that to the direct expression of wonder at, or submission to, the divine will. The nineteenth Psalm is in this respect something of an archetype and was so regarded by Bellarmin and Jeremy Taylor. The first six verses represent the impact of the sunrise on the poet's consciousness—'his going forth is from the ends of the earth'; then there is immediately following this the moral thesis, the consideration of the *Torah* or moral law, which is felt, like the sun, to enlighten the eyes; and in the final sentence, the poet considers what he has written and humbly offers his Meditation to God, 'Let the words of my mouth, and the meditation of my heart, be acceptable, in thy sight.'[2] This type of Psalm brings together in an organic form the spheres of Man, God, and Nature; there is a high degree of introspection, but at the same time there is a contemplation of outer physical reality, and finally a direct address to a divine otherness whose presence is felt to be no less real than that of the other two factors con-

---

[1] *Susurrium cum Deo* (1650).

[2] Many (though by no means all) modern critics hold that this Psalm was not originally composed as a unity, and they would divide the second part (concerned with the moral law) from the first part (dealing with the images from the realm of Nature). The obvious literary balance and cohesion of the Psalm seem to be an important argument against this view of some textual critics, as I have argued elsewhere (see 'The Analogy of Nature', *J.T.S.* (Oxford, 1955), N.S., VI, 171-2). At all events, seventeenth-century readers of the Bible were not perplexed by such speculations and, happily undisillusioned by Higher Criticism, would enjoy the Psalm as an imaginative unity, and proceed to imitate it.

cerned. It may be claimed that in this type of writing we have an example of a deeply integrated consciousness; description, intellect, and emotion, or, as Jeremy Taylor puts it, Memory, Understanding, and Will, are engaged together in a single imaginative act:

> For supposing our memory instructed with the knowledge of such mysteries and revelations as are apt to entertain the spirit, the understanding is first employed in the consideration of them, and then the will in their reception, when they are duly prepared and so transmitted; and both these in such manner, and to such purposes, that they become the magazine and great repositories of grace, and instrumental to designs of virtue.[1]

It should be noted that although the Puritans were great Psalm-singers they were not as prominent in the writing of literary Meditations based on the Psalms as were the moderate Anglicans such as Hall, Taylor, and Traherne. These men it seems were readier to use the Biblical model as a basis for creative work, and they were also more in sympathy than were the strict Puritans with the practical piety of the Psalmists. The final phrase in the passage from Jeremy Taylor just quoted refers to the Meditations as 'instrumental to designs of virtue'. And this emphasis is entirely in keeping with the practical Divinity which marked the great Caroline Anglican preachers. They were conscious of the Meditation as providing a link between the inner world of spiritual religion and the outer world of practical righteousness. In one of his later Meditations, Hall clearly relates (in one of those echoes of the nineteenth Psalm which we constantly come across in this type of writing) the observation of the heavens to the demands of a practical piety:

> The motion of this thy heaven is perpetual; so let me ever be acting somewhat of thy will: the motion of thy heaven is regular, never swerving from the due points; so let me ever walk steadily in the ways of thy will, without all diversions or variations from the line of thy law.[2]

This kind of emphasis on the devotional act as a spur to moral

---

[1] *Works*, I, 66.

[2] *Occasional Meditations* (1630), No. 1, in *Works*, ed. P. Wynter (Oxford, 1863), X, 121.

activity is not precisely Calvinist; it is more typical of the moderate Anglicans, of the 'Arminian nunnery' at Little Gidding, and of such practically oriented parish-priests as George Herbert and Thomas Traherne. We shall note in the next Chapter how Herbert made use of the Meditation-pattern in his poetry; here we may close our consideration of the prose-writers with Traherne.

Traherne was perhaps of all the religious writers of the seventeenth century the most deeply conscious of the *Psalms* as a model for writing and as a model for the good life. His *Thanksgivings* are in some passages little more than a pastiche of Psalm-poetry, and their unconventional rhythms (for this is a kind of free-verse) suggest also an adaptation of Biblical versification.[1] But his most creative and original use of the inspiration of the *Psalms* is in his *Meditations*, in which he relates how the reading of the Psalms became to him the entrance into a vision of the true beauty of the world around him, as well as the entrance into the world of divinity itself.

> When I saw those Objects celebrated in His Psalmes which GOD and Nature had proposed to me, and which I thought chance only presented to my view: you cannot imagine how unspeakably I was delighted, to see so Glorious a Person, so Great a Prince, so Divine a Sage, that was a Man after Gods own Heart by the testimony of God himself, rejoycing in the same things, meditating on the same and Praising GOD for the same. For by this I perceived we were led by one Spirit: and that following the clew of Nature into this Labyrinth I was brought into the midst of Celestial Joys. . . .[2]

He retraces the imaginative path taken by David in much the same way as the average Puritan retraced the spiritual road taken by the Apostle Paul. He tells us in Meditation 66 of the third Century, for instance, that he sees clearly how the experience of David is the normative religious experience, 'the Way of Communion with God in all Saints'. Having perceived this, he says, 'Me thoughts a New Light Darted in into all his Psalmes, and finaly spread abroad over the whole Bible.'[3] The Psalms

---

[1] *Thomas Traherne: Centuries, Poems, and Thanksgivings*, ed. H. M. Margoliouth (Oxford, 1958), I, Introduction, p. x.
[2] *The Third Century*, No. 70, *ibid.*, I, 153.
[3] *Ibid.*, p. 148.

had, throughout the Middle Ages, been regarded as a pattern for devotion, but here is a sense of *new* revelation shining in, something related to the new awareness of the outer reality fostered by the new natural science.

In considering the various kinds of Hebraism available in the seventeenth century, therefore, due prominence must be given to the literary and devotional effort based upon the reading of the *Psalms*. This indeed did not produce a gaudy Rhetoric but it produced an echo of the still small voice of God addressed to the soul and the answering murmur of the soul in prayer or meditation. It proved to be a capital source of inspiration both in prose and poetry, and particularly among the literary men (both ecclesiastical and non-ecclesiastical) who stand outside the zone of doctrinal Puritanism, or even of political Puritanism. There were of course other kinds of Hebraic literature based on other parts of the Hebrew Bible. Milton's religious poetry and combative prose tends to draw on *Judges*, *Samuel*, and *Kings* for its inspiration; Donne, tormented with problems of guilt and expiation, with thoughts of death and corruption, turned to the more involved poetry of *Job*. The essayists and moralists, as we have seen, found examples in *Ecclesiastes* and *Proverbs*. But we shall constantly return to the Book of *Psalms* as the primary source of the literature of Meditation. And it stood not only as a literary pattern but as sanction and authority also. Jeremy Taylor tells us that it is in the Psalms that we are commanded to derive 'arguments of worship and Religion' from the 'Book of Creatures'.

> And this is the cause holy Scripture commands the duty of meditation in proportion still to the excellencies of piety and holy life, to which it is highly and aptly instrumental. 'Blessed is the man that meditates in the law of the Lord day and night.'[1]

Nor should we suppose that in deriving moral arguments from birds and flowers, and from events of daily life, these writers were merely allegorists finding sermons in trees, merely seeing the objects of Nature as convenient pegs wherein to hang their neatly constructed moral ideas. There was in Traherne, in Herbert, and Jeremy Taylor, and even Hall, a genuine meeting

[1] Discourse 'Of Meditation', in *The Great Exemplar* (1649), Part I, sec. v, Discourse III.

with Nature, a radiant openness to experience. They were aware of the world around us and of the experience of our daily life, as the arena of revelation; and the revelational tone of Traherne's *Meditations* preserves them from wooden allegory. Indeed, such writers when meditating (like Hall) on a spider in the window, or (like Marvell) on a drop of dew, or (like Vaughan) on a waterfall, were not engaged in the pursuit of allegorical fancies, but in the imaginative discovery of symbols, in the search for some existential principle of unity between the outer and inner world, between the secular and the sacred. Undoubtedly, there is in this much of the medieval world-picture, with its theory of correspondence between the inner and outer realities; but we note an altogether new urgency and intensity here.

These writers whom we have considered above both overtly in their doctrines and obliquely in style and image were seeking certain insights relating to Man, God, and Nature which evidently the open Bible of the Reformation could provide. At this moment it is the stylistic aspect which interests us most. Wherever prose has tried to break down the boundaries dividing it from poetry (and *vice versa*) the example of the Hebrew Scripture with its elastic transitions from logic to rhetoric, from narrative to oracle, from hortatory to devotional, has been of service. We shall shortly consider the position from the aspect of poetry proper which in the seventeenth century likewise owed an important debt in the matter of style and structure to the Hebrew Bible. But it is worth bearing in mind that this is not only a matter of the seventeenth century. It is found earlier in the antiphonal plain-song of the Middles Ages, and later, in the writings of William Blake and Walt Whitman, the freedom of whose loose-limbed parallelistic verse has an obvious, and acknowledged Biblical background. In all such examples, the influence of the Bible has been directed to greater freedom, to the breaking down of formal boundaries, to the integration of thought and feeling, to the subjection of aesthetic to moral impulses, and to the promotion of ideas held to be greater ultimately than the writer or his work.

IV

HEBRAIC POETRY

WE HAVE been concerned so far with Biblical models for 'holy Rhetoric' and this may have led to a certain undue emphasis on stylistic flourish, height, and colour. But as a matter of fact, a Hebraic style—especially in poetry—may turn out to be simpler and less adorned, less supplied with the 'figures' of rhetoric, than a non-Hebraic style. Joseph Hall, whom we have claimed as a Hebraic writer (and who certainly considered himself as such) discussed the problem of style in his *Holy Observations* (1607) and took up a characteristically moderate position corresponding to the *Via Media* which he counselled in Theology:

> Truth hath a face both honest and comely, and lookes best in her owne colours: but above all, Divine Truth is most faire, and most scorneth to borrow beauty of mans wit or tongue . . . Againe, she would be plaine, but not base, not sluttish: she would be clad, not garishly, yet not in rags: She likes as little to be set out by a base soile, as to seeme credited with gay colours. It is no small wisdome to know her just guise, but more to follow it; and so to keep the meane, that while we please her, we discontent not the beholders.[1]

Hall here is fully conscious of the virtues of simplicity and plain-ness, for Truth 'scorneth to borrow beauty of man's wit or tongue', nevertheless he clearly has in mind something other than the negative, Puritan ideal of austerity in writing. The sort of plainness which he is seeking and which, at his best, he attained, is one which constituted in itself a genuine literary merit as that form of elocution which alone might convey the fullness of a certain kind of experience.

We are reminded of the similar standpoint of Hall's con-temporary, George Herbert—likewise an exponent of the *Via Media*—who declared in his famous 'Jordan',

[1] *Holy Observations*, No. 22. *Works, ed. cit.*, VII, 528.

Hebraic Poetry

Who sayes that fictions onely and false hair
Become a verse? Is there in Truth no beautie?

We have spoken earlier of the extreme plainness of the 'dissociated' styles in Bacon and the Puritans, but we should not conclude that the integrated and healthy imagination necessarily finds expression in a copious rhetoric. It may very well turn out in many cases to be the other way round: a dissociated Rhetoric set against a deeply imagined and emotionally controlled simplicity. It is the latter that we find in Herbert's poetry,

> Throw away thy rod,
> Throw away thy wrath:
>   O my God,
> Take the gentle path.
>
> For my heart's desire
> Unto thine is bent:
>   I aspire
> To a full consent.[1]

One of the differences between the 'Hebraic' writers and the doctrinal Puritans is that the latter flattened the poetry of the Hebrew Bible into prose (we remember Anthony Wotton's Ramist paraphrase of the twenty-third Psalm), whilst the former managed (even in prose) to preserve the poetic vibrations of the Hebrew. Herbert's poetry has its roots deep in the Psalter, and its simplicity is that of the Psalmist.[2]

In the twenty-third Psalm, which Herbert, like many another English poet before him, turned into English verse, we have those great, simple, and universal images which vibrate through all the levels of consciousness: the valley of the shadow of death, the still waters, the green pastures, the overflowing cup, the path through the unknown land. These images are, in the final analysis, profoundly ambiguous; they invite a multiple

[1] *The Works of George Herbert*, ed. F. E. Hutchinson (Oxford, 1941), p. 178.
[2] On Herbert's debt to the lyric tradition of Sidney and Campion and in particular to their limpid versions of the *Psalms*, see L. Martz, *op. cit.*, pp. 260-70. Professor Martz fails to do full justice to the *immediate* inspiration of the *Psalms* in Herbert's poetry, but there is sufficient evidence of this (if the reader conscious of the Biblical tradition requires such evidence) throughout Hutchinson's valuable Commentary to the poems.

sense exegesis, for they have the ambiguity of all primary symbolism. This richness is preserved by Herbert.

The Psalter provided Herbert with just that type of spiritual poetry, simple, passionate, and meditative, which he needed to bring his delicate yet masculine genius to full expression. The Hebrew Psalms articulate in simple primary images the human need for confession, prayer, and trust. As a literary document, they provide the prototype for that special kind of subjective poetry in which the soul addresses itself to a personal God who deals with His creatures in love and justice. He is represented as the Shepherd (xxiii, lxxx), the confidence of the everlasting hills (lxxxvii, cxxi); at the same time, he is seated in the heavens (ii), and by the voice of his thunder he causes the hills to skip like rams (cxiv). He is the great water-giver who 'causes the grass to grow for the cattle and herb for the service of man' (civ), and by analogy, he is also the giver of spiritual water 'satisfying the longing soul, and filling the hungry soul with goodness' (cvii). He appoints the light of the sun (civ), and by the same token, he 'sows' light for the righteous and gladness for the upright in heart (xcvii).

The Psalms are often spoken of as lyric poetry, and compared to the lyric poetry of other nations, for instance that of England in the Romantic Period. Such a definition has more value than most definitions of this kind. The Hebrew poet singing a song of praise, 'Sing unto the Lord a new song'—is engaged in just that spontaneous overflow of powerful and melodious feeling which we are told is the essence of lyrical poetry. But it is necessary to bear in mind a certain phenomenological difference between the lyric poems of the English romantics and the typical Hebrew Psalm: the former is essentially monologue, the latter is essentially dialogue. The *Sitz im Leben* of the romantic poet, is symbolized by the lines of Wordsworth,

> Behold her, single in the field,
> Yon solitary Highland Lass!
> Reaping and singing by herself;
> Stop here or gently pass!

The solitary reaper does not answer nor does the poet address her; on the contrary, she is herself the symbol of the poet's own essential isolation. The romantic poet will often commune with

Nature, but this is communion, not dialogue. There is blending, the abolition of separateness—again Wordsworth's stoical pantheism is typical of this tendency—but there is no distinct confrontation of self with an autonomous outer reality; there is no *dramatic* encounter. This is perhaps the reason why the romantic poets in England were unable to write true drama. Byron's *Cain* is, like his lyrics, essentially monologue.

Now, the Psalms are typically a song for two voices addressing one another in the intimate drama of the covenant-relation, the covenant that is to say as the bond between the soul and God. They are not so much the spontaneous overflow of powerful feelings as, to use the title of one of Hall's later devotional tracts, a *Susurrium cum Deo*. In such whispered dialogue the human speaker does not fill the overflowing vale with his sole unaccompanied voice, nor does he abandon his personality by a contemplative act of mystical self-effacement. He and his divine interlocutor remain confronting each other to the last, separate, and yet held together by indestructible bonds:

> O Lord, my God, I cried out to thee,
> And thou hast healed me.

Both the cry and the answered consolation are made real in the poem. There is a call and a response, giving to the poem a dramatic movement. A Psalm such as lxi or cxxx will begin 'out of the depths' of trouble and hopelessness and as a result of the exchange of vows, or of prayer and acceptance, which the Psalm celebrates, it will end on a note of comfort and assurance. This is a typical movement. In this respect it is an active rather than a contemplative type of lyric poetry; it involves a movement through dialogue from one position to another.

George Herbert's meditation poetry, like that of George Wither, is essentially of this kind, and needless to say, it goes back in many instances to his careful reading and paraphrasing of the *Psalms*. One of them is in fact entitled, *Dialogue*, but the pattern may be traced throughout the *Temple* even in less obvious examples such as the following from the poem entitled, 'An Offering.'

> Since my sadnesse
> Into gladnesse
> Lord thou dost convert,

O accept
What thou hast kept,
As thy due desert.[1]

This type of Divine Poetry in the seventeenth century is clearly more strictly *religious* than other forms of literature basing themselves on Biblical examples. For it is possible to imagine a completely secular paraphrase of the historical portions of the Bible—which would omit the theological dimension; Peele's play of *King David and Fair Bethsabe* (1599) is such a Divine Drama lacking in religious inwardness,[2] but the poetry of meditation and dialogue finds its most authentic direction in the exploration of the soul's relation to God.

It is not surprising that this very individualistic poetry expressing this essentially personal religious experience should have grown up in the era of Puritanism and of the Counter-Reformation, and yet it is worth noting that none of its exponents are thoroughgoing doctrinal Puritans. The reason is not far to seek: this Meditation-poetry as displayed in Donne, Herbert, Vaughan, and Marvell presupposes as the meditating subject an essentially moral agent standing freely and independently over against the transcendent otherness of a divine partner: such colloquy is not precisely compatible with the Calvinist sense of an unconditioned divine sovereignty which nullifies the value of human freedom. Nor is it essentially compatible with a Catholic mystical type of experience as in Crashaw where the emotional powers are uppermost and the elements of debate, of genuine struggle, are not so evident, the meditating subject seeking rather to indulge in a luxury of religious sensation. The type of meditative poetry I am trying to isolate here is more strenuous, earnest, and controlled; it brings together the various powers of the soul into a unity—the contemplative and active sides, the rational and the emotional. Herbert has such titles as *Employment*, *Discipline*, *Vertue*, all of

---

[1] *The Works of George Herbert*, ed. cit., p. 147.

[2] Lily B. Campbell, in her *Divine Poetry and Drama in Sixteenth Century England* (Cambridge, 1959), pp. 4-5, makes a useful distinction between divine poetry and devotional poetry. Of the former (of which Peele's play would be an example) she remarks, 'it is the subject-matter of the poem or drama that makes it divine poetry or divine drama and not the religious or non-religious attitude of the author'.

which stress the practical moral side of his religion, the element of significant, human choice. In the following poem, submission and self-assertion are held in a perfect balance which is at once formal and doctrinal—the final note is one of active endeavour:

> Do not beguile my heart,
>   Because thou art
> My power and wisdome. Put me not to shame,
>   Because I am
>   Thy clay that weeps, thy dust that calls.
>
> Thou art the Lord of glorie;
>   The deed and storie
> Are both thy due: but I a silly flie,
>   That live or die
>   According as the weather falls.
>
> Art thou all justice, Lord?
>   Shows not thy word
> More attributes? Am I all throat or eye,
>   To weep or crie?
>   Have I no parts but those of grief?
>
> Let not thy wrathfull power
>   Afflict my houre,
> My inch of life: or let thy gracious power
>   Contract my houre,
>   That I may climbe and finde relief.
>   (*Complaining*)[1]

Herbert is capable of a simple doctrinal gesture—of a prayerful mood lacking in dialectical strain, but his characteristic poetry reveals a certain tension owing to the juxtaposition either in sequence or in balance of the various opposing forces of the religious life. A characteristic opening line would be that of 'The Collar',

> I Struck the board, and cry'd, No more . . .

and a typical closing line would be (from the same poem)

> Me thoughts I heard one calling, *Child!*
> And I reply'd, *My Lord*.

[1] *Works, ed. cit.*, pp. 143-4.

From this constant arbitrating between the human and the divine engaged in the covenantal *rencontre*, arise the undecorated quality of the language, the strenuous and athletic quality of the verse, the leaping from point to point in the effort to arrive at a point of rest or illumination, all of which are marked characteristics of the poets mentioned in this section. It sometimes seems to me that the term 'dialogic' would be better as a means of classifying this type of poetry than 'metaphysical'. To Metaphysics after all belongs the contemplation of paradoxes: the One and the Many, Soul and Body, etc. But in the work of Marvell, for instance, such paradoxes are as often as not handled in dialogue form giving to the speculation a certain dramatic character.[1] Even Donne's non-religious poetry has this tendency to replace the pure lyric by something more colloquial, more dialogic.[2] Our concern is here with the religious poetry of the metaphysical poets, and especially that part of it which in diction, rhythm, and mood clearly reveals a biblical lineage; but it is right to be aware that this influence in the seventeenth century is both deeper and more pervasive than such a limited consideration would suggest.

[1] I have in mind such examples as 'A Dialogue Between the Soul and Body' and 'A Dialogue between the Resolved Soul and Created Pleasure'. There is possibly the influence here of the Platonic dialogue-form; but the whole subject deserves to be explored further. One thing is clear, and that is that the dialogue-form is much rarer in later periods of English poetry, when the Biblical examples had less force.

[2] As a final example one might mention also the earlier work of George Wither, a poet who at his best approached the strength of George Herbert. He achieves a dramatic, dialogue quality in such a poem as 'For a Musician' from *Hallelujah* (1641). His *Emblemes* (1635) are clearly patterned on the Meditation plan, of description, analysis, and prayer. There is no doubt that in all this he was deeply indebted to the Book of *Psalms* on which he directly based much of his poetry and prose.

His paraphrases and metaphrases of the *Psalms* form an instructive bibliography. There is *A Preparation to the Psalter* (1619); *Exercises Vpon the first Psalme. Both in Prose and Verse* (1620); *The Songs of the Old Testament* (1621); *The Psalms of David, translated into Lyrick Verse according to the scope of the original, and illustrated with a short Argument and a briefe Prayer or Meditation before and after every Psalme* (1632). George Wither represents one of the healthiest strains in seventeenth-century religious poetry and deserves a more careful consideration than space here permits.

PART TWO

The Background of Ideas

V

THE LOGOS

I

A WORD about methods. So far, we have viewed the field from the point of view of stylistics, and proposed that there was a pattern of three rhetorical phases, the Ciceronian, the anti-Ciceronian, and then (not exactly displacing the other two) the Hebraic. It would be tempting to regard this as a sort of Hegelian sequence of thesis, antithesis, and synthesis, except that the three kinds of Rhetoric or attitudes to Rhetoric described above do not always follow one another in strict historical order, but considerably overlap, and in fact it is the second, the scientific plain style, leavened with Senecan brevity and Puritan austerity, which largely prevailed at the end of the seventeenth century. Nevertheless, the Hebraic manner was more than a passing fashion, and the revival of interest in mid-seventeenth-century poetry and prose in our own day may be taken as indicating the permanent interest of its imaginative forms. Of course, those who reread Milton and Herbert today are not necessarily prepared to suspend their disbelief to the extent of reconstructing for themselves the whole ideological background of the period, and such readers may feel that the stress upon the centrality and significance of Hebraism is not absolutely dictated by the literary evidence alone.

Let us therefore dive into the deeper waters of *Geistesgeschichte* viewing the same quasi-Hegelian pattern from a direction approximating to that of intellectual history and theology. The more philosophically minded reader, will, let us hope, emerge reassured somewhat after having tested the firmness of the bottom, and will feel that he is not being tossed about for ever in the uncertain eddies of style, image, and rhythm.

But how is one to handle conceptually such a subject as Hebraism, without over-simplification or distortion? For one thing, there is no such thing as unadulterated Hebraism in the seventeenth century, or in any other Christian century: it always comes along alloyed with Hellenic thought forms and post-biblical Christian exegesis. Moreover, the Old Testament is an entire literature, a reflection of an entire civilization; it does not have a fixed and undeviating conceptual character and it is no easier to predicate of it definite theological and literary qualities than it is of an entity such as the Middle Ages, or Greek Civilization. How in such circumstances are we to avoid the danger of special pleading, the shortcoming that we have discovered in other studies of seventeenth-century dissociation? For, it is special pleading that leads Eliot to discount the positive factors of the Renaissance, and it is special pleading that leads Miss Nott to discount theology. The remedy for this is a stricter attention to the methods of phenomenology and intellectual history. The fact is that we do, in the interests of history and criticism, select the leading principles or *topoi*, as we conceive them, from out of the great mass of varied and complex phenomena that make up, say, Hellenism or Medievalism, and use these leading structures as a kind of guide through the labyrinth. Thus a central Hellenic image, that of the Platonic Chain of Being, has been made by one scholar the focus for a detailed and illuminating study of ideas in the eighteenth century.[1] The medieval allegory of the Garden of Love represents an important and leading structure, and the changes it underwent down to the sixteenth century have provided for another scholar illuminating evidence of ideological development and conflict.[2] We are entitled to do the same with Hebraism. Such a structure of ideas for instance as the Covenant of Works is no mere *shibboleth*, but a central phenomenon in Hebraism; it deserves to be given weight in any discussion. Moreover, it has the advantage that it was well understood and earnestly discussed in the very period with which we are concerned, as were many of the other principal *topoi* of Hebraism. In fact, we may rely to a great extent on the philosophical and theological literature of the period and so avoid the danger of importing false modern categories of thought into the period. We shall employ other well understood leading ideas—for instance the idea of the 'Temple of Nature' which has a strong

---

[1] A. O. Lovejoy, *The Great Chain of Being* (Cambridge, Mass., 1936).
[2] C. S. Lewis, *The Allegory of Love* (Oxford, 1936).

Hebraic overtone, and the idea of the 'Theatre of the World' which, whilst originally Hellenic, acquires in Henry More an undoubted Hebraic content. The same could be said of the 'Book of Nature' which so often, in Boyle and Thomas Browne comes to represent a parallel revelation to the Scriptures. Joseph Hall talks about the world as a great Hebrew folio in his comment on the text from *Psalm* viii, 'When I see the heavens, the moon and the stars that thou hast ordained, Lord, what is man?' This he paraphrases as follows:

> When looking over that great night-piece, and turning over the vast volume of the world, as Gerson terms it, he saw in that large folio, amongst those huge capital letters, what a little insensible dagesh-point man is, he breaks forth into an amazed exclamation, *Lord, what is man?*[1]

But it would be wrong to treat this particular *topos* as authentically Hebrew; the Book-image, it is true, has been well hebraized by Hall, but in essence it is a *logos*-image. It goes back to Plato and the Greeks and signifies essentially a rational cosmos, a cosmos which can be read as a Book, and which like human reason itself retains a permanent unalterable character. It does not imply the possibility of some dynamic process of revelation such as the Hebraic concept of *Torah* requires—for this included an unwritten law which is unfolded through History and therefore can never be read from beginning to end.

Before we come to the central topics of Hebraism therefore it will be as well to describe by way of contrast those Greek modes of thinking which were nourished either in the Middle Ages or the Renaissance. Here, the leading term and structure will be the *logos* which for the Greeks brings together the spheres of Man, God, and Nature. *Logos* is for the Greek Divine Reason, Human insight and the Order of the Cosmos all together. Beyond it there is no further wisdom to be sought; it is the beauty which lies upon the countenance of all things.

II

We are accustomed nowadays to the view that the great medieval commonplaces concerning Degree and Order, and

[1] Sermon XXX in *Works*, V, 449-50.

the medieval confidence in the validity of the hierarchies, survived into the Tudor period colouring the imaginations of Elizabethan writers and helping philosophers as well as common folk to understand their world.[1] According to Ulysses in Shakespeare's *Troilus and Cressida*,

> The heavens themselves, the planets, and this centre,
> Observe degree, priority, and place.

Whilst clearly, Shakespeare had serious reservations in this play about the traditional notions of order, there is no doubt that the wisdom of Ulysses expressed nevertheless a still living reality, both for him and his audience.

It is hardly necessary to argue that this sense of an orderly cosmos had a medieval basis. The medieval doctors, and typically Thomas Aquinas, achieved a philosophical synthesis of Christianity and Aristotle which was still very much alive for Christian humanists in England in the century of Sir Thomas More, Spenser, and Hooker. Moreover, the medieval structure of analogy and correspondence linking the different spheres of reality remained as an essential system of reference in poetry and drama. In Shakespeare's tragedy of *King Lear*, Gloucester holds to the commonplace whereby the outer world of cosmos both reflects and influences the world of human society, the microscosmos:

> These late eclipses of the sun and moon portend no good to us: . . .
> Love cools, friendship falls off, brothers divide: in cities, mutinies;
> in countries discord, in palaces treason.

If his bastard son Edmund laughs his father's old-fashioned ideas to scorn, it is because Edmund represents the disenchanted post-medieval generation for whom the orderly cosmos was no longer quite convincing. The scholastic universe of Thomas Aquinas had been rational, graduated, ordered. Whitehead speaks of the 'unbridled rationalism' of the Middle Ages;[2] the chief complaint of Galileo's critics, both lay and ecclesiastical, was not that he had outraged some mystery of faith but that he was in conflict with the highest form of reason as attested by

[1] Cf. D. Bush, *The Renaissance and English Humanism* (University of Toronto Press, 1939), *passim*; E. M. W. Tillyard, *The Elizabethan World Picture* (London, 1943), *passim*.

[2] *Science and the Modern World* (Cambridge, ed. of 1933), p. 11.

Aristotle and the traditions of the schools. Similarly Hooker's complaint against the Puritans was principally on account of 'their disparagement of Reason'.[1] The Hellenic-Christian system of thought implied in such a judgement is a *logos*-system. The world obeys a pattern, if you like, an aesthetic pattern, and he who damages the pattern runs the risk of bringing about a cosmic catastrophe—

> Take but degree away, untune that string,
> And hark what discord follows . . .

Shakespeare's image of music here is entirely in place, for order was essentially harmony: in its most charming formulation the medieval *logos* was orchestrated by the music of the spheres.

But reason is the chief ground of order. The reason of man is reflected in the moral and natural order, and religion itself was compounded of the highest reason. The beautiful symmetry of the *Nicomachean Ethics* is due to its formulation of the moral nature of man in terms of rational, *a priori* categories. A system in which the idea comes first and experience second is a *logos*-system. Philosophy in effect swallows up Theology, Science, and Ethics, for confidence in the eternal and irrefragable soundness of Philosophy is unbounded. Aristotle remarked that, 'True Philosophy is an ascending from the things which flow, and rise, and fall, to the things that are forever the same.' True philosophy, he would have said, sees the general in the particular; the temporal rooted in the timeless; particular acts of men gathered up into great and invariable laws. Aristotle does not ask what men, in fact, do or have done, but what, according to our preconceived notions of his nature, he may ideally be supposed to do. His *logos* will guide him in the right path as an ethical agent, just as the *logos* of the philosopher guides him as ethical mentor. Reason and virtue are necessarily one. And this was the complaint of Machiavelli, and after him Bacon, against the traditional Ethics, namely that it taught, not what men do, but what they ought to do.

But when we speak of the *logos* as the key to the traditional aspect of Renaissance thought, we must not only refer to Aristotle and his ordered classification of the arts and sciences. The more otherworldly philosophy of Plato is no less a *logos*-

[1] *Ibid.* p. 12.

69

system. Its aim is the contemplation of things in the light of Reason as that to which all things ultimately conform. Mind is supreme, contemplation comes before action. The final achievement of the philosopher is a state where the World and the Flesh have ceased to matter because he has transcended them and achieved a perfect peace, not the Christian 'peace which passeth all understanding', but the peace of *gnosis*, of total understanding. The influence of Platonism in the Middle Ages was calculated to moderate the harshness of primitive Christianity. It is true that Plato's negative attitude to the world of phenomena (as expressed in the *Phaedrus* and *The Republic*) might and did encourage an ascetic spirit among Christians, but the rational accommodation to, and positive appreciation of, the world as reflecting the beauty and order of the *logos* which he expresses elsewhere (in the *Timaeus*, for instance), helped the men of the Middle Ages in their search for compromises. Plato's notion of the Great Chain of Being is harmonized with the Judeo-Christian account of the Creation of the World to afford a picture of man made of the dust of the earth but linked as to his intellectual parts with the angels.[1] He has an assured medial status. It is a typical *logos*-formula, and it survives, as Professor Lovejoy has shown us, right down into the eighteenth century.

By contrast, the reading of the human situation according to the Hebrew Scripture *without* the medieval Platonic gloss is decidedly non-logistic; it 'must needs astonish human reason and make it ashamed of its own poorness'. These words are quoted from Joseph Hall's Sermon on the eighth Psalm, referred to earlier, on the text, 'When I see the heavens, the moon and the stars that thou hast ordained, Lord, what is man?' If we look at the eighth Psalm ourselves we shall see indeed that the picture of man's location in the cosmos which it presents has really no place for that assured human elevation, that stable aristocratic dignity implied by the idea of the Great Chain. When the psalmist looks at the Sun and the Stars 'which thou has ordained', he exclaims in amazement,

> What is man that thou art mindful of him?
> And the son of man that thou visitest him?

[1] Cf. Lovejoy, *op. cit.*, printing of 1948, pp. 63, 93, 97-8.

Here the son of man is no other than *Adam* made out of the red
earth, the *Adamah* of *Genesis* ii, 7. His claims to special consideration in the universe are entirely nugatory. But then immediately
and with extraordinary boldness, the Psalmist presents the
paradox of man's place in the creation:

> For thou has made him a little lower than the angels,
> And hast crowned him with glory and honour.

There is no attempt at aesthetically composing the paradox
in the form of an image of a Chain of Being which holds the
son of Adam neatly and symmetrically somewhere along the
line dividing angels from beasts, nor of rationally composing it
in the form of an ethical Middle Way (as in Aristotle's *Ethics*)
which regulates these extremes of human nature. Instead, there
is a moral and existential challenge, a peril and an insignificance
rooted in the nature of man, and capable of being assuaged
only by the nearness and unbelievable saving power of God:
'O Lord, our Lord, how excellent is thy name in all the earth!'

Hebraic anthropology yoked, in the Middle Ages and the
Renaissance, to the Greek *logos* had been made to yield a
deceptively smooth exterior: it had been robbed of its dialectical character. The great name associated with the harmonizing of Stoic and Platonic concepts with Hebraic theology is of
course that of the first-century Jewish writer, Philo of Alexandria. His whole work, indeed, the importance of which for the
Christian Middle Ages (in Clement and Origen for example)
was immense,[1] is directed to the composition of a Biblical
theology in which at all costs the violent, impetuous, and
frequently arbitrary God of the Hebrew Scriptures is made to
behave with the sweet reasonableness of the *logos*. Philo gave
to the term *logos* the central place in his system: through it, the
world becomes one of aesthetically contrived and static order,
and through it also Man can gain a more intimate and thrilling
contact with Divinity. The *logos* is planted in the soul just as it is
impressed upon the outer world. The mention of Philo reminds
us also of the *Hermetica*, a body of early medieval writing which
testifies to his formative influence and to the power and
attractiveness of his blend of Jewish, Platonic, Pythagorean,

[1] Cf. Beryl Smalley, *The Study of the Bible in the Middle Ages* (Second ed.,
1952), pp. 6-7.

and Stoic images.[1] The *Hermetica* was to take on a new life in the sixteenth century in the writings of Ficino, Pico della Mirandola and others. Here also a new ingredient was added in the form of an admixture of later Jewish mysticism, especially the *Zohar*, as understood (or more frequently, misunderstood) by the Renaissance Hebraists such as Pico and Reuchlin.[2] By now, new factors are at work. The world is one of esoteric phenomena, of mystery. But the adept's intuitive powers, his capacity for *gnosis*, are equal to the task of apprehending such a world. For this kind of philosopher, the *logos* weaves a more fantastic pattern in the brain: but the world is still seen as firmly held together by a system of analogies, of mysterious correspondences, even if they can now only be discovered by a privileged few. Order reigns supreme, and a disturbance in the stars is echoed in the microcosm. Planets, metals, and men obey an immanent principle of harmony.

All these influences, separately and together, helped to create the specific atmosphere of Renaissance thought with its happy symbiosis of Religion and Philosophy. For the optimistic and enlightened Christian philosopher, the contemplation of the cosmos was non-problematical. He was not disturbed, as were the Calvinists, by brooding terrors inspired by a God likely to damn or to elect for unexplained reasons, or for no reasons at all. Nor was he disturbed by the prospect of some unexplained interference with the normal workings of Nature. Nature was regulated by a principle of Order and Law, and this sense of an ordered cosmos inspired an appropriately glowing and serene rhetorical statement, the type of oratory which goes back to Aristotle and Cicero. As has already been stated, the typical style of the 'High' Renaissance is the Ciceronian periodic style— the normal literary correlative of the *logos*-philosophy in its various forms. It is ornate, magistral, self-complete, rational, and complacent. An extra touch of gravity is often given to it by Biblical, Hebraic echoes, but its fundamental rhythm is classical. It is well represented in the following passage from Hooker which eloquently sums up that traditional fusion of

[1] Cf. R. P. Festugière, *La Révélation d'Hermès Trismégiste*, vol. 2 (Paris, 1949), p. 585.
[2] See J. L. Blau, *The Christian Interpretation of the Cabala in the Renaissance* (New York, 1944), *passim*.

The Logos

Divinity and Natural Philosophy so characteristic of the 'High' Renaissance:

> This world's first creation, and the preservation since of things created, what is it but only so far forth a manifestation by execution what the eternal law of God is concerning things natural? And as it cometh to pass in a kingdom rightly ordered, that after a law is once published it presently takes effect far and wide, all states framing themselves thereunto, even so let us think it fareth in the natural course of the world. Since the time that God did first proclaim the edicts of His law upon it, heaven and earth have hearkened unto His voice, and their labour has been to do His will. He made a law for the rain, He gave His decree unto the sea that the waters should not pass His commandment. Now if nature should intermit her course, and leave altogether, though it were but for a while, the observation of her own laws; if those principal and mother elements of the world whereof all things in this lower world are made should lose the qualities which now they have; if the frame of that heavenly arch erected over our heads should loosen and dissolve itself; if celestial spheres should forget their wonted motions and by irregular volubility turn themselves any way as it might happen; if the prince of the lights of heaven, which now as a giant doth run his unwearied course, should as it were, through a languishing faintness, begin to stand and to rest himself; if the moon should wander from her beaten way, the times and seasons of the year blend themselves by disordered and confused mixture, the winds breathe out their last gasp, the clouds yield no rain, the earth be defeated of heavenly influence, the fruits of the earth pine away as children at the withered breasts of their mother, no longer able to yield them relief—what would become of man himself whom these things now do all serve?[1]

This majestic commonplace coming originally out of Arnobius[2] may be matched in other writers down to Pope and Berkeley in the eighteenth century, but in Hooker it achieved its most eloquent formulation. For Hooker (as for Thomas Aquinas whose pupil he was) the universe was an ordered and rational system, and the moral order derives its sanction from the inviolable regularity of the cosmos. His *Ecclesiastical Polity* is really a sustained oration on this theme which is basically the

[1] *Of the Lawes of Ecclesiasticall Politie* (1597), Book I.

[2] *Ad Gent.* I, 2. See R. Hooker, *Works*, ed. Keble (seventh ed., Oxford, 1888), I, 208.

stoic theme of natural law. The world is supported by a structure of analogy—Man, God, and Nature eternally obeying
together the rhythm of natural law. It is stable and balanced,
like a Greek work of art. In spite of the many Biblical echoes in
the quoted extract (from *Job* xxviii, 26; *Psalms* xix, 5; and civ,
19), we do not find here the scriptural world of change and
miracle, of creative acts, of superhuman tasks imposed on the
unwilling clay by an inexorable deity. It is, as has been said,
rather a universe of law and order.

But changes are already on the way. On the face of it, the
question as to what would happen 'if nature should intermit
her course', is for Hooker merely rhetorical: it is part of the
topos which he is here rehandling. Yet, surely there is an undertone of uneasiness. If anything may be learned from comparing
this with the parallel passage already referred to in Shakespeare's play of *Troilus and Cressida*, it would seem that this
picture of the return of chaos, of anarchy broken loose is the
echo of an unacknowledged and horrifying suspicion, the
suspicion that the *logos* is not as stable as it seems, that it is
perhaps about to crumble.

> but when the planets
> In evil mixture to disorder wander,
> What plagues, and what portents, what mutiny,
> What raging of the sea, shaking of earth,
> Commotion in the winds, frights changes, horrors,
> Divert and crack, rend and deracinate
> The unity and married calm of states
> Quite from their fixure!

Ulysses' vision of the breakdown of order carries with it much
of Shakespeare's disillusioned and embittered sense of life in
this play. Would it be too much to suppose that Hooker, like
Shakespeare, had a fearful intuition of those revolutionary
changes in men's thinking soon to be announced in the philosophy of Bacon and already manifest in the Purtian 'disparagement of Reason' and the Copernican revision of the cosmos,
and that such thoughts compelled the great and terrifying image
of the heavenly arch loosening and dissolving itself? The vision
of *sophia*, of the *logos*, is still there hovering over the uncreated
void, but there are new dangers and challenges all about. The
account of these will occupy us in the next Chapter.

74

VI

THE COUNTER-RENAISSANCE

I

THERE IS a disposition now to recognize that the sixteenth-century phase of the Renaissance was not all Sweetness and Light. It is true that in the writings of Sir Thomas More, Erasmus, Hooker, and Spenser, the Renaissance presents a picture of Christian humanism securely buttressed by Aristotle, Cicero, and Thomas Aquinas. But against this trend (though sometimes subtly infolded with it) there was also a desperate challenge to the traditional philosophy, a breakdown of confidence in the medieval world-picture, and the growth of a powerful interest in tangible proof and experiment to the exclusion of received authority. Professor Hiram Haydn has called this movement, the 'Counter-Renaissance'.[1]

In the humanist field, this counter-movement is characterized by the denial of limit, by excessive stress on Love and Honour, and by intense individualism; in the field of natural philosophy, by empiricism, an emphasis on utility, and the lust for power; and in the field of Divinity, by excessive reliance on Faith as against Reason and Morality, a stress on human depravity, and on the immediate experience of divine illumination. Common to all these manifestations is the empirical factor, the demand for unmediated experience, whether in the field of Man, God, or Nature. One is struck by such a figure as Luther, brooding, violent, turbulent, a rebel against Reason which for him has ceased to be the handmaid to Divinity (which it was for Aquinas) and has become instead, 'the Devil's harlot'. Impelled by a strong ideological antisemitism, Luther strove to expel the Epistle of James from the University because of its Judaic insistence on the Law of Works. Here the attempt to disturb the traditional Hellenic-Hebraic synthesis of the Middle Ages is

---

[1] H. Haydn, *The Counter-Renaissance* (New York, 1950), pp. 67 f.

carried back into the New Testament itself. Telesio in science breaks away from the tradition of natural law. Valla in his avowal of the primacy of appetite and in his frank utilitarianism marks the desertion of the traditional ethics according to which the law of our nature is coextensive with Right Reason. Above all, Machiavelli's political philosophy clearly disjoins moral from practical considerations thus giving to the anthropological sciences a new and radical independence of theology. In such instances, the unified world-view of the Middle Ages is revealed as breaking down. We become aware of the Renaissance not merely as an era of novelty but of terrible and destructive novelty, in short, of revolt.

> Then everything includes itself in power,
> Power into will, will into appetite;
> And appetite, an universal wolf,
> So double seconded with will and power,
> Must make perforce an universal prey,
> And last eat up himself.[1]

In this play of Shakespeare, the denial of limit finds its most striking expression in the words of the hero Troilus speaking of the passion of love in a way calculated to overthrow the elegant categories of medieval and Renaissance Platonism.

This is the monstruosity in love, lady, that the will is infinite, and the execution confined; that the desire is boundless, and the act a slave to limit.

It is not necessary to summarize the literary examples of this trend since this has already been done by others, and specifically by Professor Haydn himself, and also since this study is concerned not so much with the Counter-Renaissance itself as with the seventeenth-century aftermath, that is with the attempt to heal the breaches caused by the Counter-Renaissance. We shall really be concerned with one major figure, and that is Bacon, but before we turn to him, two striking Counter-Renaissance literary portraits may be mentioned at this point since they will have a certain symbolic value in helping us to map out the history of ideas during this epoch: they are Marlowe's Faustus and Shakespeare's Hamlet.

Marlowe's hero, unsatisfied, ambitious, tearing aside tradi-

---

[1] *Troilus and Cressida*, Act i, scene iii.

tional restraints in his search for new knowledge and experience, exchanging the promise of eternity for twenty-four years of 'all voluptuousness', is a central example of the trend we are considering, fashioned forth by a great man of imagination. He turns back to the ancients, to the 'old philosophers', but not to achieve serenity and spiritual elevation, but rather to find in Helen of Troy a more intense and concentrated appeal to his senses. The classicism of the Counter-Renaissance is a revolutionary classicism: it involves a complete transvaluation of values. Shakespeare's Hamlet is indeed a more balanced portrait, for he embodies the ideal of the Tudor knight and gentleman, active, courteous, public-spirited, and obedient to the laws of God and Man. But the crisis which he undergoes overthrows this side of his personality: it makes of him a figure of brooding intensities. He evokes the traditional Christian-humanist picture of man elevated high up in the cosmic Chain but only to shatter it as an impossible illusion.

> What a piece of work is a man! How noble in reason! How infinite in faculty! in form, in moving, how express and admirable! in action how like an angel! in apprehension how like a god! the beauty of the world! the paragon of animals! And yet, to me, what is this quintessence of dust?

Disillusionment is complete.

The new philosophy which Hamlet and his friend Horatio had both learned at Wittemberg and which is referred to in the play is the new extreme stoicism of the time. This is not the traditional Ciceronian stoicism with its stress on natural law and public responsibility, the doctrine which had served so well the needs of a sunnier generation of Renaissance Christian humanists, but a more radical humanism derived from Seneca and others which stressed the introversion of the stoic personality, unsubjected to a religious or social code, and seeking confidence and security within the narrow sanctum of the well-ordered mind.[1] Horatio, more an antique Roman than a Dane, is said to achieve just this: he is 'as one in suffering all that suffers nothing'. But Hamlet himself suffers everything; whilst taking the stoic path of inwardness, he is unable, burdened as he is with ethical responsibilities and a sense of filial duty, to

[1] Cf. L. Zanta, *La Renaissance du Stoïcisme au XVIe Siècle*, (1914), p. 336.

reach the calm position of *apatheia* and the happy acceptance of suicide as a solution to life's problems, which the stoics had recommended. Perhaps the intervening centuries of Christian experience had ultimately rendered such an achievement impossible for the neo-Stoics of the late sixteenth century. Certainly, Lipsius, the author of the famous *Two Books of Constancie*, was amongst the most inconstant of stoics. With Hamlet, what we recognize is not the calm inviolability of the ancient stoic, but rather a desperate search for certainty, and an intense and consuming self-awareness. He illustrates the crisis of the Counter-Renaissance.

II

In turning to Francis Bacon and his position as a major representative of the phase discussed in this Chapter, 'the inheritor and final expositor of Counter-Renaissance science',[1] we are struck by the fact that in comparison with Hamlet or Dr. Faustus, Bacon is not a disordered, anguished spirit. He performs the grandiose gestures of the *logos*, assuming for his world a certain completeness and symmetry. In this he was like Calvin, another great apostle of the Counter-Renaissance, who came to overthrow the rational theological systems of the Middle Ages and replace them by an unbounded stress on the experience of Divine Grace as the centre and circumference of the religious life. Yet he too composed his ideas in the form of a comprehensive and reasoned Summa Theologiae—his *Institutes* —which could be taken, and indeed often were taken, as a substitute for the great *Summa* of Thomas Aquinas. Bacon too came to overthrow 'Philosophy' in the broader sense through an unbounded emphasis on empiricism and induction, and yet he aspired to write an *Instauratio Magna*, a new comprehensive unitary system capable of being matched with that of Aristotle. Thus in the *De Augmentis*, when discussing the three Philosophies of Man, God, and Nature, he observes that they are 'like the branches of a tree which are united in a common trunk'. The argument for the traditional, medieval, unitary philosophy could hardly be put in a neater fashion, and it requires some-

[1] Haydn, op. cit., p. 250. Professor Haydn's full and perceptive discussion of Bacon (pp. 250-76) is much to be commended.

thing of an effort to remind oneself that it was Bacon and no other who announced the radical severance of Philosophy and Theology. This is an expression of the revolutionary secularism of the Counter-Renaissance. He claims that without such a separation, no real progress can be made in the physical sciences, for the confusion of the two spheres was the crime of the kabbalists, Paracelsus and Fludd; it is that which leads to what he calls 'the Idols of the Theatre'.

Now it is worth asking whether Bacon announces this separation of Theology from Philosophy as a philosophical principle or as a scientific convenience. If the latter, is one really entitled to attach such a fundamental significance to Bacon as the great seculariser? Or would he in that case not simply be saying, 'Let us release the scientist in his day-to-day laboratory work, from a pre-occupation with matters of religion; scientists have enough to do, just as builders and shipwrights have, without being expected to train as theologians'? This point of view, whilst not exactly inspiring, is unlikely to create terror and dismay. But in fact it does not correspond to the revelational tone and the august scope of Bacon's plan. The truth is that whilst on the one hand Bacon is narrowing philosophy down to a system of induction and empiricism, he is at the same time giving to scientific research an inflated value by imputing to it an inclusive philosophical truth and validity. This is a most remarkable philosophical manœuvre but it also marks the end of Philosophy in the accepted sense as the 'Wisdom of the Whole'. It marks the abandonment of the *logos*.

The fact is that the basic preoccupations of medieval Christian philosophy and of sixteenth-century Christian humanism have really ceased to matter for Bacon. He objects to the 'corruption of philosophy by superstition and an admixture of theology' claiming that this is bad for both, and in an attempt to rid philosophy (meaning Science) of what he terms the 'Idols of the Theatre', he splits up the Four Causes which Aristotle had recognized and removes Final Causes entirely from Physics, making it clear that further inquiry into them would be sterile and unprofitable. The mechanical philosopher never asks, Why, or, To what End, but only, How. When he considers the heavens, the moon and the stars 'which Thou hast ordained', he is not moved to wonder at their relevance to the plans of providence

79

as a whole. Thus, the dependency of all material causes upon God's creative act, and their incorporation in the vast, purposive system of natural law, the vision which inspired Ralegh and Hooker—all this Bacon accepts, acknowledges, and passes over. The religious teleology which had been characteristic of philosophical thought hitherto, is now relegated to the sphere of Faith, and Faith is finally separated from Reason. Like Montaigne, another great figure of the Counter-Renaissance, in his *Apology for Raymond de Sebonde*, Bacon bids us render to Faith that which belongs to Faith, and to Reason, which has now gathered up into itself all the business, pleasure, and profit of this world, that which belongs to Reason. And Reason in Bacon's sense is no longer the *recta ratio*, the broad light of a reasoned accommodation between the unseen and the visible worlds, but a *lumen siccum*, the dry practical light of a new pragmatism.

Bacon's philosophical procedure may be defined as a series of dichotomies, each intended to cure a certain disease of the Intellect or the Imagination. Reason is separated from Faith and Fables (a cure for the Idols of the Theatre); objective truth is separated from subjective feeling (a cure for the Idols of the Cave); and Philosophy is separated from Poetry and Rhetoric, and the troublesome associations of words (a cure for the Idols of the Market-Place).[1] By means of such dichotomies, the human mind is left free to confront a new bleaker vision of the natural world. The onlooker, crossing the boundary between the traditional, aesthetically balanced world of the *logos* and the new world perceived by Bacon might well be shocked by the change, by the sudden egress into the sphere of the spectral Albion, of single-vision, and might say with Hamlet:

> this goodly frame the earth, seems to me a sterile promontory; this most excellent canopy the air, look you, this brave o'erhanging firmament, this majestical roof fretted with golden fire, why it appeareth nothing to me but a foul and pestilent congregation of vapours.[2]

---

[1] *Novum Organum*, Bk. I, sect. xxxix-lxvii. See *Works*, IV, 53 f. There is a fourth Idol, that of the Tribe, by which he intends the false views and impressions 'of the whole tribe or race of mankind'. Browne's *Pseudodoxia Epidemica* (Vulgar Errors) may be regarded as an elaboration of this theme.

[2] *Hamlet*, Act II, scene ii.

Naturally, Hamlet is suffering from a neurosis, and we would not go to him for a measured appraisal of the advantages or disadvantages of the new narrowed and dichotomized view of the universe. But his neurosis is itself an interesting symptom of the profound and disturbing changes which were taking place in his intellectual environment: it tells us how critical they were. Order and Beauty have *for practical purposes* disappeared from the cosmos; 'The Starry Heavens are fled from the mighty limbs of Albion.' The only factor with which the Natural Philosopher is concerned is the naked contact between the unfettered human will and a material universe stripped of its divine secrets.

We may ask at this point whether Bacon is really so very modern? It is sometimes pointed out that, in separating Faith from Reason, Bacon is obeying a very ancient Christian instinct, giving to Caesar that which is Caesar's and to God that which is God's, and also that he is following the nominalist, 'double-truth' tradition of the later Middle Ages in William of Ockham and his disciples, which likewise laid down a radical separation of matters of Faith from Matters of Reason and sense-experience. Both these objections must be partially admitted. Indeed the gospels and even more the Epistles of *Paul* had insisted that 'flesh and blood cannot inherit the kingdom of heaven' and had rigidly divided the mysteries of faith from the carnal reason of the Old Adam. Bacon too in attacking the school of Paracelsus and Fludd for their 'unwholesome mixture of things human and divine', had complained that this was bad, not only for philosophy, but for religion as well. It led to heresy. And he continued, 'Very meet it is therefore that we be sober-minded, and give to faith that only which is faith's'.[1]

Bacon's appeal for a faith purified from this-worldly philosophy is in line with the evangelical spirit of Calvinism and Lutheranism, and marks an attempt to revert to an uncompromising Pauline Christianity. But we should remember that the spirit of compromise had entered Christianity very early, if not in the New Testament itself. The Epistle of *James*, already referred to, has as Luther recognized, a decidedly non-evangelical insistence on the saving power of good works, that is, of

[1] *Works*, IV, 66.

practical goodness. Above all, medieval Christianity had sought and found compromises which served well to accommodate the Christian community to the life of this world; Faith and Reason had married with the blessing of the Church on their union. Even Augustine, who turned his back on heathen culture and philosophy in an attempt to reach the purity of the gospel, devoted his major intellectual efforts to the comprehension of the Christian view of history and to the visualizing of the relation between man's pilgrimage in this world of principalities and powers and the unseen order which is beyond. In spite of the radical separation of spheres taught in the New Testament, the overwhelming sentiment of Christian orthodoxy has been that an accommodation must be found. The Book of *Genesis* taught that God created the world and declared it to be good; it can therefore not be abandoned to the rule of the Devil. It is this very fundamental Jewish doctrine working explicitly and implicitly within the structure of Christian thought and feeling which saved medieval Christianity from the dangers of manicheeism, from the complete division of spheres.

As for the philosophical separation of Faith and Reason in the nominalists, we should remember, as Huizinga points out, that for the Middle Ages, 'nominalism has never been anything but a reaction, an opposition, a counter-current vainly disputing the ground with the fundamental tendencies of the medieval spirit'.[1] What held sway in the Middle Ages was the 'realistic' concept of the world, fact joined always to symbol, a world upheld by the *logos*, and rendered significant by Divine Truth, Beauty, and Order. Natural Philosophy and Divinity were in this respect at one, and could be felt as one in each and every manifestation of natural law.

Bacon's overt intention, then, is to design a neutralized Nature capable of being handled efficiently by the scientist and stripped of the obscurities of medieval realism and imaginative fantasies of all kinds. He protests against the introduction of Biblical motifs and images into Natural Philosophy by Fludd and Paracelsus. But the strange thing is that Bacon was himself a man of imagination, a poet, as Shelley insisted, and though he fought back against this impulse in himself, the fact is that

[1] J. Huizinga, *The Waning of the Middle Ages* (1919, English edition, London, 1955), p. 206.

the Idols of the Cave, the Theatre, and the Market-Place, were the ghosts of his own mind. When he complains that 'words do shoot back upon the understanding of the wisest and mightily entangle and pervert the judgement',[1] it is not difficult to detect the note of self-admonition, to guess at the mental and emotional barriers which had to be overcome before he could curb his imaginative impulses and force himself into the Procrustean bed of a rigorous empiricism. The truth is that Bacon was not naturally an empiric; it is well known how impatient he was of the hard, day-to-day labours of the laboratory. He complains from time to time (as surely no professional scientist would) about having to do menial tasks which were 'beneath the dignity of an undertaking like mine'. Of course he made the effort. In spite of his 'ambition of the understanding' and his impatience to arrive at the great imaginative synthesis or the dramatic result, he did, in such works as his *Natural History*, set himself the formidable task of gathering the straw, making the bricks, and putting up the building itself. Yet there is no doubt that his genius did not lie that way. Whilst proclaiming that the programme of Science must be one of rigid empiricism, he himself stands before us supremely as the man of Imagination, whispering his dream into the ear of the scientists. He is the first of the moderns, but he is also the Fallen Angel of the pre-scientific universe. He dismisses the neo-platonic speculations of the sixteenth-century men of magic and mystery, of Bruno, of John Dee, Pico, and Paracelsus. Yet he is close enough to them to betray more than a hint of the outlook that he is repudiating. Note for instance this curious sentence from the *Novum Organum*:

> For every tangible that we are acquainted with contains an invisible and intangible spirit which it wraps and clothes as with a garment.[2]

Passages of that kind must have sounded oddly to the men of the later seventeenth century, the *virtuosi* of the Royal Society, when they came to sift the writings of the great Verulam.

I should like to argue here quite seriously that Bacon was not so much a philosopher as a magician. He owes more than a little in expression and terminology to the alchemists. In this

[1] *Works*, III, 396-7.   [2] *Ibid.*, IV, 195.

he truly resembles Marlowe's Dr. Faustus. Bacon's stress on Magic, indeed, and the central place he gives it have not often been appreciated. In the *De Augmentis Scientiarum* (Bk. III, ch. 4-5), Bacon tells us something about Metaphysics, a term which he uses in a rather special way. To Metaphysics belongs two kinds of inquiry, the first is the inquiry into Final Causes, but this he says is 'barren and like a virgin consecrated to God' (we note the interesting anti-papist implication of this image): the second, and more important, is the inquiry into the 'essential forms' of Nature. This has nothing to do with the medieval or Aristotelian 'formal cause'; if an anachronism may be forgiven, what Bacon is trying to suggest is something like the energy of the atom, or radiation, the basic forces of Nature (Telesio may have helped to suggest the notion of the 'forces' of Nature). These 'forms' he tells us are the secret of gravity, heat, and density, and if we could get at them, they would be 'of all the parts of knowledge the most worthy of inquiry'. They provide a short cut across the barren fields of empiricism. 'This part of Metaphysic', he says, 'has the advantage that it enfranchises the power of men to the greatest liberty, and leads it to the widest and most extensive field of operation.' Now could these forms, or forces be got at? The answer is that they could, and that the practical exploration and application of these ultimate basic forces of Nature was the business of 'Natural Magic'. That is the subject of Book III, ch. 5 of the *De Augmentis*.

There are, in fact, according to Bacon, two parts to the 'practical doctrine of nature'; the first is applied Physics which is concerned with the simple rules of Matter and Motion. The characteristic application of this was in Mechanics. Now Bacon's stress on mechanical physics has generally been regarded as his chief contribution to the development of science and perhaps in a manner of speaking it was. But in these sections of the *De Augmentis* Bacon is speaking of a greater matter than Mechanics, namely applied Metaphysics, or Natural Magic. It is greater because it will enable mankind to effect all physical possibilities for 'whosoever knows any Form knows also the utmost possibility of superinducing that nature upon every variety of matter'. This, he hastens to inform us, has nothing to do with practice of the natural magicians of the sixteenth century which dealt only with occult properties, with 'credulous and superstitious traditions and observations concerning sympathies and antipathies, hidden and specific properties, with experiments for the most part frivolous'. He himself defines Magic as being properly,

> the science which applies the knowledge of hidden forms to the production of wonderful operations; and by uniting (as they say) actives with passives, displays the wonderful works of nature.[1]

He will have no truck with light Magic, Alchemy, Astrology, and the rest, but he hankers after the same results for which the practitioners of such arts has been ambitious: absolute power, the conversion of quicksilver into gold, and the prolongation of life—all this he thinks may be possible through the control of the hidden forces of a neutralized Nature. Marlowe's Dr. Faustus is in this respect just such a man as Bacon; he has dismissed Heaven and Hell as 'trifles and mere old wives' tales'; there is for him no reality beyond the here and now; but Magic remains, offering him the tantalizing promise of supreme power over this new 'despiritualized' universe:

> Oh, what a world of profit and delight,
> Of power, of honour, of omnipotence
> Is promis'd to the studious artisan!
> All things that move between the quiet poles
> Shall be at my command: emperors and kings
> Are but obey'd in their several provinces,
> Nor can they raise the wind, or rend the clouds;
> But his dominion that exceeds in this,
> Stretcheth as far as doth the mind of man;
> A sound magician is a mighty god. . . .

Can anyone doubt that Bacon has taken over from the magicians this Faustian (and, of course, quite irrational) dream of unlimited human power of Nature? The follies of the magicians, their inability to grasp the limitations of human power and intellect, are bound up with their intoxicating vision of the mysterious, vital properties infused into the world of matter. Magical effects could be produced, 'actives' could be applied to 'passives', because of the endless analogies and affinities

---

[1] *Ibid.*, p. 367. Ellis writes (*Ibid.*, I, 573 n.) that the expression *magnalia naturae* used here 'is a favourite phrase with Paracelsus'.

linking all the different spheres of existence. Their 'Magic' is merely the extravagant offspring of a fundamentally religious and poetical view of the world. They went wrong by allowing their faith in the reality of the unseen to overflow its bounds; but Bacon's confusion is even more radical. He dismisses (or tries to dismiss) the poetical and metaphysical basis of sixteenth-century magic and aims at magical power for its own sake. He tends to replace the analogical structure of thought which had constituted the faith of the magicians, with a blind faith in the unlimited capacity of man himself standing over against the world. But the result he hopes for is the same! This is not nominalism, but something new and dynamic—not the formal separation of spheres, but the transference of the energies of Faith into the region of technology. Bacon makes Physics not a technique but a religion, and Induction becomes for him not so much a useful mechanism for the discovery of certain limited axioms, but rather a mystic path, an ultimate revelation and a millennial hope. And let it be said that this part of Bacon's philosophy, this pseudo-religious faith in the possibilities of the scientific method has worked even more powerfully (howbeit surreptitiously) in the history of modern science and modern civilization, than his immensely influential stress upon a mechanical Physics, and indeed to this day when the mechanical account of natural law has proved its inadequacy, Bacon's Faustian dream of magical power over the world continues to possess us and drive us on. It is in that sense that Bacon is, as Whitehead has well said, the architect of the modern mind.

III

Having reached this point, I should like to say that I am not sure if the term 'Counter-Renaissance' is any longer very helpful. If that term denotes the break-up of old certainties, the spirit of revolt, distress, conflict, scepticism, the feverish search for direct experiential truth, then it fits Bacon well. But is there not some more positive driving-force here as well, some additional demon, some ground of zeal which we have not so far satisfactorily explained? He pictures himself in a famous passage as Columbus setting out on that wonderful voyage across the Atlantic. Whence this *élan*, this extraordinary sense of mission, this feeling of immense opportunity? This does not quite belong to the philosophers of the sixteenth century.[1] Perhaps we shall get at it by looking for a moment or two at Bacon's Philosophy of Man, a branch of his writings as important as his Philosophy of Nature, for human utility stands as the final object of his method, the new 'Final Cause' so to speak, in his universe.

It is by now a truism to speak of Bacon's debt to Machiavelli and his echoing of the stoicism of the ancients. His disenchanted realism is clearly in the line of Machiavelli; he learned from the Florentine his realistic, empirical approach to political and ethical questions. One branch of study which Bacon proposes for himself would be concerned with 'frauds, cautels, impostures and vices' which he would handle more seriously and wisely than they had been handled before, taking the example of 'Machiavelli and others that write what men do, and not what they ought to do.' (*Advancement of Learning*, Bk. II). Like Machiavelli, he turned to the ancient historians and biographers for evidence of what men did, and he wrote his *Essays*, rather in the way that he wrote his *Natural History*, that is in order to record in an unimpassioned and unidealistic fashion the principles governing human conduct, both privately and in society. Bacon, in short, divides Ethics from Theology, and makes of it a pragmatic science, just as he divides Theology from Nature in his Natural Philosophy.

Similarly, he follows the Stoics, not Cicero but Seneca, and more immediately, Montaigne, in considering matters of individual psychology and ethics. He uses the introspective art of Montaigne, though with less ease and charm. 'He seems often, indeed,' says one critic, 'to have written with his head severed and placed cleanly before him on the table, an inch or two beyond the farther edge of his manuscript.'[2] The aim will be, through the study of human behaviour and through introspection, to reduce the knowledge of human nature in all its aspects to the condition approaching nearest to a practical art

[1] Professor Haydn notes also, after quoting Bacon in a characteristically exalted mood, that 'he leaves the Counter-Renaissance utterly behind' and that he raises 'its enthusiasm for "things as they are" to the level of a religious reverence' (*op. cit.*, p. 274).

[2] G. Tillotson, 'Words for Princes' in *Essays in Criticism and Research* (Cambridge, 1942), p. 31.

or science. An otherworldly destiny for man is entirely outside the field of concern.

An excellent example of what has just been said would be Bacon's Essay 'Of Death'. He follows Montaigne, who had of course written at great length on the same topic, in treating Death without any reference to 'the other side'. All the emphasis is on this life. The problem for consideration is the fear of death which is common to all men, to what extent this fear reduces our professional efficiency, and how it may be overcome by training. He is concerned with the art of dying. A series of historical examples are brought to show how unconcernedly men had submitted to death from time to time, and Seneca is quoted as saying that death may even be sought as an escape from boredom. He goes on, very much in the style of Seneca, or Marcus Aurelius,

> It is as natural to die as to be born; and to a little infant, perhaps, the one is as painful as the other.

Here is something like the stoical *apatheia*, or *ataraxia*, the attitude of wise passiveness or indifference which the Stoic tried to cultivate as part of his search for tranquillity and self-command. All this Bacon had digested along with the stoic introversion and the stoic or Senecan style with its strict control over feelings and imagination.

But does this take us so very far with Bacon? It explains his style and technique, and certainly he was seeking self-command, but he has in his *Essays* a further aim which is very far from stoical. Bacon's whole determined plan of self-mastery is directed at an object which mattered little to the real Stoics, namely worldly success and greatness. Shakespeare's Brutus is of a truer stoic breed: he offends us by his sublime self-sufficiency, his complacent virtue, his rigid equanimity, but Antony justly acquits him of envy and personal ambition. Even Hamlet is more of a Stoic in this respect than Bacon; his inner search is infinitely more important to him than the political objective or even the just solution of his family feud; his true personality is revealed in soliloquy, in the drama of arrested action, of meditation. With Bacon, however, ethical discipline and the search for inner integrity come second to the power objective, to Health, Empire, Estate, Great Place. These very unstoical objectives provide the deep background rhythm of the *Essays*. He reminds us in this respect of no one more than Dreiser's Titan, the type of the power-seeker and conquistador of the modern world.

Now does this driving force in Bacon belong strictly to the Counter-Renaissance? The capacity for action, even violent action in the pursuit of honour is of course highly characteristic of one extreme form of Renaissance Humanism. Shakespeare's Troilus, Fortinbras, Laertes and even Hamlet himself in some moods, are men of thoughtless impetuosity, they are men

> Whose spirit with divine ambition puffed
> Makes mouths at the invisible event,
> Exposing what is mortal and unsure
> To all that fortune, death and danger dare,
> Even for an egg-shell. . . .

But Bacon is not such a one; he does not make mouths at the invisible event; he is no daredevil, no dice-thrower with destiny. For him the active power-impulse is yoked to a sense of immense responsibility, to a plan of world conquest, of millennial change. It is, in however strange and perverted a way, a religious impulse.

The reader will perhaps have guessed that the point to which we are driving once again is Hebraism—a distorted Hebraism, one cut free from Covenant responsibilities and ethical restraints, but nevertheless the active impulse of Hebraism seeking through historical change and human endeavour the fulfilment of a messianic hope. This is far from the patient suffering of stoicism, from the intellectual ideal of Platonism, or the recklessness of the Renaissance devotees of honour. Bacon's drift is rather that of John Eliot, one of the Fathers of the American colonies when he declared, 'Up and be doing for the Lord is with thee.' Bacon has kept the Hebraic imperative, but in attaching himself to a Machiavellian politic and a Senecan ethic, he has struck off the theological proposition which supports it.

The Baconian *anthropos* is not really explicable in terms of Counter-Renaissance humanism at all. Humanism, I take it, whether in Valla, or Pico, or Montaigne leads logically to a contemplation of Man's perfected nature, his *qualities*, physical, moral, or imaginative. Its desired end is the fullest realization of Man's nature, in a word, his emancipation. Now strictly speaking, the Baconian Man standing over against Nature does not seek emancipation: he seeks Power. The realization of his own nature in perfected freedom is no necessary part of his aim. On the contrary, his aim involves the *subordination* of his nature to his purpose—his pseudo-divine purpose. Whence comes this zeal of enterprise, this determined bending of the personality to a task conceived to be of transcendent worth? Surely this is not Hellenism or Renaissance Humanism, at all. It is rather part of the dynamic rhythm set up in the Reformation era by the Hebraic doctrine of election and covenant, a doctrine which Bacon (quite literally) learned at his mother's knee.[1] From his Calvinistic background, Bacon derived that zeal for 'doing', for 'justification', which brought other more theologically minded Puritans across the Atlantic to New England and eventually drove them westwards until they had conquered the last frontier. That secularization of the Puritan spirit of industry which seems to have occurred in America somewhere along the line dividing Cotton Mather from Benjamin Franklin is already fully anticipated in Francis Bacon.

Bacon's philosophy thus represents a determined crossing of Renaissance Humanism and Reformation Puritanism. Whilst objecting to the obscurantists who mingled Theology with Philosophy, he brought about, in a way, a new combination of the two. The fundamental factor governing this new combination is action; it came to replace a different medieval and Renaissance synthesis of Hebraic and Hellenistic motives whose fundamental term had been contemplation. In overthrowing the religious categories of that universe which a more leisured, a more relaxed, and a more aristocratic generation of men had designed, he thus replaced a basically logistic, by a basically pragmatic system. Hebraism enters on both sides of the equation.

It is worth remarking by way of conclusion that Bacon's quotations from the Bible are more numerous than those from

[1] Of Bacon's mother, R. W. Church writes, 'She was passionately religious according to the uncompromising religion which the exiles had brought back with them from Geneva, Strassburg, and Zurich, and which saw in Calvin's theology a solution of all the difficulties, and in his discipline a remedy for all the evils, of mankind.' *Bacon* (London, 1886), p. 5.

any other source. He is in this respect obviously a child of the Reformation, for whom the direct contact with the Biblical text is a primary experience. Often he uses a biblical quotation to support some scientific proposition, as in the Second Book of *The Advancement of Learning*, where he quotes, 'I know that whatever God does, it shall be forever; nothing can be put to it, nor anything taken from it.' This is brought to confirm his view 'that the *quantum* of Nature is eternal.'[1] The text here is used allegorically rather in the Puritan manner and is reduced to a bare logical argument. In this way, Scripture is made applicable to the affairs of life though at the cost of its spiritual content and poetry. Also like that of a Puritan is his austere treatment of the mysteries of faith which, he says, are 'not to be attained but by inspiration and revelation from God'.[2] The Bible in such instances must be accepted as a bare and dogmatic statement. To exercise the human imagination about the text would be a presumption. The Bible is too sacred for interpretation; and yet his handling of the text often has the curious effect of completely subverting it. He quotes, 'The spirit of Man is the lamp of God, wherewith he searches the inwardness of all secrets.' Here is a text which surely echoes through all the corridors of the soul: it became a primary focus of inspiration later on for the Cambridge Platonists who were to achieve a healthier Hebraism than either Bacon or the Puritans. For Bacon this text is used to underpin the argument for an omnipotent and omniscient humanity! 'Nothing parcel of the world is denied to man's inquiry and invention', is his comment.[3] Here is a conclusion to take the breath away. It is the Bible used to sweep away all theistic considerations, and to rid the cosmos of all its divine mystery.

With the help of Scripture imagery and rhetoric a Biblical cast is given to Bacon's philosophical writings. Science in his sense becomes a sort of religious enterprise. The urgent demand for inquiry and invention, cut off from all moral sanctions and all limitary feelings of awe, becomes a pseudo-religious impulse, a sacred task, a serious call, supported by appropriate prooftexts. This atmosphere of Hebraic intensity, this ever present sense of a missionary enterprise in the cause of the aggrandise-

[1] *Works*, III, 348.   [2] *Ibid.*, 479.   [3] *Ibid.*, 265.

ment of Man and his Empire over Nature, betray a confusion of spheres more radical than that of the Hebraic enthusiasts of the Paracelsan school whom Bacon accuses of corrupting Philosophy through an admixture of Theology. With greater presumption than theirs, Bacon is prepared to draw upon the Hebrew oracles and call his imaginary scientific academy designed for 'the enlarging of the bounds of human Empire, to the effecting of all things possible' by the name of Solomon's House. The august scriptural associations are obvious; it is decidedly for Bacon the exalted edifice from which salvation and light would go forth to mankind.

VII

THE COVENANT

I

HAVING ARRIVED at the conclusion that for Bacon Hebraism constituted an important driving-force and that there was also in this respect a link between him and the new middle-class spirit of Puritan enterprise, let us beware of contradictions. Earlier we spoke of the plain style of Bacon and the Puritans as contrasted with the richer poetic styles of Browne, Milton, and Jeremy Taylor. These latter were, we said, Hebraic, whilst Puritan plainness is to be sought rather in the austerities of the gospels and in the Pauline repudiation of the old law and the 'old Adam'. What then do we mean by Hebraism? How can it be both itself and its own opposite? And likewise what do we mean by Puritanism? How can it stand both for Hebraism and the evangelical repudiation of Hebraism?

An answer might be intimated along the lines of Blake's mythology. Puritanism and Baconianism are, as Blake would say, Albion fallen into the sleep of Ulro, of deadly error and the cold, unimaginative world of 'perverted and single vision'. But Albion is still always the 'spectre' of Jerusalem, of ideal unity, of the fullest development of the senses and the Imagination, the harmony and peace of Eden (*Jerusalem*, sect. 15). The dialectic of Blake's system is certainly helpful and should not be lightly dismissed by the student of ideas. We may consider the major revolutions of ideas from the Renaissance onwards as a drama in which the main actors are, so to speak, Jerusalem and Albion, Albion being taken in this context as the genius of western Man linked with bonds of love and obedience to Jerusalem, but occasionally inclined to break free. These acts of insurrection do not disprove the bond; on the contrary they paradoxically confirm it, for the very zeal and dedicated purpose of Albion in tearing aside the veil of the sanctuary are themselves derived from, and only to be explained by, the divine powers contained in Jerusalem.

93

These hints are alluring but they can do little more than illuminate the road of strict analysis and research into historical origins. Moreover, with Blake we have to beware of a certain shifting quality in the very meaning of his symbols. We are not always entitled to assume that he consistently means by Jerusalem and Albion what we would have him mean by them.[1] We shall have to define Hebraism and Puritanism for ourselves.

There can be no doubt that the stern Puritan saint at war with the World, the Flesh, and the Devil, stands to outward view at a great distance from either Judaism or Biblical Hebraism. The God of the Hebrews was after all one whose Temple was built with hands, and whose claims on men were addressed to them in their flesh and blood character as mortal creatures of passion and instinct. It has been said by one perceptive author, J. G. Dow, writing on 'Hebrew and Puritan', that 'the Puritans wanted that fulness of life which made David dance before the Ark and enabled Solomon to deck an earlier bower of Acrasia'.[2] He goes on:

> We are at once struck with the outward splendour of Judaism as contrasted with the austerity and bareness of Puritanism; and the contrast between the sensuous magnificence of the Temple-service and the wan, cold, colourless worship of a Puritan church is an index of the radical distinction between the Puritan and the Hebrew mind.[3]

This explains, according to Dow, why the Puritans never produced a religious poetry. That indeed was one of the essential differences between Hebrew and Puritan. When we turn from the Jewish prophets to the Puritan preachers, we find that 'we have descended on a sudden from poetry to casuistry, from prophecy to pettifogging'.[4] And whilst the Puritan insensitivity to the complex or symbolic quality of words helped to create conditions in which a clear, unambiguous prose-style could be developed, on the debit side it meant

---

[1] See below, Epilogue.
[2] *The Jewish Quarterly Review*, III (London, 1891), 52-84. Citation from p. 75.
[3] *Ibid.*, pp. 76-7.
[4] *Ibid.*, p. 78.

undoubtedly the impoverishment of the powers of the imagination, 'a touch of frost to the imaginative life of the soul'.[1]

For the Puritan, to be zealous meant harshly to reject the World; it meant an eternal self-denying ordinance; it meant no theatres, little music, sobriety in dress, and a concentration upon the inner life, a 'walking with the spirit'. For the Hebrew, zeal meant action in the realm of history, a sense of personal and national dedication, a social and cultural life galvanized by a central sanctifying purpose, an experience of God which expressed itself in a rich ceremonial and a multifarious literature. The far-off divine event to which the whole creation moved was not in the world to come but in this world. The theme of salvation was for the Hebrew, the theme of History, not of Metahistory.

To understand the extent and nature of the differences between the two, and at the same time to employ a theological terminology which would have been understood by the men of the seventeenth century, we may distinguish between the Hebrew 'righteousness of works' and the Calvinist (and ultimately Pauline) 'righteousness of faith'; between the Hebrew stress on Birth and Creation and the Calvinist (and ultimately Pauline) stress on Rebirth and Redemption, between the Hebrew stress on the law and the commandments and the Calvinist (and ultimately Pauline) stress on Grace.

What is meant by the righteousness of works? For this term is not only important as a term of abuse in the Protestant assault on Romanism, it is also a central issue in the debate between Calvinist and Arminian, Jesuit and Jansenist. In a well-known Hebrew poem, the first Psalm, the righteous man is described as being

> Like a tree planted by rivers of water,
> That bringeth forth his fruit in his season;
> His leaf also shall not wither;
> And whatsoever he doeth shall prosper.

The first thing to be noted is that the righteous man, the *Sadik*, is imaginatively defined by the life of the natural world; he is like a tree planted by rivers of water. Both the reference to man as a tree and to *Torah*, or saving Truth, as a fountain of

[1] Cf. Matthew Arnold, 'The Study of Poetry'. See above, Introduction.

95

water have an insistent frequency in the Hebrew Bible (e.g. *Deut.* xxxii, 2; *Psalm* lxxii, 6; etc.). Water does not come, as it were, automatically in the Land of Israel, and when it does come it is felt to be a direct and peculiar blessing of God. In the Old Testament, punishment and reward are generally associated with the cessation or granting of rain (e.g. *Deut.* xi, 14-17; *Zech.* xiv, 17), so much so that the Hebrew religion has been called a rain-theology.[1] Nevertheless it is 'natural' for rain to fall and vegetation to grow—in the sense that if these things did not happen, life itself would cease to be possible. The miraculous is somehow inseparable from the organic life of man and nature. Similarly, righteousness though nourished in a mysterious way is nevertheless a flowering of potentialities with which we are already endowed owing to the kind of form and substance that we are. Righteousness does not involve leaving the world behind, or despising our natural abilities; it is rather a matter of raising them to the highest power:

> The commandment which I command thee to-day is not too hard for thee, neither is it far off. It is not in heaven that thou shouldest say: Who shall go up for us to heaven and bring it unto us, and make us to hear it, that we may do it. . . . But the word is very nigh unto thee, in thy mouth and in thy heart, that thou mayst do it.
>
> (*Deut.* xxx, 11 f.)

One notices the repeated emphasis on doing. A righteousness unrelated to action would have been meaningless to the ancient Hebrew. Priest and Prophet might place their emphasis differently: one might stress the conservation of the values of tradition, whilst the other might see the challenge rather in terms of dynamic progress, but in either case righteousness was a matter of practical performance, and the practical discipline of the Law was for both the very foundation of the religious life. In the pharisaic phase of Judaism the observance of the law reached a stage of elaborate particularity. But there was nothing altogether novel about this. The prophet Ezekiel and the author of *Psalm* cxix were hardly less pharisaic than Rabbi Gamaliel.

[1] B. Duhm, quoted by H. Wheeler Robinson, *Religious Ideas of the Old Testament* (1913 ed., London, 1949), p. 73.

The righteousness of faith as taught in the gospels is very much a reaction against this. We are not at this moment concerned with the causes of this reaction, though this might take us into some interesting by-paths of history and literature. But we are concerned, briefly, with its result.

> Then said they unto him, What shall we do, that we might work the works of God, Jesus answered and said unto them, This is the work of God, that ye believe in him whom he hath sent . . . the bread of God is he which cometh down from heaven, and giveth life unto the world.
>
> *(John* vi, 28 f.)

St. Paul enforces and consolidates the doctrine of the 'righteousness of faith'. Eternal life is guaranteed to those who believe and denied to those who do not. The Law is the false road of righteousness 'for ye are not under the law, but under Grace'.

The differences between these two conceptions of righteousness, enter the seventeenth century as the theme of the debate between the Arminians and the Calvinists. The Arminians, or many of them, inclined to the Pelagian heresy which stressed the natural ability of man to achieve righteousness through the exercise of his free-will. They also no doubt drew on the Ciceronian tradition of the Renaissance, for Cicero with something of the stoic pride recognized the power of man to achieve *virtus*, even if (unlike a Hebrew moralist) he did not recognize such virtue as being ultimately owing to the Grace of God. Certainly Greek and Roman wisdom as brought forth in the Renaissance helped the Arminians to formulate their creed, but in substance the righteousness of Works (and I take it this is where the Pelagian heresy leads) is attributable to the legacy of Hebraism. The passion for right-doing is, as Matthew Arnold repeatedly urged, the great ethical motive of the prophets of Israel. In putting their emphasis here, the Pelagian heretics, of whom Jeremy Taylor was one, and Milton possibly another, were truly close to the spirit and doctrine of the Old Testament. The Calvinists were correspondingly far from it. For them as for Paul, righteousness is achieved by Faith, and Faith is achieved when the Old Adam has been destroyed and Man has been reborn through Grace.

Grace, or *charis*, is of course a special word and an extra-ordinarily difficult word in the New Testament. No doubt it has a great many undertones and a great many revealing differences of emphasis, and if we here simplify its meaning by concentrating on the transcendent and other-worldly character of Grace in the evangelical Christian tradition, it is because its meaning is undoubtedly flattened out in this way later on in Calvinism. It occupies a sphere beyond that of Nature. 'Nothing is more at variance with the Grace of God than man's natural ability,' said Calvin.[1] The nearest Old Testament word to Grace is *hesed*; though generally translated as 'Loving kindness', *hesed* is an extremely difficult word in the Old Testament too. It has been rendered by one recent writer 'Covenant love'[2] and that is perhaps as near as we can get. We could say that *hesed* is closely related to the creation and conservation of the world ('The world is built by Grace' is probably the correct rendering of *Psalm* lxxxix, 2) and the creation of Man in the Divine Image. The same *hesed* binds father to child and husband to wife often in despite of the recalcitrance or disobedience of its object. (*Lamentations* iii, 22; *Hosea* ii, 19; *Deut.* vii, 9). It is indeed Covenant-love, and it is rooted in natural relationships. Grace is thus closely bound up not with re-birth and re-creation, but with Birth and Creation; it is a sign of the unbelievable nearness of God; without it the godward adventure would be meaning-less, just as without it the blessings of God seen in every shower of rain and every blade of grass would be meaningless also. And Righteousness is the human testimony to the manifest reality of this Covenant-love.

The Hebrew Covenant or *Brith* therefore whilst being essen-tially a 'Covenant of Works' as Christian theologians have always recognized, is nevertheless rooted in Covenant Love or Grace. As in the Father-Child relationship or the Husband-Wife relationship—both of which are so frequently used in the Old Testament as images of the Divine Covenant with men—love and duty, mercy and judgement, go together and are inseparable from one another. Obligation is rooted in uncon-ditioned Love: Love is rooted in unconditioned Obligation. 'As a man chasteneth his son, so the Lord thy God chasteneth thee.

[1] Comment. ad 2 *Corinthians* x.
[2] N. Snaith, *Mercy and Sacrifice* (London, 1953), pp. 80 f.

Therefore shalt thou keep the commandments of the Lord thy God, to walk in his ways, and to fear him.' (*Deut.* viii, 5-6.) What has happened in the Pauline theology is that Covenant Love has been somehow separated from Covenant Obligation, and the former has taken on a supernatural character: Grace has become a special and barely human privilege unconnected with Works. 'And if by Grace, then is it no more of works: otherwise grace is no more grace. But if it be of works, then is it no more grace: otherwise work is no more work.' (*Romans* xi, 6.) This is the Pauline 'election of Grace' which became for Puritan theologians the basis of the so-called 'Covenant of Grace', the spiritual gift of rebirth and regeneration, the entry into which guaranteed the death of the Old Adam and the promise of eternal life.

It should not be thought that this stress on Grace led to a liberation from the sense of sin, a walking with the spirit in pure freedom. This indeed was the spiritual experience of certain groups of antinomians in the mid-seventeenth century in England and the American colonies,[1] but such deviations were looked on with horror by the orthodox. As with Paul himself, the Puritans having thrown off the shackles of the Law, submitted themselves to an even more rigorous moral discipline than that demanded by the 'Covenant of Works'. The Law had recognized Man as a creature of blood and passions and had legislated accordingly: the Covenant of Grace legislated for Man as reborn in the Spirit. All that belonged to the Old Adam had to be overcome. There is a paradox here, and it belongs to the heart of Puritanism. Spirit and Flesh have been divided as they never were in the Old Testament, but the Old Adam now newly revealed by the light of Grace has to be rooted out and mortified by means of a discipline more rigorous than that envisaged in the Law of Moses (*Romans* vii, 18; viii, 13). This is the dualism of the Greek yoked to the righteous zeal of the Hebrew. The flesh is full of evil concupiscence and original sin and must consequently be mortified: 'O wretched man that I am! who shall deliver me from the body of this death?' The pathos of this cry is echoed through centuries of Christian

[1] For an interesting account of this, see Gertrude Huehns, *Autinomianism in English History 1640-1660* (London, 1951), and Perry Miller, *The New England Mind* (New York, 1939), ch. 13, *passim.*

martyrdom and sacrifice. St. Paul keeps before his followers the flaming example of his own tremendous self-conquest:

> But I keep under my body, and bring it into subjection: lest that by any means, when I have preached to others, I myself should be a castaway.
>
> (1 *Corinthians* ix, 27)

This principle is carried forward through Augustine and the sixteenth-century reformers and explains the moral intensities of the English Puritans of the seventeenth century.[1] It also explains the violence of the reaction to Puritanism which is felt later on both in England and America when its restrictive moral code came to be overthrown. Victorian prudery is certainly the legacy of English Puritanism, but post-Victorian licence is its legacy no less. The Covenant of Grace suggests therefore on the one hand a very exalted concept of human possibilities, a reaching beyond the norms of human nature to a rarefied and spiritual state, an agonizing and thrilling contact between the believer and his personal Saviour, an opening of the heart to mysteries which are beyond this life. On the other hand, it suggests a depressingly low valuation of human nature ('But if it be of works, then is no more grace'); such Grace cannot be extended to Man simply as he is created, for Man is unbelievably corrupt, depraved, full of evil concupiscence; in him dwelleth no good thing (*Romans* vii, 18). This is what we may term religious polarization: instead of seeing every man as an incarnation, an *imago dei*, we have a situation in which there is one single incarnation. The human race is in principle unworthy of salvation, but very special arrangements are made

---

[1] It is hardly necessary to prove that the Calvinistic Puritans regarded themselves in a special sense as the disciples of Paul, just as the Quakers saw themselves as the followers of the author of the fourth gospel. Calvin looked upon Paul's epistle to the Romans as the entry 'unto all the most secret treasures of the Scriptures'. (*Argument* prefixed to his Commentary on *Romans*.) It was the book with which he commenced his exegetical labours. Bunyan tells us in *Grace Abounding* that the decisive stage of his spiritual history was reached when he began to read the Pauline sections of the New Testament. W. Haller notes (*The Rise of Puritanism*, New York, 1938, p. 86): 'Calvin's most important effect upon the preachers was to send them posting back to scripture, particularly to the epistles of Paul, to Paul's life as recorded in Acts, and so to the gospels and to the rest of holy writ.'

whereby through Grace we may be able to transcend our natural human condition and so attain, though not in the flesh, the promise of salvation. Calvin announces the paradox clearly in the Second Book of the *Institutes*:

> Our inquities, like a cloud intervening between Him and us, having utterly alienated us from the kingdom of heaven, none but a person reaching to him could be the medium of restoring peace. But who could thus reach to him? . . . The case was certainly desperate, if the Godhead itself did not descend to us, it being impossible for us to ascend. Thus the Son of God behoved to become our Emmanuel, i.e., God with us; and in such a way, that by mutual union his divinity and our nature might be combined; otherwise, neither was the proximity near enough nor the affinity strong enough, to give us hope that God would dwell with us; so great was the repugnance between our pollution and the spotless purity of God.
>
> (Bk. II, ch. 12)

On the one side, the whole Creation is lost in the murk of Original Sin; on the other side, a purely metaphysical corporation is instituted, detached from the normal process of living, and consisting of those who are joined by faith to the community of Jesus. For Calvin there is no universal touch of election, 'Those who dream of some seed of election implanted in their hearts from their birth by the agency of which they are even inclined to piety and the fear of God, are not supported by the authority of Scripture. . . .'[1] Now the stress upon the utterly transcendent nature of God; the purely spiritual character of our relation to him; his distance from the world, which becomes a place of evil under the dominion of Satan; the necessity for some Mediator to overcome this distance by standing between 'our pollution and the spotless purity of God', these are in essence not Hebraic, but Greek and Gnostic modes of thinking. The Jewish Messiah, a politico-religious leader of the type of David, takes on now the character of a supernatural *Soter* or *Paraclete*.[2] By way of reciprocation, the Devil—not exactly a

[1] *Institutes*, III, 24 (10).
[2] On the general differences between the Jewish and Christian doctrines of the Messiah, see J. Klausner, *The Messianic Idea in Israel* (English translation, by W. F. Stinespring, London, 1956) pp. 519-31.

major personality in the Hebrew Scriptures—assumes rather gigantic proportions as the cosmic antagonist of the *Messiah*: but he is an immanent as well as a transcendent Devil, for he works evil in our bones and members in an undying warfare against the operations of Grace; he is the great red Dragon of the Apocalypse, the accuser, who can only be assuaged by the blood of the Lamb (*Revelation* xii, 3 f.).

These are the aspects of Christian doctrine which receive major emphasis in Calvinism and subsequently in the different Puritan societies in England and the New World. The dichotomy of Flesh and Spirit, which had its affinities in the Hellenic philosophies of St. Paul's time, emerged in its harshest and most extreme form in the disjunctive logic of the Puritan followers of Calvin in the seventeenth century. Man is either saved or (more probably) damned; if the former, then he is of the elect and his relation to the world is existentially unimportant; if the latter, then he has, correctly speaking, no vision of heaven and no contact with the angels. Richard Baxter says in his blunt fashion, 'the godly loveth not the world nor the things of the world, and the wicked loveth not God, nor the things of God, as such'.[1]

Such dichotomizing is curiously parallel to other trends in the Counter-Renaissance. The Calvinist doctrine of total human depravity is, as has often been shown, analogous to the Machiavellian 'naturalism' with its cynical view of human nature (cf. *The Prince*, ch. 17). Like Machiavelli, Calvin sees in the notion of human free-will a mere illusion. There is a similarity also between the function of Fortune in Machiavelli's philosophy of history and the place of Predestination in the Calvinist system. For both, human destiny is given over to the rule of an arbitrary, and even capricious agency far removed from the slightest concern with human motive or effort.[2]

The ethical side of Calvinism with its tendency to negate the value of this-worldly effort, of mere 'Works' has marked affinities with the stoic *apatheia* and *ataraxia*. Paul asked the Corinthians why they went to law with one another and did not rather 'suffer themselves to be defrauded'! This is *ataraxia* in its

---

[1] *The Saints' Everlasting Rest* (Edition of 1658), p. 833. From a supplementary note, dated January 15, 1657.

[2] Hiram Haydn, *op. cit.*, p. 439.

most extreme form. The possible link between Paul and the stoical philosophers of his time does not interest us here, but there is undoubtedly a link between emergent Protestantism in the sixteenth century trying to get back to the primitive doctrine of the apostle, and the neo-stoical movement of the late Renaissance.[1] Melanchthon embraced the ethical system of stoicism as applicable to the 'exterior man' whilst reserving the interior sanctum of the heart for the operations of Grace.[2] On the practical side they have much in common. The Puritans later on were generally opposed to the humanist revival of ancient thought, but they sometimes made an exception in favour of Stoicism and in particular of Seneca's teachings. Comenius (who was close in spirit to the English Puritans) reserved a place for Seneca in the school room in spite of the generally anti-humanist bias of his *Great Didactic*. Milton's observations on Cromwell and Fairfax point chiefly to their stoical bearing and reserve.[3]

The attraction of such analogies is very great. We could pursue a similar parallel between the Puritan emphasis on Grace and the new mystical neo-platonism of the sixteenth and seventeenth centuries. The stress on transcendent 'Ideas' and the after-life with the correspondent attitude to this world as a place of death and decay results in a philosophical polarization comparable to the religious polarization of Calvinism; and in the literature of the period they often flow together.[4] But all these analogies, though dazzling enough, often obscure more than they enlighten. If we consider the position thoughtfully, we must report that Cromwell (as Marvell pictured him) 'through adventurous War urging his active star' was not in the least like a Stoic hero or a Platonic mystic either of antiquity or modernity. He reminds us neither of Lipsius, Montaigne, nor Shakespeare's Brutus. Surely the Puritan attitude to the external order is ultimately the opposite of Stoic apathy! Apathy is just one minor chord in Puritanism. The dominant note is

[1] Cf. M. Higgins, 'The Development of the "Senecal Man",' *Review of English Studies*, XXIII (Oxford, 1947), 24 seq.

[2] L. Zanta, *op. cit.*, p. 71.

[3] *Works, op. cit.*, VIII, 215 f.

[4] Cf. R. W. Battenhouse, 'Doctrine of Man in Calvin and in Renaissance Platonism', *J.H.I.*, IX (1948), 447-71.

sounded in what R. H. Tawney calls the 'daemonic energy' with which 'the Puritan flings himself into practical activities'.[1]

Besides the New Testament passivity of the Puritan ('why do ye not rather suffer yourselves to be defrauded') there is also powerfully and paradoxically enfolded with it a large measure of Old Testament activism. The Puritans were in fact more often fighters, captains of industry and commerce than they were contemplative mystics. Puritanism came to overthrow the *logos* philosophy with its combination of Aristotle and Genesis, and its ethic of the Middle Way, and replaced it with a new Judeo-Hellenic dialectic of its own. It succeeded in linking the dynamic appeal of the Old Testament, especially its doctrine of election with the religion of the gospels. 'Calvin', it has been said, 'carries back the idea of free grace into the law, and interprets the latter by the former.'[2] The doctrine of election, on the direct analogy of the election of Israel as recounted in the Old Testament, is centrally located in Calvinism. It gives the 'Saint' a sense of chosenness and mission which could have, and indeed did have, the most extraordinary practical consequences. Calvinism became the religion of the new rising Middle Class and stimulated their zest for enterprise, for an economic structure giving the maximum of freedom and opportunity for the individual now thrust forward into the world to fight and conquer.

In Calvin's own system, the doctrine of election was intended to have a spiritual application only, but such powerful psychological drives, once released, cannot be confined in dogmatic barriers. John Knox, Cromwell, and the Puritans who pushed into the American midwest, felt themselves the chosen vessels of the historical and political purposes of Providence. Whilst despising the world, the Puritan hero felt nevertheless that it was given him to exploit. There is a theological inconsistency here, but then these forces were not nourished by theology. They were nourished by something much more potent, namely the direct, unmediated, imaginative contact with the English Bible. This was the primary religious experience of the new era. And the English Bible placed in the hands of all by the

[1] *Religion and the Rise of Capitalism* (1926 ed., London, 1938), p. 180.
[2] W. Adams Brown in Hastings, *Encyclopaedia of Religion and Ethics*, s.v. 'Covenant Theology', IV, 219-20.

Reformation included both the Old Testament and the New. On the one hand, the English Protestant, and specifically the Puritan who represented Protestantism in its most radical form, would feel himself to be a follower of the evangelists and the apostle Paul fighting against the law of Works (with which he identified Roman Catholicism) and the 'Jewish' priestly ceremonial of the Church. In this sense his was a religion of the gospel. But on the other hand, there was the strong imaginative constraint of the Old Testament. Had they not, like the Judges of Israel been summoned to destroy the idols of the heathen and break down their altars? How could they fail to identify themselves with the Israel of old when the Lord's people were called to do vengeance on their enemies, when the battle was carried over into the political arena?

Calvin himself has been scrupulous in defining the boundaries between the civil and religious authority. He insisted on the complete autonomy of the Church in its sphere, but he insisted likewise on the unconditional obedience due to the civil magistrate in his sphere. This is the doctrine of separated spheres and it is the gist of the final chapter of the *Institutes*. But it did not survive the revolutionary tide of Puritanism in the mid-seventeenth century. Nor did it last long for Calvin himself, because his system eventually emerged as a theocracy. In Scotland, Puritanism took on the character of a seditious conspiracy, an attempt to overthrow the existing political order and replace it likewise by a theocracy. But whether in Geneva, in Scotland, in England, or in the North American colonies, the tide of Calvinist spirituality swept over from the ecclesiastical into the civil sphere; and the important and disappointing fact to be noted is that with all allowance made for a certain contribution to the growth of modern democracy, the Puritan effort in the civil sphere failed to result in any high ideal of civil polity. The psychological pattern here is a trifle complex; but briefly one may say that the powerful drives released by the doctrine of election overflowed the boundaries erected between God and the World, thus bringing into the secular sphere a kind of effort geared to a highly spiritual motor-mechanism; nevertheless, the Calvinist separation of Nature and Grace was not forgotten and it continued to determine the thoroughly amoral and unspiritual content of that effort itself.[1]

This is the spectral Albion once more—a fragmented spirituality. It came of taking from the Hebrew Scripture its doctrine of election whilst failing to grasp the universal setting of that doctrine and the original moral purpose which informed it. It is perhaps true that the dynamic power which the sense of election afforded was (and is) in some ways the greater for its having been detached from its original content and moral ends. That would explain the tremendous forward impulse which Puritanism gave to the civilization of the West in commerce, science, and industry. But being a severed fragment of some primal unity, it revealed in these spheres a diabolical as well as an angelic potency.

II

It has been suggested that the idea of chosenness is what gives to Puritanism its special Hebraic character. But mere election does not cover the case satisfactorily. After all, election of itself may be compatible with a passive response on the part of the person or persons elected. It does not suggest the full dynamic quality of the relationship, the aspect of urgent human participation which belongs to the core of Puritanism, as indeed it belongs to the heart of Hebraism. The more inclusive and satisfactory term here is 'Covenant'. We do not come across this word so much in Calvin's writings, but in the seventeenth century, and typically in such a work as William Ames's *The Marrow of Sacred Divinity* (1642), the Covenant-idea becomes a central, and almost, one might say, an all-embracing theological concept. The Covenant-idea became for Puritans the central

[1] A. S. P. Woodhouse shows (*Puritanism and Liberty*, London, 1938, Introduction, p. 85) how a new secularization of the State is authorized by Puritanism in place of the hierarchical, sanctified order which obtained before the Reformation. In the vacuum created by the despiritualization of the political order, various modern kinds of State could flourish, including the Machiavellian type. (See also below in the sections on Hobbes.) A modern version of the doctrine of election combined with a considerable measure of political inhumanity is to be found in the South African policy of *apartheid*. The inspiration for that is doubtless to be traced to the same theological sources we are considering here.

feature of the analogy with Israel. In England the congrega-
tionalists pledged their faith in Covenant-form. In Scotland, a
formal Covenant was entered into by the people in the presence
of their rulers as in Old Testament times (cf. *Jeremiah* xxxiv).
In New England later on, under the leadership of men like
John Winthrop and Thomas Hooker, the societies undertook a
similar public Covenant in addition to the special spiritual
Covenant governing the lives of the elect.[1] The religious life and
the social life are founded on agreement, obligation, on the
responsible undertaking of free agents conscious of the tremendous significance of their decisions.

We are not here concerned with the political and social
consequences of the Covenant-doctrine; if we were we should
probably find that it led not only in the direction of American
democracy but also no less in the direction of revolutionary
communism. At this stage we are more concerned with the new
'Gestalt' itself, with the new sense of oneself and one's relation
to God and the World which the Covenant, as brought forward
by the Puritans from Hebraic sources, seemed to authorize.

In the Covenant-doctrine, Man is seen to be created from
nothing. He starts out merely as dust, with no claims whatever
to any specially assigned place in a cosmic Chain. In this
sense, the Covenant preserves the sense of an enormous, indeed
apparently unbridgeable, distance between an omnipotent
Creator and his human creation. On the other hand, impotent
and without claims as he is, Man is miraculously elected to be
the partner of Deity in an historical enterprise. His life is invested not merely with purpose but with divine purpose; and
within the categories of the Covenant, he and his Divine
Creator enter into mutual obligations to one another. This is
the audacious claim of the Hebrew Religion; to the Greeks
it would have seemed an example of incredible *hubris*. The
doctrine is in some sense taken over into Christianity from its
inception, and is found in Thomas Aquinas, in the later Middle
Ages, but its full possibilities are not realized until it is awakened
by the Reformation rediscovery of Scripture, and kindled into
intense life by the Puritans.

The tremendous sense of liberation, as well as the tremendous

[1] Cf. Perry Miller, 'Preparation for Salvation in New England', *J.H.I.*,
IV (1943), 254-5, *The New England Mind*, I, 419 f.

sense of responsibility which went with the doctrine of Covenant, are difficult to grasp at the present day, when we have left the atmosphere of Puritan spirituality far behind us, but the effects are still with us in our zeal for technological advance and in the various movements for social and political reform which followed in the wake of Puritanism. In essence, the Covenant-idea gives a meaning and value to life in this world, quite different from that fostered by Hellenic thought patterns. It introduces a sense of urgency and an impetus for boundless activity which are the marks of the Hebrew Religion as against the more contemplative ideals fostered under the influence of Greek Philosophy. It is the Hebraic alternative to the *logos*. The *logos* offers illumination, the recognition that the nature of things corresponds to the nature of the mind. The excitement is that of seeing one's own reflection, so to speak, in the mirror of nature. The Covenant leads us back to a dramatic encounter, a confrontation of our own individuality with a transcendent otherness—an I/Thou confrontation. The Chain of Being, to take one typical *logos*—formula, is a *picture* of relationships in the cosmos. It is static. It lacks the time-dimension. The Covenant by contrast is a *drama*—a drama of election and salvation. It is essentially a statement about historical ends and means.[1] Moreover, it gives Man a more paradoxical and exciting role in the order of things than did the traditional ethics of the Golden Mean. Perhaps that is why it erupted so powerfully in the period of the Renaissance and the Counter-Renaissance,

---

[1] On the centrality of the Covenant in Old Testament thinking and in its theopolity, there is now a vast literature; see G. E. Wright, *The Old Testament Against its Environment* (London, 1951), pp. 54 f., M. Buber, *Königtum Gottes* (Berlin, 1932), pp. 111-35 (ch. 7), and W. Eichrodt, *Theologie des Alten Testaments*, I (Leipzig, 1933), *passim*. Tillich remarks justly that 'the Covenant-symbol is applied not only to the relation between God and the nation but also to the relation between God and Nature' (*Biblical Religion and the Search for Ultimate Reality*, Chicago, 1955, p. 40). It is generally recognized that the Israelite, in replacing mythical time by historical time, gave pattern and significance to the latter by visualizing it as a Covenant-drama in which the acts of God and the responses of Man have reference both to Covenant beginnings and Covenant ends. Creation itself is a Covenant-act, and has reference to an ultimate consummation without which mere Creation as such would be meaningless. For further discussion, see also A. Neher, *L'Essence du Prophétisme* (Paris, 1955), pp. 116-45. Mr. Neher's handling of the 'Alliance' is perhaps the most lucid and helpful to date.

when the 'discovery of Man' had found expression in so many other striking ways.

The doctrine of Covenant in its modern, dynamic form (for at this moment I omit discussion of the employment of the Covenant-idea in traditional Christian philosophy and the natural-law school) was brought forward by the Puritans, but in so far as the Puritans continued to attach to it their evangelical notions of piety, its healthier possibilities, its more civilizing possibilities, shall we say—could not be realized. In the form of the 'Covenant of Grace' it served to intensify many of the dissociative forces in seventeenth-century life: it produced a climate in which enormous energy could be released in the economic and political spheres by the Puritan believer urged on by his sense of election and mission. But in the system of Calvinism that energy will not be ethically controlled, since the Kingdom of God is not to be constructed out of the materials of this world. Consequently it finds itself free from ethical restraints, and this results all too often in ugliness (the ugliness of the Industrial Revolution for instance) and in the pursuit of power for its own sake. This is the spectral Albion separated from its true Emanation in Jerusalem. The new climate of middle-class enterprise and Puritan spirituality, the paradoxical combination of extreme worldliness and extreme otherworldliness, have been made familiar to us by the writings of Weber and Tawney. And we are aware that seventeenth-century Puritanism was in a way more disagreeable, because more *actively* inhuman, than the ascetic Middle Ages, with its contemplative atmosphere.

It is hardly necessary to say that this kind of morally dissociated activism of the Puritan movement, as it is described to us by the social historians, is no part of the original Old Testament form of the Covenant-idea. The Biblical *Brith* had yielded a psychology characterized by the passion and thirst for righteousness of the Hebrew prophets. Its climate was ethical and its preordained aim was the liberation of mankind from tyranny and its sanctification in the service of God. 'For I the Lord love justice, I hate robbery for burnt-offering; and I will direct their work in truth, and I will make an everlasting covenant with them.' (*Isaiah* lxi, 8.) Moreover the Hebrew prophets and lawgivers looked always to a universal Covenant.

Though there is no doubt ever of the special Covenant-responsibilities of Israel, these are explicable only in terms of a wider Covenant embracing mankind as a whole. In the later chapters of *Isaiah* the universal aspects of the Israelite Covenant are the theme of a series of impassioned oracles.

> I the Lord have called thee in righteousness, and will hold thine hand, and will keep thee, and give thee for a covenant of the people, for a light of the Gentiles.
>
> (*Isaiah* xlii, 6)

The Covenants with Israel (originally the patriarchal Covenants, and subsequently the Sinaitic Covenant) are themselves environed by a more embracing Covenant-formula, that entered into with the sons of Noah (*Genesis* ix, *passim*), that is, with the human race as a whole. And if the beginnings of the Covenant have this universal scope, its foreordained end likewise is one which includes the vision of peace and blessing for a mankind finally obedient to the voice of God, who is the God of Israel but no less imperatively 'God of the spirits of all flesh.' The Puritans based their Covenant-doctrine on an analogy with a privative Covenant between God and Israel. For them the election of Israel (*sc.* themselves) carried with it as a corollary the damnation of the non-believers, those who were not elected into the Covenant of Grace. This is the notorious Calvinist theme of election for reprobation, and would have occasioned considerable surprise to the Hebrew prophets. The special tasks given to Israel in the providential plan of salvation were more often conceived as a burden than a privilege (and evidently this has been fully confirmed by the pattern of Jewish history): Amos reminded his audience (iii, 2) that since God had chosen Israel they must consequently expect greater punishments than other people. Special functions did not automatically carry with them a special quantity of Grace: on the contrary when Jonah was sent to Nineveh to save the misguided inhabitants, it was they who found Grace whilst the chosen vessel was sent away discomfited. Grace indeed is Covenant-love but it is by no means confined to Israel; it is God's way of working with the Creation as a whole with which he has entered upon a vast Covenant plan. In seizing upon the notion of 'special calling', of a restrictive or exclusive Covenant

The Covenant

as their theological basis, the Puritans were again, as in so
many other ways, guilty of fragmenting, of splitting-up the
spiritual wholes of which Hebraism is composed, and those
fragmented parts of Hebraism, intensified, and disengaged
from their context, gave rise to the dissociative trends in
Puritanism.

To those who in the seventeenth century grasped something
of the Hebrew doctrine of salvation in terms of Covenant, who
grasped it, that is, in its more authentic less dissociated forms—
and as we shall see there were not a few who did—the idea
became not merely, or primarily, a force for great technological
advances, but an ethical inspiration, a means of mobilizing our
powers under the stress of an urgent, compelling, and exalted
ideal. In this sense, the Covenant held within it the possibility
of a healthier integration of Society (for Society is bound by
Covenant just as the individual is bound therewith to his
Creator) as well as a healthier integration of the human personality itself as a compound of flesh and spirit, as the vessel
of creaturely impulses and immortal longings and possibilities.
Above all, the Covenant-idea in its authentic form brought
together the spheres of Man, God and Nature, severed by the
anarchy of the Counter-Renaissance revolt against order, and
bestowed upon them a common purpose jointly undertaken.
Thus the possibility of a new unity was held out to men. The
Covenant could come to replace the *logos*, to offer a hope of
spiritual integration on new lines significantly different from
those of traditional Christian humanism.

It is possible to discern such a new theme of unity in a number
of English writers of the mid-seventeenth century. It would be
too much to say that the theme was clearly beheld, that this life-
purpose was definitely grasped, but the pattern may be glimpsed with significant iteration. As a corrective to the Counter-
Renaissance Natural Philosophy, we glimpse the Hebrew
doctrine of Creation; as a corrective to the new Anthropology,
we find the Hebrew doctrine of Salvation, and as a corrective to the narrower forms of evangelical piety, we discern the
Hebrew doctrine of Revelation. The syntax by which these
three, Revelation, Salvation, and Creation are bound together
is that of the *Brith* or Covenant. It has been claimed by the
twentieth-century Jewish philosopher, Franz Rosenzweig that

III

the three orders of reality, Man, God, and Nature, only become meaningful in this way, that is in the light of Biblical experience, and that Greek Philosophy whilst claiming to be the wisdom of the whole was in fact only a wisdom of Nature.[1] It reduced everything to the World, to the *cosmos*, so that Man and God became shadows of the World—hence the Greek emphasis on order and symmetry which may be more properly predicated of the World than of Man or God. But by seeing the whole in terms of the *cosmos*, the Greeks failed to see even the *cosmos* in its true character. The *logos* is ultimately a deception.

Nature viewed not as *cosmos* but as Creation, is for Hebraism no less a theme of the Covenant-doctrine than Man or God. The prophet Jeremiah speaks of 'my covenant of the day, and my covenant of the night' (xxxiii, 20). Nature becomes subject to the Divine Law and the Divine Purpose: it takes upon itself the sign of the Covenant (*Genesis* ix, 15-16). It partakes in the historical programme of the Covenant and is destined, like Man, to be redeemed.[2] Like human society, it is visualized as the sphere of change and miracle (cf. *Isaiah* xi, 6 f.) rather than of meaningless static order. Such a Creation partakes with man of the excitement and sense of urgency that go with the Covenant. Nature becomes indeed the region of adventure, and man, coeval with it, and yet raised above it by his special tasks and responsibilities, is the great adventurer. In such a climate, the eruption of modern science, as a special manifestation of the Covenant-spirit, becomes easier to understand.

It is this special manifestation of Hebraism that we noted in the work of Bacon and in his unlicensed, Faustian dream of power. He expresses often this sense of adventure as in the passage in which he compares himself to Columbus setting out on his famous voyage of exploration. Nature is not static but dynamic, full of momentous possibilities for him who may grasp them. But this Baconian spirit represents, like Puritanism itself

[1] See Nahum N. Glatzer, *Franz Rosenzweig: His Life and Thought* (New York, 1953), pp. 191, 198. Rosenzweig's existential teaching is fully displayed in his central work *Der Stern der Erlösung* (Frankfort a.M., 1921).

[2] This is not always recognized by Biblical scholars otherwise alive to the implications of the Hebrew covenant theology. But see W. Eichrodt, *Theologie des Alten Testaments*, II (1935), 81-2; E. C. Rust, *Nature and Man in Biblical Thought* (London, 1953), p. 64; Johs. Pedersen, *Israel III-IV* (English version, Copenhagen, 1940), pp. 617-18.

(which collaterally inspired Bacon to a great extent), a dissociated and perverted form of Hebraism. Bacon had not the
Hebraic vision of a sanctified nature (sanctified by worship
and sacrifice) and of a far-off divine event—other than simply
human self-aggrandisement—to which the whole creation
moves. The ethical context of Hebraism is missing in Bacon.
But it was glimpsed in the writings on Natural Philosophy of
Robert Boyle, Thomas Browne, Henry More, and the later
alchemists.

The next sections of this work will be devoted to the more
positive forms of Hebraism which were to be found in the middle
of the seventeenth century among naturalists, men of letters,
anthropologists, and divines. These will be represented as in a
sense belonging to Jerusalem, the emanation of Albion. They
closely follow in the wake of the discoveries of Bacon and the
Puritans. But they are also in reaction against them and are
seeking a more integrated and ethically exalted ideal, and this
they drew in a great measure from Hebrew sources, as will be
shown. The whole complex of ideas and impulses which I have
gathered together in this chapter were never, I think, grasped
in quite this way by any one of the seventeenth-century writers
with whom I shall be dealing. Nevertheless the account given
here is not simply an importation into the seventeenth-century
field of a modern reading of Old Testament theology. The
pattern can be traced in the writings of our representatives of
'Jerusalem' in different degrees and with differences of emphasis. Milton's writings show a peculiarly intense concentration of Hebraism: for him, England was a Covenant-nation
having tasks and opportunities similar in detail to those of Israel
of old. There is something here of the privative Covenant which
served to distort Milton's sense of history: but he sensed the
ethical context, the passion for righteousness which is inseparable from the Hebrew notion of Covenant. The Levellers taking
a broader view stressed the need for a new society founded on
religious principles. In their campaign for Agreements of the
People, they brought into the region of politics something of the
Hebraic idea of a community sanctified by Covenant-rights and
mutual obligations.[1] They did not adhere to the Puritan separa-

[1] Cf. J. W. Gough, *The Social Contract* (Oxford, 2nd Edition, 1957), p. 95.

tion of Nature and Grace; their idea of a Covenant-community included in itself both the secular and religious aspects of freedom. Anthropology had momentarily come to terms with Revelation; and that precisely is the Hebrew notion of community. Later on there is a reaction in favour of Albion again: we shall see in Hobbes a kind of half-way house between the Hebraic and non-Hebraic versions of the social Covenant. Thus, the ideological history of the century takes on a dialectical pattern as a struggle between what we have (taking certain liberties with Blake's mythological system) termed the forces of Jerusalem and Albion. And these are not angels and demons battling in the central blue but forces of unity and disunity struggling for mastery over men's minds and actions.

It would be incorrect to identify the positive or unitive forces of the period too narrowly with the influence of Israel or with the Jewish factor in western culture. There were too many remnants of Hellenism for that—too much of Plato, Aristotle, and Cicero. Among our representatives of a positive Hebraism will be, for instance, the Cambridge Platonists and no one would wish to deny that group's major debt to Hellenism. Again the idea of social contract in the Levellers, in Hobbes, and even in the Puritans owes much to the Epicurean *syntheke* or primordial compact, described also by Lucretius (*De Rerum Nat.* v, 922 f.). But it is the influence of the Hebraic *Brith* which gives the idea in Western Europe its revolutionary force as well as its atmosphere of dedication and high purpose. Through this investing of it with divine purpose, Hebraism bestows an ideal significance on what, in the Epicurean and Lucretian scheme, had been just a convenient arrangement for the sake of limited advantages.

With the writers whom I shall propose as the representatives of a unitary, associative tendency, many elements of different cultures will be noted, but it will be claimed that the Jewish factor, or to take a word of more universal significance—the factor of Jerusalem—is pre-eminent. It was for them the solvent, the catalyst, which promised to make possible a new and more dynamic order in place of the old philosophies. It represented a new unitary principle which could be invoked instead of the old inadequate unity of the *logos*.

PART THREE

Milton

VIII

MANNA IN THE WILDERNESS

WE HAVE asked the question, 'What was Puritanism?' Let us now ask the question, 'Who were the Puritans?' This, it seems, is a difficult question, because, whilst everyone has a fairly strong feeling (usually one of dislike) which helps him to identify Puritanism, a distribution of the title among various seventeenth-century English writers would certainly raise controversy. Was Marvell, compounding with the new order in 1660, a Puritan; was Bishop Hall, suffering sequestration at Norwich at the hands of the Parliament in his seventy-first year; above all, was Milton who wrote his *Comus* as a retort to the Puritan onslaught on Masques and Plays?[1] Was he a Puritan? The answer in each case seems to be yes and no!

Contemporary attempts at definition seem to have been as contradictory as our own. Malvolio in Shakespeare's *Twelfth Night*, with his middle class ambition, his sobriety in dress, his sanctimoniousness, his hypocrisy (recognized by Henry More and later, by George Eliot as the besetting sin of Puritans) seems a likely candidate, and so Maria terms him 'a kind of Puritan'; but she herself shortly withdraws the suggestion saying, 'the devil a Puritan that he is or anything constantly but a time-pleaser'. No one I think would deny the title to the right wing and centre of the parliamentary party in the Revolution of 1642-46, that is to the Presbyterians and the Independents, but a difficulty arises with some of their opponents, ministers of the episcopal party, who were often good doctrinal Calvinists, or with some of the revolutionary Puritans to the left of the centre such as the Levellers, Diggers, Quakers, Antinomians who were very far from doctrinal Calvinism or any Protestant orthodoxy whatever.

---

[1] William Prynne's *Histriomastix* of 1632 stimulated a number of writers such as Carew to retort by producing new masques. Milton with his *Comus* (1634), it seems, was one of them.

It has been suggested that the common factor in true Puritanism is 'the effort to erect the holy community'.[1] This is a vague enough definition which could easily include the Catholic Church Militant, as well as Bunyan's Bedford meeting. The point is that the paradoxical nature of the Puritan faith stultifies all definitions. In one sense, Milton, with his sense of mission, his fanatical zeal for the 'holy community' represents the quintessence of Puritanism. In another sense, his humanism, his tolerance, his luxury of image, and his delight in the things of this world both in poetry and in life, are at the opposite extreme from the evangelical narrowness of Puritanism.

For practical purposes, the best thing to do is to distinguish between the doctrinal Puritans,[2] including many on the royalist side or many quite uncommitted in the political struggle such as John Davenant, George Abbot, and George Carleton, and the political or revolutionary Puritans who, whether or not they subscribed to Calvinist orthodoxy, were driven on by the inner force of the election or Covenant-idea which, as has been shown, had taken shape in the atmosphere of Calvinist theology. Common to both types or varieties, the doctrinal and the political Puritans, is a vivid sense of 'personal' mission and responsibility. The personal factor, the sense of the world's destiny balancing on one's least word, thought, or action, are the common ground of Puritanism in all its forms. For the doctrinal Puritans, this resulted in an intense inwardness, a concentration upon the inner life where the operations of Grace might be registered, and this would involve a kind of retirement from the world. For the revolutionary Puritans, on the contrary, the sense of personal commitment combined with the doctrine of predestination gave their enterprises a peculiar momentousness, a specially determined character—'for who would not courageously fight, that is beforehand assured of victory'.[3] It gave them a sense of exemption from tradition and precedent, from mere historical conformity. Far from wishing to retire from the world, they

[1] A. E. Barker, *Milton and the Puritan Dilemma. 1641-1660* (University of Toronto, 1942), p. xxi.

[2] For a sensible use of this term and an account of the 'doctrinal Puritans' amongst the episcopal party, see J. B. Marsden, *The History of the Early Puritans* (London, 1850), pp. 371 f., 382.

[3] John Downame, *A Guide to Godlynesse* (1622), Bk. I, 52.

were more inclined to think of themselves as world-reformers, heralds of salvation and change.

Where is Milton in all this? Clearly, he is not a doctrinal, but a political or revolutionary Puritan, holding fast to the Good Old Cause in 1660 when nearly all the others had already lost heart. He has that sense of personal mission and dedication, that sublime inwardness, one would almost say egoism, which made the Puritans our first diarists and psychological novelists. His whole poetic work is one continued autobiography in which the dealings of God with John Milton constantly shine through as the major theme. Thus, speaking through the mouth of his hero, Samson, he laments his blindness, linking it by image to the world's Creation.

> O first created Beam, and thou great Word,
> Let there be light, and light was over all,
> Why am I thus bereav'd thy prime decree?
>
> *(Samson Agonistes,* lines 83-5)

The personal, lyrical element is, in the last analysis, the specific differential of Milton's style in epic and drama. He is never absent from his characters, all of whom, Adam, Satan, Samson, Messiah, Comus, and the Lady, express like a changing dream-landscape, the anguish, the protest, the aspiration, the faith of their author. Milton is in this sense, the first romantic poet. Or rather, it would be true to say that romanticism would not have been possible had Milton not brought into poetry the possibility of an imaginative universe circumscribed by the author's individuality. The subject of his poem is himself. In this sense *Paradise Lost* is the prototype of Wordsworth's *Prelude* and Shelley's *Prometheus Unbound*. Finally, what marks Milton as a Puritan is that quality of 'seriousness'—the word carrying its full theological and moral weight—so important for all evaluation of eighteenth- or nineteenth-century literature. God does not trifle with John Milton and Milton does not trifle with his reader. If it be concluded that the English genius expresses itself primarily in the comedies of Shakespeare and in Chaucer's *Canterbury Tales*, then it must be admitted that Milton and Wordsworth with their exemption from the comic spirit represent a sad deviation from the normal. But then literary history is made up of such deviations, and it is surely mere literary atavism to regard the 'merrie England' tradition of the Middle Ages as somehow more authentic than the Puritan seriousness of the seventeenth century. Students of American literature have never forgotten its Puritan origins, but students of English literature have been less quick to discern behind the moral earnestness of Wordsworth, of George Eliot, of John Stuart Mill (to take three widely separated instances) the influence of the great 'serious' writers of the seventeenth century, Puritan and non-Puritan.

The present intention is to show, against the background of Puritan piety and seriousness, the emergence of a particular constellation which we have termed 'Hebraism'. It is by no means co-extensive with Puritanism; on the contrary its true character has often been obscured by a too simplistic equation between Hebraism and Puritanism; and yet it is impossible to think of its emergence into modern life and literature except in the context of Puritan seriousness.

Milton's strongly Hebraic use of the Covenant-idea has not, so far as I am aware, been fully described as yet.[1] Unlike Shakespeare in the chronicle-plays, he does not think of society as somehow determined by order and tradition. He has in mind rather (like the democratic Levellers) a concept of the dynamic power of change vested in the people. He speaks almost like a modern democrat of 'the liberty and right of free-born men to be governed as seems to them best'. But in fact Milton was no democrat and he has been wrongly represented as such by latter-day zealots for democracy. In *The Ready and Easy Way to Establish a Free Commonwealth*, published on the eve of the Restoration, he appeals for a kind of perpetual senate of the ablest and wisest to govern in the name of what Matthew Arnold would have called the 'national best-self'. By way of analogy he refers to 'the supreme council of seaventie call'd the *Sanhedrin*, founded by *Moses*'[2] and to the Areopagus in Athens. He has in

---

[1] 'Covenant' is a key-term and a key-concept in Milton's writings. In the Index to the Columbia edition, the citations in which it occurs occupy nearly six columns. The union between King and subject is a holy covenant (*Of Reformation*); Milton covenants with the reader to fulfil his promise of writing a great poem (*The Reason of Church Government*); every covenant between man and man may be called a Covenant of God (*The Doctrine and Discipline of Divorce*, Book I, ch. 13); above all, marriage is a Covenant of God (*ibid.*).   [2] *Works*, VI, 128.

mind a patriarchal and theocentric form of government, but founded in, and sanctioned by, popular consent. This conjunction of authority and freedom, law and liberty, this theocentric humanism with all the tensions that such a faith requires, is no temporary phase of Milton's thought, but a deep and permanent feature; it belongs to the heart of his Hebraic message. For the Israelite experience of freedom (archetypally the 'going out of Egypt') is essentially bound up with the experience of total obligation, that is, with the *subordination of freedom* to the law and the commandments. This is the pattern of all Hebrew Covenant-formulae.

The term 'freedom' occurring so often in Milton's writing has thus to be understood in close alliance with the term 'law', and his use of 'law' has to be carefully differentiated—in spite of many similarities—from the 'natural law' of the Stoics, to which, for instance, the Levellers often appealed. Law was not, for Milton, a property of human nature, or if so, it was one which, like Samson's locks (an image in which the notion of law frequently presents itself to Milton) might quickly be alienated through folly and disobedience. It is 'natural' to us in so far as we choose to obey it. This is different from the view of Hooker and other traditional Christian humanists for whom the moral law has the inevitability of the 'eternal' laws of Nature. Milton sees law as having a kind of independence. It has in its action something of human personality rather than natural impersonality. It is a revealed will not a mechanism.

> The hidden wayes of his providence we adore & search not; but the law is his reveled wil, his complete, his evident and certain will; herein *he appears to us as it were in human shape, enters into cov'nant with us*, swears to keep it, binds himself like a just Lawgiver to his own prescriptions, gives himself to be understood by men, judges and is judg'd, measures and is commensurat to right reason.[1]

The mutuality which marks the covenantal encounter between the human and divine wills is here brilliantly, even daringly, expressed. God 'judges and is judg'd'. It is that personal aspect of Law which makes it ultimately compatible with Freedom. He is here dealing with the old Jewish law on Divorce

---

[1] 'The Doctrine and Discipline of Divorce' in *Works*, III, 440 (my italics).

and Adultery and not only must the obviously Hebraic term 'Covenant' be noted, but the last term 'right reason' must also be understood in a specific Hebraic sense. It is not for Milton (nor for the Cambridge Platonists) a purely stoic term. It does not imply quite the stoic rational deportment, nor the self-adaptation to a perfectly ordered *cosmos* suggested by the traditional use of *recta ratio* in the Christian Middle Ages. It implies obedience to the behest of a personal God: it implies a respect for the human intelligence as brought into relationship with the divine will through Covenant responsibility in such a way that neither the unconditioned nature of the Divine sovereignty, nor the freedom of the human agent is obscured. It thus becomes for Milton a violation of 'right reason' for Adam in *Paradise Lost* to partake of the forbidden fruit, an action which would scarcely constitute a breach of *orthos logos* considered in any philosophical sense.

As the inevitable corollary of Law and Reason there is always as we have said—Freedom. And here more than any where else Milton shows his distance from doctrinal Puritanism. For Calvin, the notion of Adam's freedom to obey or disobey was a 'frigid fiction'[1] though some Calvinists made a distinction between freedom before the Fall (which they granted) and freedom after the Fall (which they denied under the harsh rule of predestination). Milton, it is fairly evident, did not accept this quibble. In *Paradise Lost*, Adam's free-will has the widest possible significance. It becomes a symbol for human freedom in general and for a moral responsibility placed on all men.

> for how
> Can hearts not free, be tri'd whether they serve
> Willing or no, who will but what they must
> By destinie, and can no other choose?

(Book V, 531-4)

Milton's Covenant-theology is indeed a theology of Works. He leans in this sense to the Arminians who had been so severely censured at the Synod of Dort in 1618, and like them he shows the determined crossing of the Renaissance faith in Man with the Reformation experience of God. The specific environment of this combination is Hebraic. 'See I have set before thee

---

[1] *Institutes*, III, 23 (7).

this day life and good, and death and evil.' Moral action is meaningless without free choice. This gives to human nature and human history the character of peril, of infinite risk. But without such risk, human existence would indeed be a 'frigid fiction', an achievement of robots. It is along these lines that Milton learns to justify the ways of God to Man.

> I made him just and right,
> Sufficient to have stood, though free to fall.
>
> (*Paradise Lost*, Bk. III, 98-9)

So far we have briefly considered what may be termed the personal dimension of Milton's Hebraism. But Biblical theology is not merely or principally a path to individual salvation by Works: the individual challenge is there of course and the individual response also (as in the *Psalms*); but the Covenant gives to Salvation a collective force and reference; it broadens it into a national and even an international theme. Israel is called upon to be 'a Kingdom of priests and a holy nation'. Nothing testifies more strongly to the influence of the Hebraic type of experience on Milton than the patriotic aspect of his teaching. For Milton, the sacred community is above all the English People marvellously chosen to be the heralds of salvation for the human race. There is nothing in Calvinism to warrant this, nor indeed does it spring from any of the accepted orthodoxies of the Reformation; it is rather a conjunction of the Covenant-idea with Renaissance nationalism, and it is one for which Milton found his warrant above all in the Old Testament Scripture, which pointed to a national community bound by Covenant-bonds to its divine king. 'Why else was this nation chosen before any other,' he asks, 'that out of her, *as out of Sion*, should be proclam'd and sounded forth the first tidings and trumpet of Reformation to all *Europe*?'[1] Here in his religious

---

[1] *Areopagitica*, in *Works*, IV, 340. E. M. W. Tillyard emphasizes Milton's religious patriotism in his book, *The English Epic and its Background* (London, 1954), p. 384. Naturally Milton was not the first Protestant, nor the first Puritan, to express a vigorous pride in his own country. The tradition may be said to begin with John Foxe, the Protestant martyrologist. But Milton differs from the general run of patriotic humanists and divines in fastening on to his national pride, the ideology of election and mission. It was not his Church or sect which constituted for him the sacred community, but his nation.

patriotism is Milton's most intimate link with the Hebraic notion of a sacred community.

The patriotic element in Milton's sensibility is one of the means by which he comes to harmonize and control the Renaissance and Reformation drives within him. The great moral task to which he felt the People of England were called, was one in pursuance of which they might be nourished by the cultural riches of their own native land. These were part of its panoply of battle, part of its spiritual resources. The poet is free to pour out his richest strains, for his music, even if it celebrates human things, even if it deals with matters of worldly concern is at all times the music of a chosen people, and hence a potent religious music. Indeed the poet is supremely chosen, for he it is who shows to the blind and labouring many, the great destiny which Providence has appointed for them; he is the trumpet of revelation in the same way and perhaps, Milton seems to suggest, in the very same degree as the prophets and poets of ancient Israel. He is one of the 'selected heralds of peace, and dispensers of treasure inestimable'.[1]

The strong consciousness of the nation as the vessel of spiritual and cultural values, and of the national tie as binding all members of the community together in a common spiritual destiny is undoubtedly a genuine Old Testament feature in Milton.[2] It is Hebraism which had taught him that the whole man is involved in the religious life, that his national and religious affiliations are not separate things but rather aspects of an organic unity and related to one another as body is to soul. Blake's patriotism, which ran to rather crazy extremes, was nourished by similar religious sources. There is no doubt that Milton's mind like Blake's is working here along the lines of a direct analogy with Israel. He claims a biblical sanction for the new republican form of government, since in setting it up the People of England have made God their king and supreme governor 'in the conformity as neer as may be of his ancient government'.[3] There is a crucial error here, an error which may be defined briefly as that of detaching the Covenant from

---

[1] *The Reason of Church Government*, Bk. II. *Works*, III, 230.

[2] Cf. Johs. Pedersen, *Israel Its Life and Culture*, I-II (English version, Copenhagen, 1926), pp. 56-7, 475.

[3] *Tenure of Kings and Magistrates. Works*, V, 39.

the normal historical process. The Covenant does not come to overthrow history, it comes to fulfil it. Hence in Hebraism, tradition is never despised. Milton by foisting on his contemporaries a particular messianic task unwarranted by the tradition of his people, and based on a too narrow and too exact analogy with ancient Israel was guilty of a quixotic misjudgement of reality. His revolutionary Hebraism was carried to a point at which he was blinded to the nature of the society in which he lived and to the specific conditions of its history. And history was later to take its revenge on him and show him all too clearly that England was not prepared to undertake any messianic tasks and adventures. The analogy with Israel could not be carried as far as that.

He went wrong of course, but then the history of Hebraism in the West has been one of men going wrong by making false equations. The amazing thing about Milton was not that in one or two particulars he got it wrong, but that to so very great an extent he got it right! His understanding of Hebraism was both deep and exact and he had assimilated it to himself in an extraordinary degree. His patriotism is part of that acceptance of the life of the world and the senses which distinguishes Milton's Hebraic piety from the non-Hebraic piety of the general run of Puritan 'saints'. The main implication of Milton's religious patriotism—and the events of the Restoration do not in any way invalidate it—is that there is no essential barrier between Man viewed as a natural creature born of physical parents in a physical and national environment and Man as the child of God called to a high and immortal destiny. There is in brief no Calvinist disjunction of Nature and Grace—that is the positive implication of his patriotism. It is tempting to see in the drops of spring-water from the river Severn which are used in the masque *Comus* to release the Lady from her enchantment, the symbol of Milton's very human love of his own country. If we read the symbol aright (and Masques were always supposed to have an allegorical code of this kind) then what he is saying is that the very physical attachment to one's homeland, and the blessing that flows from it, are a potent factor in the history of Salvation and Redemption.

One perceptive critic, Miss M. M. Mahood, has recognized that Milton, like certain other religious poets of his age, represents 'the seventeenth century attempt at reintegration'. She speaks of a 'theocentric humanism' which 'does not demur at the full and uninhibited use of natural gifts'.[1] As in the present study, the this-worldly affirmations of Milton are shown as linking him spiritually to other serious-minded writers such as Thomas Browne, Henry More, Vaughan, and Herbert, who like him were trying to reconcile the faith of the Reformation with the new knowledge and humanism of the Renaissance to produce a unitary and integrated philosophy of life. 'Milton', she says, 'rejected the Baconian antithesis of Faith and Reason.' With all this one would eagerly concur. But Miss Mahood bases her theory on the rather slender ground of what she terms 'the Baroque faith in man and nature'.[2] The 'sensuous complexity' of the Baroque recognized the World and the Flesh at the same time as it made a godward affirmation of man's destiny in the world. This is an important factor for many of the poets of the mid-seventeenth century and serves to link Milton with the metaphysical poets—a valuable counterpoise to the discussion of Milton by other critics such as Mr. Crutwell and Miss Nott. On the other hand, one wonders whether the stress on the Baroque, by which Miss Mahood means to indicate the whole range of Counter-Reformation literature and art and the kind of sensibility that went with it, is not likely to put Milton, for one, seriously out of focus. After all, he was not merely by accident a Protestant; he was by temperament, and with the whole force of his mind, opposed to the Catholic ceremonial and to the typical imagery associated with the 'Baroque' in religion. One should search for a deeper common ground than this, a more authentic inspiration. Such I think may be found in the new surge of thought and feeling which flowed in upon Milton (and no doubt also on the Baroque artists too) from the Hebrew Scriptures. And here, moreover, we have the advantage of dealing with a source and an influence explicitly attested on every page and in every poem of the authors under discussion.

Here, in Reformation Hebraism, is the true ground of that dynamic confidence in human possibility as itself guaranteed by a divine promise, of the leap into faith which never demands

[1] M. M. Mahood, *Poetry and Humanism* (London, 1950), p. 19.
[2] *Ibid.*, p. 145.

the abandonment of our human condition. For the world is itself not a static world of death but a divine Creation: human life is not a dreary prologue to the true life everlasting, but the history of Salvation and Redemption; and God is not arbitrary and unknowable, but a God who reveals himself at all time to men through the law and the commandments.[1]

[1] Miss Mahood's comment on Vaughan's poem *The Retreate* might serve as a summary of what has been said in this section about the critical importance of the Hebraic factor, for without quite realizing it perhaps, she has made use of the system of imagery of the Hebrew Bible for describing the world-view of one of her 'Baroque' poets. 'For Vaughan, life is not the exile by the waters of Babylon that it seemed to Christina Rossetti; it is a pilgrimage to a known shrine, the journey into the Promised Land. The way lies through the wilderness, but even there God sends manna from the sky, and water from the rock, and guides his people as a pillar of cloud by day and a pillar of fire by night' (p. 294). The Hebraic concept of human life as the history of salvation could hardly be better put.

IX

JOB OR SENECA?

I

WHAT HAS often hindered a correct appreciation of Milton's Hebraism has been the assumption that we have, in *Paradise Lost* for instance, a traditional blending of Greek and Hebrew themes. In the Invocation to the Muse at the beginning of Book I, Sinai is juxtaposed with Olympus: in a famous passage in Book IV, the Garden of Eden is paralleled with Enna

> where *Proserpin* gath'ring flours
> Her self a fairer Floure by gloomie *Dis*
> Was gatherd.

The Muse to whom the poet turns for inspiration at the beginning of Book VII is Urania, the Christian Venus blent with the figure of Wisdom or Sapience from *Proverbs* viii, 23-30. Urania establishes a link between Milton and the Renaissance tradition of harmonistics, that easy synthesis of Hellenic and Hebraic themes which we noted in connexion with Hooker and the Christian Platonists of the sixteenth century. We hear of her in Ficino, then in Du Bartas, and again in Spenser.[1] Milton was certainly acquainted with the literary and philosophical currents suggested by those names. Like Spenser and Sir Walter Ralegh also, he was in touch with that Renaissance tradition of Biblical paraphrase and exegesis (represented chiefly by Benedict Pererius) in which classical mythology and Biblical story walk hand in hand in peaceful co-existence.[2] All this was very suited to the temper of the 'High Renaissance' and like so much else

[1] See Lily B. Campbell, *Divine Poetry and Drama in Sixteenth Century England*, pp. 1, 75-80, 87-92.

[2] Cf. A. Williams, 'Milton and the Renaissance Commentaries on *Genesis*', *M.P.*, XXXVII (1939-40), pp. 263-78. G. McColley, 'Paradise Lost', *H.T.R.*, XXXIII (1939), pp. 181-235.

in that cultural epoch, it had its medieval origins.[1] In this case, the tradition of literary harmonistics goes back to Clement of Alexandria and to Jerome who had claimed that the Bible was written in Greek hexameters! It was decidedly a tradition of accommodation, of non-revolutionary Hebraism.

To see how much all this applies, or does not apply, to Milton we have only to compare his use of this tradition with Spenser's. There is, of course, no doubt of Milton's general affinities with 'our sage and serious Spenser' to whom he pays tribute in more than one place in his writings. *Paradise Lost*, in particular, if not exactly Spenserian in style, has the *collected* quality, the magnificence, even the complacency, which we associate with the great Christian humanists of the sixteenth-century phase of the Renaissance in England. Order and calm seem here to triumph, and the classical rotundity of the Virgilian epic style reinforces the impression of collected majesty and order. The long periodic sentence with which the poem opens is entirely characteristic.

> Of Mans First Disobedience, and the Fruit
> Of that Forbidden Tree, whose mortal taste
> Brought Death into the World, and all our woe,
> With loss of *Eden*, till one greater Man
> Restore us, and regain the blissful Seat,
> Sing Heav'nly Muse, that on the secret top
> Of *Oreb*, or of *Sinai*, didst inspire
> That Shepherd, who first taught the chosen Seed,
> In the Beginning how the Heav'ns and Earth
> Rose out of *Chaos*: or if *Sion* Hill
> Delight thee more, and *Siloa's* Brook that flow'd
> Fast by the Oracle of God; I thence
> Invoke thy aid to my advent'rous Song,
> That with no middle flight intends to soar
> Above the *Aonian* Mount, while it pursues
> Things unattempted yet, in prose or Rhime.

The ordered harmony of this, the majestic tone, the symbiosis of classical form and Hebraic subject-matter suggest that here we have the continuation of that Christian humanism so marked in Spenser. We are almost inclined to agree with Mr.

[1] See E. R. Curtius, *European Literature and the Latin Middle Ages* (London, 1953), pp. 219-20, 446-8.

C. S. Lewis who says of Milton's discussion of Biblical and Classical models for poetry in *The Reason of Church Government*,

> The truth probably is that there is no struggle, and therefore no victory on either side, There is *fusion*, or integration. The Christian and classical elements are not being kept in watertight compartments, but being organized together to produce a whole.[1]

And of *Paradise Lost* as a poem expressive of the tradition of Christian humanism going right back through the sixteenth century to the Middle Ages, no one has written more eloquently than Mr. Lewis. He tells us that it is, like Spenser's poetry and the speech of Ulysses in Shakespeare's play, a poem celebrating Order, Degree, and the Hierarchies.

> The Hierarchical idea is not merely stuck on to his poem at points where doctrine demands it: it is the indwelling life of the whole work. . . .[2]

Now, I should like to argue that whilst there is a certain truth in this, at least in reference to *Paradise Lost*, the most traditionally based of Milton's poems, it is at best a half-truth. The comparison with Spenser's romantic epic *The Faerie Queene* (to which Milton was certainly indebted) obscures more than it illuminates. Let us take a closer look at this blending of Greek and Hebrew images which occurs in both poems. In *The Faerie Queene* we find at one place the Biblical Deborah exchanging reminiscences with Homer's Penthesilia; they are represented as two parallel models of female prowess. The point is that the images are *confluent* and *reciprocal*: there is no tension between them.

> For all too long I burne with enuy sore,
> To heare the warlike feates, which *Homere* spake
> Of bold *Penthesilee*, which made a lake
> Of *Greekish* bloud so oft in *Troian* plaine;
> But when I read, how stout *Debora* strake
> Proud *Sisera*, and how *Camill'* hath slaine
> The huge *Orsilochus* I swell with great disdaine.
>
> (Book III, Canto IV)

[1] *A Preface to Paradise Lost* (Oxford, 1942), p. 5.
[2] *Ibid.*, p. 78.

The apparent discounting of Homer in favour of the Bible is a mere formality, a pose; here is indeed fusion, as Mr. Lewis would say. The conjunction of Greek and Hebraic themes is non-problematical. Britomart, the heroine of this third book of Spenser's epic, is herself a perfect pattern (and one is tempted to add, a perfectly lifeless pattern) of assured Christian Philosophy, a combination of Christian chastity and Aristotelian temperance. Faith and Reason have come to rest in one another's arms. Now, this is not in the least the way we are made to feel about the chief characters in *Paradise Lost*, or its author. There is the same superficial harmonizing, but beneath there are awful chasms, perilous gulfs, dangers, and difficulties. The author tries to bring together the Renaissance and Reformation worlds in terms of the old well-tried machinery of harmonistics, as in the hexaemeral literature,[1] but the combination of themes and images, here issues from a more personal centre of crisis and illumination:

> Not that faire field
> Of *Enna* where *Proserpin* gath'ring flours
> Her self a fairer Floure by gloomie *Dis*
> Was gather'd, which cost Ceres all that pain
> To seek her through the world; nor that sweet Grove
> Of *Daphne* by *Orontes*, and th' inspir'd
> *Castalian* Spring might with this Paradise
> Of *Eden* strive . . .
>
> (Book IV, 268-75)

Proserpin is not Eve, because Eve chooses: Proserpin is gathered like a flower. We are reminded, it is true, later on of this same passage when Eve is herself described as the 'fairest unsupported Flour' in the Garden of Eden (Book IX, 432) and thus the two figures and the two images are closely intertwined. But there is nevertheless a certain opposition between them. The figures in the Garden of Eden are marked, according to the continuation of the passage quoted above, by 'sanctitude severe and Pure/ Severe, but in true filial freedom plac't'. They are morally responsible figures, and Eve can only ironically be represented as 'unsupported'; in fact she herself is held to be the mistress of

[1] Cf. B. Rajan, *Paradise Lost and the Seventeenth Century Reader* (London, 1947), pp. 40-3.

her destiny in no less a degree than Adam. This is the central doctrine of *Paradise Lost*. The passage quoted above has a deeply nostalgic tone, it betrays a longing for the sunny idyll of Greece, for the Pagan world in which human destiny is still undifferentiated from the rhythm of Nature. 'Not that fair field of Enna'. The negative frame in which the image is syntactically disposed is not adventitious. It comes to tell us that though we might long for the fatalism or pantheism of the Pagan world, we are required to see human existence in more challenging and realistic terms, in terms of righteousness, obedience, and responsibility. The Covenant teaching of the Book of *Genesis* is being urged against the more charming but morally less invigorating world of classicism.

Paradise Lost is, at bottom, only unevenly harmonious. In bringing together the religious and secular experience of his Age, Milton could not, like Spenser, refer himself to ready-made Aristotelian or Thomistic formulae. He had encountered, as Spenser had not, the full destructive blasts of the Counter-Renaissance, and thus, he was involved in the situation at a depth where lines of communication did not, as yet, exist. Consequently, there were times when communication failed, when his Puritanism gained control and threatened to dash in pieces the gold and silver ornaments of his Hellenic culture, or when conversely, the Renaissance enchantments (as with Dr. Faustus) threatened to make short work of his Puritan conscience. Milton, in his writing, we may say, is always in mortal peril: Spenser never. The luxurious picture of the Bowre of Bliss in Spenser's poem may momentarily imperil the moral stability of the reader, as it does of Guyon, but the author, supported by Aristotle and his doctrine of the Golden Mean, is always in full control of the situation. There is no real danger: that is the advantage of having the *logos* at one's back. In Milton, on the other hand, the great speeches of Satan, like the great speech of Comus, threaten to subvert the moral foundations of the poem for reader and author alike.

Milton's central difficulty (call it moral, or call it aesthetic) in writing the Christian epic is to achieve a proper combination of Power and Goodness, to focus Deborah and Penthesilia in one image. The epic-hero, in Vergil or Homer, is essentially a power-figure, and the epic is meaningless without such a figure.

To harmonize this with the Christian ideal of Goodness (so far removed from Roman *virtus*, or even *pietas*) involves the basic question of what exactly is Christian Goodness if you do not have, like Spenser, the traditional compromises to fall back on. If Goodness is to be identified with saintly ataraxy as in the Jesus of *Paradise Regained*—in some valiant attempt to return to the primitive ideal of the gospel ('whosoever shall smite thee on thy right cheek, turn to him the other also'), then it will inevitably become disjoined from Power, and the Imagination seeking its proper satisfaction in a power-figure will find it, if necessary, by self-identification with the Devil. Milton's difficulty here arises it would seem from the evangelical insistence on the purity of the gospel which is primary to the religious experience of the Reformation. The New Testament ideal ('My Kingdom is not of this world') is one with which the poet's imagination inevitably will have certain difficulties. In strictly New Testament terms, 'the Kingdom can no longer be fought or striven for in an earthly effort. It can only be prayed, waited, and suffered for'.[1] If almost any would-be epic writer would find difficulty with this, then how much more a poet of such earth-bound, sensuous endowment as Milton! And so the protest of the Imagination finds expression in these magnificent epic similes in which Satan is presented as an adventurous seaman sailing round the Cape of Hope (IV, 160 f.), as King

---

[1] R. J. Z. Werblowsky, *Lucifer and Prometheus* (London, 1952), p. 74, and see also G. W. Knight, *The Chariot of Wrath* (London, 1942), p. 130.

Mr. Werblowsky in his psychological study of the genesis and rise of Satan as a phenomenon in the history of Christianity as well as in Milton's poem, points to the need felt for psychological compensation arising from the emphasis in Christian theology on 'Divine Goodness holiness and mercy' at the expense of God's 'at times daemonic power'. Thus the devil becomes an 'autonomous complex' gathering to himself the Promethean qualities of assertiveness, energy, and rebellion, all of which have become detached from the conception of the godly. We may note that in the Old Testament there is not this same disjunction: in the Book of *Job* Satan is one of the 'sons of God'. His manners are not very good, but then those of the angel of death—another member of the Divine family—are probably worse. Blake has the same trouble with the exclusion of the daemonic from the Christian conception of God. His question when looking at the Tiger, 'Did he who made the Lamb make thee?' is evidently a real and not a rhetorical question. See Kathleen Raine, 'Who made the Tyger?' *Encounter* (London, June, 1954).

Arthur (I, 580 f.), as 'the Sun new ris'n', as—most amazingly of all—Moses, the leader of the Israelites, summoning the plague of locusts (I, 338). Here the ideal of the Renaissance, the humanistic, assertive ideal, has found a momentary personification. Among the fallen angels indeed we must include the poets and musicians of the Renaissance who

> Retreated in a silent valley, sing
> With notes Angelical to many a Harp
> Thir own Heroic deeds and hapless fall
> By doom of Battel; and complain that Fate
> Free Vertue should enthrall to Force or Chance.
>
> (P.L. II, 547-51)

Here is the wistful, nostalgic note once again as the Pagan ideal of courage and 'Virtue'—inevitably defeated—is nevertheless mourned by the poets and singers—the author himself included in their ranks.

The whole difficulty about the identity of the epic hero in *Paradise Lost* is an indication of the tension, the conflict, the uncertainty beneath the assured, majestic façade of the poem. We are not bound to agree with the Satanists in awarding to Satan the title of epic hero, but the fact that so many writers from Blake onwards have felt this way about him shows that some potent imaginative forces are as it were running amuck in the poem. The poem, is in a certain sense, out of control: the order which Milton is seeking—and no one would deny that he is *seeking* order—is no established logistic order, but a shifting personal value, constantly threatened with some new factor, some new challenge. In the middle sections of the poem, under the aegis of a more wholesome spirituality, Milton does achieve a combination of Power and Goodness, in such a figure, for instance as Abdiel, heroically resisting the seductions of Satan (Book V, 800 f.) Here Energy and Goodness have found their integration, for a moment, in a personality far removed from the ideal of passive non-resistance to evil. And in Books V and VI the role of epic-hero is taken over by the Messiah, riding 'the chariot of paternal Deitie' and gazing 'full of wrauth upon his enemies'. But the Jesus of these epic battles is at a great distance from the Christ of the New Testament; he carries with him more of the suggestion of the Old Testament God of battles, the Old

Testament conjunction of righteousness and ferocious power: 'For he put on righteousness as a breastplate, and an helmet of salvation upon his head; and he put on the garments of vengeance for clothing, and was clad with zeal as a cloke.' (*Isaiah* lix, 17.)

If at the beginning of the poem we have (in Satan) Power disjoined from Goodness, and in the middle their temporary conjunction in Abdiel and Jesus, at the end of the poem we have Goodness disjoined from Power. Adam (and really Milton) seems to despair of an order of society in which human values and desires can be reconciled with the otherworldly behests of a Puritan God. He lays his stress on a sort of Calvinistic inwardness, a Covenant of Grace, in accordance with which the outer world is abandoned to its sinful devices. Milton has evidently been obliged by historical developments (the latter part of the poem was of course written after the Restoration) to give up his aspiration towards an organic, religious culture, towards a messianic nationalism, a divine republic, in which Power and Goodness have met, in which Judgement has returned unto Righteousness. For him, as for Adam, this kind of Paradise is, it would seem, irretrievably lost, and so, he is thrown upon the inward resources of his spirit and the passive virtue of faith. It is a personal rather than a national salvation that he is now bound to assert. And it is at this point that Adam's stoicism also comes to the fore as he resolves on a temperate course of stoical resignation, and patiently attends his dissolution (XI, 523-48). In the final Book, the more characteristically Christian consolations are emphasized, when Michael describes how the Law, the Covenant of Works, will be replaced by—

> a better Cov'nant, disciplin'd
> From shadowie Types to Truth, from Flesh to Spirit,
> From imposition of strict Laws, to free
> Acceptance of large Grace, from servil fear
> To filial, works of Law to works of Faith.
> And therefore shall not *Moses*, though of God
> Highly belov'd, being but the Minister
> Of Law, his people into *Canaan* lead;
> But *Joshua* whom the Gentiles *Jesus* call,
> His Name and Office bearing, who shall quell
> The adversarie Serpent, and bring back

> Through the worlds wilderness long wanderd man
> Safe to eternal Paradise of rest.
>
> (XII, 302-14)

This return to Paradise is the pious sentiment on which the epic closes, but it is a Paradise 'recovered from within'[1]—it is the Saints' Everlasting Rest, not the rich locality of Eden with its birds and waterfalls, and its naked, lustrous humanity, for Milton has become conscious at this stage of agonizing re-appraisal, of the vanity and emptiness of the world and of worldly things. He has come in short very near to Calvinism and to the negative philosophy of *Paradise Regained*.

II

The kind of dissociated Goodness celebrated at the end of *Paradise Lost* leads us forward, as most critics would agree, to the poet of *Paradise Regained* (1671).[2] There we have the same combination of Stoic self-sufficiency and Puritan austerity, in short the negative ethic of the Counter-Renaissance. Above all, the hero is essentially introverted, obsessively self-involved, and seeking through self-command a certain freedom from active responsibility. This is essentially a reflection of Milton's mood at this stage of his life as he despairs of combining in any other way the secular and religious elements of his cultural background. All that is left of the august tradition of Christian humanism with its magnificent pattern and ordered harmony seems to be the still, small voice of such a philosophical guide as Marcus Aurelius whose words (from the Second Book of his *Meditations*) may stand as a gloss upon the teaching of the Archangel Michael in the last two Books of *Paradise Lost* and that of the 'epic' hero of *Paradise Regained* as he undergoes trial and temptation in the wilderness.

> What then is that which is able to conduct a man? One thing and only one, philosophy. But this consists in keeping the daemon within a man free from violence and unharmed, superior to pains and pleasures, doing nothing without a purpose, nor yet falsely

---

[1] Cf. B. Rajan, *op. cit.*, p. 91, and E. M. W. Tillyard, *Milton* (London 1930), p. 291.
[2] Cf. E. M. W. Tillyard, *Milton*, pp. 301-2.

and with hypocrisy, not feeling the need of another man's doing or
not doing anything; and besides, accepting all that happens, and
all that is allotted, as coming from thence, wherever it is, from
whence he himself came; and finally waiting for death with a
cheerful mind, as being nothing else than a dissolution of the
elements of which every living being is compounded.

(Book II, No. 17)

Jesus operates in the face of trial with these stoic doctrines of
ataraxia and *apatheia*; there is, of course, more to it than that—
there is a touch of Aristotelian magnanimity also[1]—but what he
offers basically to Satan is the blank wall of indifference. Even
the positive aim (announced at the end of Book II) of 'guiding
the Nations in the way of Truth' is prefixed by, and enclosed in,
a stoical formula, the formula which Jesus uses to reject the
offer of public responsibilities and kingship:

> he who reigns within himself, and rules
> Passions, Desires and Fears, is more a King;
> Which every wise and vertuous man attains;

The problematic nature of Milton's stoicism is revealed,
however, when Satan offers to Jesus the consolations of Philosophy in the Fourth Book, in other words when stoicism—
secular philosophy—becomes the explicit issue as a temptation,
as the symbol of ancient Humanism in its Renaissance form.
This, Jesus (and Milton) rejects instantly in favour of 'light
from above' accusing the Stoics of 'philosophic pride'. He goes
on:

> Much of the Soul they talk, but all awrie,
> And in themselves seek vertue, and to themselves
> All glory arrogate, to God give none,
> Rather accuse him under usual names,
> Fortune and Fate, as one regardless quite
> Of mortal things.

Here is the religious criticism of stoicism—but it is a sign of
the asphyxiating conflicts out of which the poem was born
that this speech should be given to a hero who has hitherto
spoken and acted as the most emphatic and unyielding Stoic in

---

[1] Merritt Y. Hughes, 'The Christ of *Paradise Regained* and the Renaissance
Heroic Tradition,' *S.P.*, XXXV, pp. 258 f.

all modern literature! Clearly this poem does not provide a happy synthesis of Reformed Religion and Renaissance Stoicism. Stoicism, as a psychological principle rather than a philosophical system, represents an important chord; it comes to reinforce the religious inwardness which is the keynote of the poem, the insistence on Faith rather than Works, passive suffering, fortitude, resistance to the allurements of the World, the Flesh, and the Devil. On these quite non-epical ideals the hero bases his behaviour. He refuses to act, even in the sense of making his ideals prevail in society and politics (as an earlier Renaissance humanist might). The active principle is voiced instead by Satan who comes to express the Renaissance drive for active self-assertion, in opposition to the Reformation desire for a self-sufficient religious experience. 'Through Satan', says Mr. Wilson Knight, 'Milton tries to persuade this adamantine Christ to assume flesh and blood, to come down from his lonely pinnacle of irrelevant righteousness, and reign.' But of course he does not come down. Milton's Puritan conscience would not, at this point, permit such a solution. 'The poem offers no synthesis.'[1] Power and Goodness are here not reconciled; the Renaissance power-thrust is instead allotted (as in Marlowe's play) to Satan, who rules the world in defiance of God, and the Reformation assertion of Goodness is appropriated to Jesus who promises no effectual application of it to the business of this world. The Hebraic integration of the two in the form of an active hero obedient to the Covenant of Works is lacking. What we have instead are the basic disjunctions which belong to the violent or revolutionary phase of the Renaissance, the phase associated with Calvin, Machiavelli, and the neo-Stoics.

To correspond with the dissociated 'Counter-Renaissance' character of the poem's inspiration, we notice here also in *Paradise Regained* the style of Puritan austerity in contrast with the richer imaginative ground swell of *Paradise Lost*.[2] There are a number of passages of vivid imagery in *Paradise Regained*, such as, for instance, the epic similes in Book IV relating the final temptation of Satan to the fight of Hercules and Antaeus, and

[1] *The Chariot of Wrath*, pp. 109, 115.
[2] This aspect of the style of *Paradise Regained* is often noted. See, for instance, K. Muir, *John Milton* (London, 1955), p. 166; John Bailey, *Milton* (London 1915), pp. 208-10.

to the manner of the Sphinx in proposing her riddle (IV, 562-80). Here we feel Milton is making use of the whole imaginative register of *Paradise Lost*; but it is only for a few moments. The poem as a whole employs a drier, more colourless diction and a logical manner of exposition, in contrast with the imaginative profusion, the grandeur, the impassioned ode-like eloquence of *Paradise Lost*. It is a poem of renunciation. It is not without significance that the opening lines of the poem echo St. Paul's epistle to the Romans, the source for the Puritan practice of the plain style. In entire conformity with this Pauline inspiration, Jesus in this poem is shown to reject those very humanistic ideals on which Milton had, so to say, staked his existence. The glory of Greece and Rome, the wisdom of Plato, the delights of Classical poetry (symbolized perhaps by the luxurious feast that Satan prepares to tempt the hero) all these must be set aside by the true Christian warrior. The strength of the poem may very well lie in this very quality of passionate self-denial; it affords a dramatic tension, a kind of dread seriousness to the poem. But it yields a negative Rhetoric. The stoical restraints which operate in the hero's conduct and speech also serve to strengthen this quality of its style. In fact the poem would do perfectly to illustrate (in verse) the movement away from the aureate style of the High Renaissance which we described earlier on (Chapter II) and it serves to remind us also that Milton was in his college days a disciple of Bacon, looking forward to a complete liberation of modern Man from the shackles of scholasticism and tradition. *Paradise Regained* represents the modern Baconian and Puritan revolt against the tradition of classical Rhetoric and of the *bonus rhetor*. The 'Oratory of Greece and Rome' he condemns as meretricious ('varnish on a harlot's cheek') and claims that the style of the Scriptures is truer because plainer:

> In them is plainest taught, and easiest learnt,
> What makes a Nation happy, and keeps it so,
> What ruins Kingdoms, and lays Cities flat;
> These only with our Law best form a King.
>
> (IV, 361-4)

These lines, as regards rhythm and phraseology, are deliberately pitched in a minor key, and the end-stopping of the lines (marked throughout the poem) gives an abbreviated, clipped, and one might even say, prosaic character to the statement.

Milton's three most considerable poems, *Paradise Lost, Paradise Regained*, and *Samson Agonistes* would, in fact, serve well to illustrate the pattern proposed earlier on in connexion with the history of prose rhetoric in the sixteenth and seventeenth centuries (Chapters I-III). Here again in Milton's poetry we have three phases (whether or not they were historically consecutive is unimportant) which we may denominate in Hegelian fashion: thesis, antithesis, and synthesis. The traditional epic form, the heavy style of orotundity in *Paradise Lost*, is comparable to the grand style in prose which we discerned in Hooker: the style of *Paradise Regained* reminds us of the Puritan and Baconian revolt against this—the new realism: whilst the style of *Samson Agonistes* represents Milton's ultimate synthesis. It is the most completely realized of Milton's poems and also, we will now add, the most genuinely Hebraic.

III

Samson Agonistes in spite of many deep similarities to the dramas of Aeschylus and Sophocles,[1] gives us no static figure of Prometheus bound to a rock, nor a passively suffering Oedipus come to end his days at Colonnus, but a dynamic Old Testament hero, tempestuous, powerful and directing his last throb of energy to the service of God and People. Moreover, Samson's virtues are not those of evangelical piety.[2] They express themselves finally in heroic action. There is no need in this play for a diabolical power-figure such as Satan or Comus, for the hero himself embodies all the qualities of assertiveness and rebellion. Power and Goodness are finally reconciled in the service of a redeemer God; action and self-control are united in a definitely

[1] Cf. W. R. Parker, *Milton's Debt to Greek Tragedy in Samson Agonistes* (John Hopkins, 1937), and A. W. Verity's (still helpful) Introduction to his edition of *Samson Agonistes* (Cambridge, 1892).

[2] It is difficult to relate Milton's Samson to the tradition which saw in this Old Testament hero a Christ-figure, a saint or martyr in the Christian sense. The critics who take this line (e.g. F. M. Krouse, *Milton's Samson and the Christian Tradition*, Princeton, 1949; T. S. K. Scott-Craig, 'Miltonic Tragedy and Christian Vision', in N. A. Scott, *The Tragic Vision and the Christian Faith*, New York, 1957) seem to be guilty of special pleading.

Hebraic fashion. Sainthood is no contemplative virtue unexercised and unbreathed, nor is it incompatible with human lapses and failings. In Samson's case, the sins of the flesh are the cause of his downfall; the Old Testament heroes are fallible (like ourselves) but they are driven on by their call to active exploits and sacrifice. All this is illustrated by *Samson Agonistes*. At the same time, to correspond with this more vigorous spirituality, the poem has a Hebrew imaginative resonance and a Hebrew verse form.[1] It lacks the Latin sonority of *Paradise Lost* and yet it has something of its exalted tone; it lacks the plainness and rigour of *Paradise Regained* and yet it has something of its dramatic tension. It presents a synthesis of the two styles, and the key to its integration of them is the use of the manner and rhythm of Hebrew Psalm, Wisdom, and Oracle.

Critics have often recognized the looser organization and freer prosody of *Samson Agonistes* in comparison with Milton's other major poems,[2] relating it variously to Old English accentual poetry, Greek Drama, and the examples of the Italian lyric poets and dramatists of the sixteenth century.[3] There is clearly much truth in all these notions; Milton was certainly alive to the Greek and Italian pattern in the composition of his Choruses, as he himself tells us in the paragraphs prefixed to the poem, but we need not doubt his even greater sensitivity, especially when dealing with a Hebrew subject, to the Hebrew Scriptures, which in *Paradise Regained* he points to as the true model for poets—'Sion's songs, to all true tasts excelling/Where God is prais'd aright, and Godlike men.' The Hebrew style is to be discovered, it seems to me, throughout *Samson Agonistes* as

[1] This is recognized by J. F. Kermode in his article, '*Samson Agonistes* and Hebrew Prosody', *The Durham University Journal* (March, 1953), pp. 59-63.

[2] For an account of Milton's use of free rhythms in *Samson Agonistes* see Robert Bridges' *Milton's Prosody*, revised ed. (Oxford, 1921), pp. 50-66. Bridges relates this to the native English love for variety and freedom, for 'natural stress rhythms'. He has in mind something like the accentual verse developed (or rediscovered) by his friend, G. M. Hopkins. For a similar view, see D. Bush, *English Literature in the Earlier Seventeenth Century*, p. 396.

[3] On Italian models (Tasso, Guarini, and Andreini) for the Choruses in *Samson Agonistes* see F. T. Prince's *The Italian Element in Milton's Verse* (Oxford, 1954), pp. 146-68. In his valuable and sensitive discussion, Prince is careful to point out, however, that 'there is no precise parallel in Italian poetry to all the prosodic features of the choruses' (p. 146).

the key to its prosody, and typically in the following examples
all of which are marked by the use of Biblical rhythms:

> The Sun to me is dark
> And silent as the Moon.
>
> (86-7)
>
> Just are the ways of God
> And justifiable to Men.
>
> (293-4)
>
> O how comely it is and how reviving
> To the Spirits of just men long opprest!
> When God into the hands of thir deliverer
> Puts invincible might
> To quell the mighty of the Earth, th'oppressour,
> The brute and boist'rous force of violent men
> Hardy and industrious to support
> Tyrannic power, but raging to pursue
> The righteous and all such as honour Truth.
>
> (1268-76)

It is surely as impossible not to hear the rhythm of the English
Bible in such passages as it would be not to catch the rhythms
of Vergil in *Paradise Lost*. Nor is the stylistic debt to the Bible
narrowly confined to the technicalities of the parallelism or the
diction of the *Psalms* (very noticeable in the last of the above-
quoted passages): the elastic transitions from short lyrical lines
to longer meditative units, the essentially free movement of the
poetry, free from the formalities of rhyme, or even the easier
bonds of blank-verse, all this is in keeping with the Hebraic
literary inspiration. Milton had an extraordinary gift for
assimilating diverse influences, and making the result his own.
Here he has brought together much of the spirit of the Greek,
the Italian, and the English, but the essential unity, the inform-
ing principle is Hebraic.

The same will apply to the system of ideas and emotions in
this dramatic poem. There are many strains, many sources,
many varied influences, but who can doubt that the overriding
spirit, as expressed by the Chorus in the last-quoted passage
is the belief in Divine Justice, in the significance of righteousness,
in the principle of salvation working through the warp and
woof of history towards a divinely ordered conclusion. It is

not necessary to seek exact Biblical parallels, for the faith
expressed here, the language, and the imagery are constantly
iterated in all parts of the Bible and perhaps chiefly in the
Psalter—the following extract from the eighteenth Psalm in the
Authorized Version, may be set beside the last-quoted passage
above from *Samson Agonistes:*

> The Lord liveth; and blessed be my rock;
> And let the God of my salvation be exalted.
> It is God that avengeth me,
> And subdueth the people under me.
> He delivereth me from mine enemies:
> Yea, thou liftest me up above those that rise up against me:
> Thou hast delivered me from the violent man.
> Therefore will I give thanks unto thee, O Lord among the
>   heathen,
> And sing praises unto thy name.

The affinity both in idea and language is not to be doubted.
And it is in the confidence of this strong Biblical inspiration
that Milton in this play comes to grips once again—and perhaps
for the last time, with the Hellenic spirit, the Hellenic spirit in
its most specific and relevantly contemporary form. Stoicism
had always been for Milton a refuge in time of trouble, and
more than that, a spiritual discipline. If in the closing books of
Paradise Lost what had chiefly impressed him, as we have said,
had been the stoical acceptance of death, the negative ethic of
Marcus Aurelius, as in the lines,

> So maist thou live, till like ripe Fruit thou drop
> Into thy Mothers lap, or be with ease
> Gatherd, not harshly pluckt, for death mature—
>
> $\qquad\qquad\qquad\qquad$ (P.L. XI, 532-4)

elsewhere stoicism had provided an ethical discipline of a more
life-accepting kind, it had nerved him to face the battles of life.
'They also serve who only stand and wait.' But at all times
stoicism exercised a powerful compulsion over him, as it did
over so many other protestants of the late Renaissance period.[1]
  Here in *Samson Agonistes*, by omitting all the middle period
of Samson's career (*Judges* xiv to xvi, 20), and concentrating on

[1] Cf. J. H. Hanford, quoted by E. M. W. Tillyard, *Milton* (London, 1930),
p. 352.

the final episode (xvi, 21-30), thus locating the drama in the last hours of Samson's life, he is enabled to study (like Shakespeare and Chapman before him) the dramatic possibilities of stoical passiveness, fortitude, and readiness for death. The fatalism expressed by the Chorus at one place, 'Tax not divine disposal' (line 210) reminds us of Cleanthes' hymn to Zeus:

> Lead, O Zeus, and lead me Destiny,
> Whither your high disposal bids me go.

Seen in this light, Samson's actions culminating in his suicide (how stoical!) could be interpreted as those of a Clermont D'Ambois—as in Chapman's play—who 'joins himself with the Universe' and merges with 'great Necessity' until ripe for death, he finally takes his life in a characteristic 'Senecal' gesture.[1] But does this really, or in any important sense, express the theme of Milton's play? It is surely no more than a subdued counterpointing, a kind of antithesis to the main theme, that theme expressed in the lines

> Just are the ways of God,
> And justifiable to Men.

For the Stoic is really not interested in the problems of theodicy, the justification of God's ways to men. For Epictetus, God is in all things, including Man himself, but no moral drama is played out. God does not confront Man in a personal dialogue relationship as in this poem of Milton. Morality is confined to the introhuman sphere as an aspect of Man's control over his own emotions and appetites. In the sphere of History likewise there is no room for a theodicy, for there Fortune is supreme, and Fortune does not have to explain herself to anyone. Indeed, the consideration of God's ways to Man is scarcely a theme for stoicism. The sphere of God, real and ever-present though it is, is a sphere of indifference to human desires and human sufferings. The human voice cannot enter there. Similarly, the human personality itself is in its way impenetrable by God. The integration, completeness, and tranquillity which a man achieves are qualities which belong to himself alone and which he maintains against Fortune, as long as circumstances, decency, and honour

[1] Cf. M. Higgins, 'The Development of the "Senecal Man" ', *R.E.S.*, XXIII (1947), 24-33.

permit, after which he holds in his own hands the means of his own dissolution. All this made a powerful appeal to Milton's egoism. He was not willing to forfeit the key to inward peace and order which stoicism seemed to afford. But at the same time, he was bound by an even more imperious need of his nature to explore the moral relations between men and between Man and God, to justify God's ways to Man. The Covenant-faith requires a mutuality, a personal, moral bond as that which arbitrates between the human and divine order, as that which explains human destiny. God 'judges and is judg'd'. A Stoic would not have been so much indifferent to such considerations as shocked at the presumption that a human being should demand that God should, so to speak, account for himself in moral terms. 'Why am I thus bereaved your prime decree?' Milton's hero demands of God. Milton's Hebraic Covenant-faith demanded no less. Where was he to find the proper kind of formulation for this kind of question and where was he to find the proper answer which should at the same time leave room for the exercise of the stoic virtues of patience, the stoic inwardness? The answer is—in the book of *Job*.

IV

Many critics have observed the similarity between the suffering of Samson in Milton's play and that of Job challenging God for an explanation of his unmatched afflictions.[1] Again, the dialogue in *Job* comes near the dramatic with the alternation of speeches by Job and his comforters, and the final speech of God answering Job out of the whirlwind. Milton seems to have taken note of this in patterning the speeches in *Samson Agonistes*: there are Samson and his tempters (Harapha, Dalila): Samson and his comforters (Manoa and the Chorus); and the approximation to the shattering Divine word of *Job*, ch. xxxviii, in the mighty roar of the climax, the collapse of the temple of Dagon 'As with the force of winds and waters pent.' Even if Milton had not expressed so often his interest in this book of the Bible, we would be prompted to see a certain resemblance

[1] Cf. J. H. Hanford, '*Samson Agonistes* and Milton in Old Age' in *Studies in Shakespeare, Milton and Donne* (New York, 1925), pp. 167-89; Verity, *op. cit.*, Introduction, p. liii.

to it, both in the plot and structure of Milton's dramatic composition. Above all the central theme of Job, the vindication of God's ways to suffering man, is that of *Samson Agonistes*. *Job* is the Book of the Bible most crucially concerned with the problems of discovering a meaning and significance in suffering and discerning a finally positive Divine plan, a providential pattern, in the history of tribulation. There is an alternation of despairing complaint, resignation, and assured triumphant faith, the movement from the depth of trouble to faith and trust. Job even in the midst of his sufferings can declare,

> For I know that my Redeemer liveth,
> And that he shall stand at the latter day upon the earth:
> And though after my skin worms destroy this body,
> Yet in my flesh shall I see God.

Similarly, Milton's hero 'Eyeless in Gaza at the mill with slaves' can nevertheless affirm in answer to the taunts of Harapha,

> My trust is in the living God, who gave me,
> At my nativity this strength, diffus'd
> No less through all my sinews, joints and bones,
> Then thine, while I preserv'd these locks unshorn,
> The pledge of my unviolated vow.
>
> (1140-6)

The response to suffering in either case is not the Stoic retirement into the inner sanctum where the victim may reach equanimity and indifference, freedom from emotion. Here there is by contrast a passionate reaching out from the enclosure of the isolated individuality towards an otherness which is nevertheless a person ready to respond to human emotion, to human supplication—a God of Terror but also a God of Pity. There is thus a kind of inner dialogue behind and beneath the outward dialogue of the characters in the Drama. And this *Susurrium cum Deo*, in which the hero challenges his God for an answer to life's problems, is what connects *Samson Agonistes* with the dialogue poetry of George Herbert and the other metaphysical poets. Stoical self-sufficiency ultimately nullifies dialogue: it knows only monologue, the dread ultimate, claustrophobic horror of the room, lit, locked, and windowless. It is from this that Milton makes his escape in this poem. And he makes his escape by discovering, or rather rediscovering, for himself, the significance of the Covenant, as that which amazingly permits a genuine meeting between the human impotence, and divine omnipotence. 'I know that my Redeemer liveth . . . and though after my skin worms destroy this body, Yet in my flesh shall I see God.' This had been the special character of the final epiphany in *Job*, the astonishing lyrical climax in which God speaks to Job out of the whirlwind (xxxviii-xli). God has the last word, but the mere fact that he condescends to address that word to Man, gives to the human personality a value that counts as triumph. Job's sufferings become part of the experience of the Covenant dialogue itself, like the sufferings of Israel himself in history; they become a mark of triumph, of election.

Milton in this poem, perhaps through a degree of self-identification with the hero, is exploring the theme of elective suffering, of individual fate which is not meaningless, but rather a witness to Divine Providence. His hero dies, but not in a gesture of readiness for dissolution in the face of an indifferent Fate, but in a final act of witness to the reality of God's promise and of his nearness to his chosen ones.

> With God not parted from him, as was feard,
> But favouring and assisting to the end.
>
> (1719-20)

His death is ultimately a justification of God's ways to man; it is punishment, expiation, and triumph all together. In the overthrow of his enemies, and those of his nation, he brings about the promised deliverance, and thus testifies to the purposes of the Providence which has chosen him for its instrument. No doubt Milton is expressing here in his old age the enduring appeal for him of the stoic philosophy of readiness for death— we could not conceive of him writing a dramatic poem at this stage in which the hero, like Job, should remain alive at the end—but the stoic theme has been swallowed up in a greater theme. Death has been swallowed up in victory. The end of the play is purposeful action.

X

MILTON AND THE HERESIES

I

FEW PEOPLE are alarmed these days by the word heresy, and even in 1823 the discovery of Milton's highly heretical work of theology, the *De Doctrina Christiana*, served to enhance his reputation for a generation glad to find so august a rebel in the ranks of the 'Devil's party'. Today whilst some are disposed to sidestep the *De Doctrina* as a sort of late Miltonian extravagance, and confidently maintain the substantial orthodoxy of the great poems,[1] the majority of readers feel that for a poet inclined to be a little too solemn about his religion, his heresies offer a certain light relief and make him endearingly akin to ourselves in many ways. His views on divorce and the freedom of the Press after all are well ahead of his time, and if they are the fruit of heresy, well so much the better for heresy.

It may therefore seem not a little reactionary, and not a little uncharitable to Milton, to suggest that though he was by Christian standards a heretic, his deviations form a pattern amongst themselves, a coherent system of belief and action. This pattern is not that of modern democracy, or humanism, though it may remind us of them in some ways—but it is that

[1] Especially C. S. Lewis, *op. cit.*, pp. 83-90. But Milton's orthodoxy was suspected by eighteenth-century writers who were completely ignorant of the heretical contents of the *De Doctrina*. It is now generally accepted, following the publication of M. Kelley, *This Great Argument* (Princeton, 1941), that the composition of *Paradise Lost* and the *De Doctrina* belong to the same period, and that, doctrinally, they are consonant with one another. One may add as a minor (literary) note to the controversy about Milton's orthodoxy in *Paradise Lost* that many details (such as the angels eating food) are taken by the average reader as permissible poetic licence which, if theologically pressed, reveal themselves as heretical. Milton was probably conscious that the poem, simply by virtue of being a poem, provided a screen for his more daring speculations, but there is no reason why the modern reader enlightened by acquaintance with the *De Doctrina Christiana* should respect the author's self-camouflaging intent.

of an ancient pre-Christian religious culture. When properly understood, his so-called heresies will be found to form a structure identifiable in large measure with what, in this study, has been termed, Hebraism.

We may start off with the Hebraic concept of the organic relation between Body and Soul. Salvation, it has been said, was offered to man in his physical earth-bound character. It is to the Old Adam that the Word of God is addressed. The significant phases of the spiritual life are in the Old Testament not termed Regeneration but Return (*Hosea* xiv, 2-8; *Joel* ii, 12-14). Salvation comes with the renewal of a Covenant-bond which has never in fact been abrogated, but only foolishly or wickedly ignored. For Hosea the return of Israel to God is exactly paralleled by the return of his faithless wife Gomer whom he had not ceased to love, and who had, through all her backslidings, remained bound to him by the Covenant of Marriage. Thus the Covenant of God with Israel and, more broadly, of the Creature with his Creator is organically rooted in history and in the human condition. We cannot be 'reborn' to it—for we have been held in its bonds from birth: it is that which gives to our earthly pilgrimage from the womb to the grave its godward significance. True, it challenges us to realize potentialities beyond those of simple natural instinct; but the sign of the Covenant is not castration; it is circumcision; its symbol is not celibacy, but marriage. Life-energy, instinct, sensibility, are controlled but never violated. In fact, it is in and through the active life of the body that we achieve a proper awareness of our creaturely status, and thus of our real relationship to God. 'I was cast upon thee from the womb,' says the Psalmist, and elsewhere, (*Psalm* vi):

> Return, O Lord deliver my soul:
> Oh save me for thy mercies' sake. ('Mercy' here is *Hesed*, or Covenant-love).
> For in death there is no remembrance of thee:
> In the grave who shall give thee thanks?

The *nefesh* or 'soul' of the first line is more properly 'life'—that which animates the physical body itself. It is not detachable from it nor thought ever to subsist without it. Discussing the doctrine of Man in the Old Testament, one modern Christian writer has said:

> The physical form . . . is not set in contrast with psychical attributes (as by ourselves); the whole animated body, whether bones and flesh, or the peripheral and central organs, have psychical and therefore moral qualities, by a sort of diffused consciousness.[1]

And this is how Milton expresses himself on this subject in the *De Doctrina Christiana*:

> *man became a living soul* [*Genesis* ii, 7]; whence it may be inferred . . . that man is a living being, intrinsically and properly one and individual, not compound or separable, not, according to the common opinion, made up and framed of two distinct and different natures, as of soul and body, but that the whole man is soul, and the soul man, that is to say, a body, or substance individual, animated, sensitive, and rational. . . .[2]

Milton has indeed understood the Hebrew of his text very well. This passage is quoted by Professor Saurat in a section devoted to Milton's 'Materialism', a doctrine which he held in common with that interesting sectarian writer, Richard Overton, and which can be illustrated, as Saurat shows, both from Milton's prose and verse. Materialism is an old medieval heresy—or at least a variety of medieval philosophy—for we find Thomas Aquinas in his *De Ente et Essentia* controverting the view of Avicebron (actually the Jewish poet and philosopher, Solomon Ibn Gabirol) in his *Fons Vitae*, that souls and other intelligibles have a material essence. Matter was, for this Jewish philosopher, an emanation of the Divine.[3] In *Paradise Lost*, the angels are represented as material (though of finer material than that from

[1] H. Wheeler Robinson, *Record and Revelation* (Oxford, 1938), p. 331. The more dynamic, ecstatic activities of the soul are usually indicated in Hebrew by the term *Ruah* (Wind/Spirit), as in *Numbers* xxvii, 18, *Psalm* lxxviii, 39, etc. But although the 'Ruah' may be less firmly and organically rooted in the body than the 'Nefesh' it is no metaphysical property, but a natural phenomenon like the wind itself which blows about the world sometimes as a normal breeze, but sometimes with unpredictable violence. For discussion of the different Hebrew terms for Soul, see Pedersen, *op. cit.*, pp. 99-181.

[2] Milton, *Works*, XV, 41.

[3] Cf. I. Husik, *A History of Mediaeval Jewish Philosophy* (Philadelphia, 1946), p. 64 f.

which man is formed); soul is an exhalation from the body nourished by the food which the body has absorbed. The angels thus partake and enjoy the food that Adam sets before them, their spiritual substance, no less than man's rational soul, requiring solid sustenance.[1]

> and food alike those pure
> Intelligential substances require
> As doth your Rational; and both contain
> Within them every lower facultie
> Of sense, whereby they hear, see, smell, touch, taste,
> Tasting concoct, digest, assimilate,
> And corporeal to incorporeal turn.
>
> (V, 407-13)

This conception of Milton's does not involve so much the materialization of spirit as the spiritualization of matter, and in the *De Doctrina*, it is systematically worked out on the basis of the idea that the First Substance out of which the world was created was drawn out of God himself, the idea of *omnia ex deo*[2]—

---

[1] Cf. D. Saurat, *Milton Man and Thinker* (London, ed. of 1946), p. 117. Henry More placed a similar stress on Matter and Flesh as part of the perfection of our nature, and his thought on this subject has a similar Hebraic background. See M. H. Nicolson, 'Milton and the *Conjectura Cabbalistica*', *P.Q.* VI (1927), p. 14.

[2] Professor Saurat relates this to Milton's supposed knowledge of the Kabbalah (*op. cit.*, pp. 233, 242); but there is no need to look so far either for this or for his free-will doctrine. Milton's acquaintance with the Hebrew Bible as well as with some of the classical Rabbinic writings would account for such ideas. For the idea under discussion, cf. the classical *Midrash Bereshit Rabba*, ch. 13, 'The Holy One Blessed be He took dust from beneath the Throne of Glory and therewith the earth was made,' or, *Pirke d'Rabbi Eliezer*, ch. 3, 'From what source was the earth created? From the snow which is beneath the Throne of Glory. . . .' Milton need not to be supposed to have gone to the original for these rabbinic *loci*; he could have met them in a much more accessible intermediate source, namely Maimonides, *Guide to the Perplexed*, Part II, ch. 26. As for the occult literature of Judaism, Milton evidently had no access to the *Zohar* itself, and the few conceptions or attitudes which he derived from such sources came to him intermediately (and in far from accurate form) from Reuchlin, and his own near-contemporary, Robert Fludd. For a useful note on this topic, see R. J. Z. Werblowsky, 'Milton and the *Conjectura Cabbalistica*', Journal of the Warburg and Courtauld Institutes, XVIII (London, 1955), 90-113.

from which it follows that Matter is essentially good rather than bad as in the Platonic view and generally in Greek philosophy.

This positive attitude to the material universe was taken by Milton from various parts of the Hebrew tradition, but perhaps we need look no further than the first chapter of *Genesis*, 'And God saw everything that he had made and behold it was very good.'!

Milton's tendency to abolish the distinction between Matter and Spirit is referred to by Professor Sewell as part of Milton's 'holism'.[1] This it seems to me is a most valuable term in this connexion. He speaks of 'a constant attempt to get rid of dualities and divisions in divine and temporal existences' and relates it to a number of other 'heretical' tendencies in Milton's thought. Closely related to Milton's 'materialism', for instance, is his 'mortalism' (likewise held in common with Richard Overton in his *Mans Mortallitie*, and entertained at one time by Sir Thomas Browne), the idea that the soul and body die together, the whole man being as in the Hebrew Bible an intrinsic compound of body and spirit. Likewise, Milton holds in the *De Doctrina* that body and soul are jointly generated, the soul being contained potentially in the seed. But the most radical 'heresy' of all flows from the application of the holistic principle to the sphere of Divinity. He dismisses all the accumulated Trinitarian dogmas of the Church, and whilst preserving a high divine function and status (as of an archangel) for the Son, denies (*De Doctrina*, ch. 5) that he is co-essential or co-equal with the Father. Such Arian speculations are not so obviously present in *Paradise Lost* but it is noticeable that here the tendency is to present the Divine World as essentially a unitary structure—a hierarchy with God the Father as alone and supreme from all eternity (cf. VIII, 405 f.). The Son executes the wishes of the Father and functions in the symmetry of Heaven as the counterpart of Satan. He is alternately presented as the Chief of the General Staff and the Ambassador Plenipotentiary, but in the last analysis the wishes and designs of Deity are to be sought in the mind of Heaven's King and there alone. In *Paradise Regained*, Jesus is presented as the heroic man struggling

[1] A. Sewell, *A Study in Milton's Christian Doctrine* (London, 1939), pp. 163, 182-3.

against temptation, and, far from functioning as the Second Person in the Trinity, he functions as the victorious successor of Adam in *Paradise Lost*, redeeming and making good through his moral resistance to temptation (and not as in the normal Christian emphasis, through his Crucifixion) for the failure of Adam before him (cf. *Paradise Regained*, I, 1-4). This is not to say that the account of the Temptation in the wilderness which Milton gives in *Paradise Regained* is markedly at variance with the traditional exegesis of the gospel narratives: it is not.[1] But the choice of that particular episode as the central event in the history of Redemption is indicative of Milton's desire to naturalize, or one might nowadays say, 'demythologize' the gospel narrative.

Had the *De Doctrina* with its Arian teachings been published during the Puritan Commonwealth, it is interesting to speculate on the possible outcome. Perhaps Milton would have suffered the atrocious fate of Servetus (another Hebraizing anti-trinitarian heretic) in Geneva a hundred years earlier: on the other hand, there were certainly other speculative minds in Milton's time working in the same direction without incurring violent opposition. Mr. Sewell points to a similar Arian streak amongst the Cambridge Platonists.[2] They too tended, like Milton, to omit abstruse theology involving such matters as the hypostatic union and the homoousia, and concentrated rather on the simple and organic relations between Man, the World, and God.

Holism if consistently applied would also involve the abolition—or at least the attenuation—of the principle of cosmic evil. In a unitary world there is scarcely room for a high and mighty Antagonist. It is only with the begetting of the Son, and with that the hypostatization of the good and gentle aspects of Divinity, that transcendent evil comes into existence as a separate entity. It is only when you suppose a heavenly Lamb, that you must balance it with a heavenly Tiger. In the Old Testament Scripture, God is the author both of Good and Evil (*Isaiah* xlv, 7)—Evil that is to say in the sense of Suffering or Temptation—whilst Man is the author of his own Sin and

---

[1] See E. M. Pope, *Paradise Regained: The Tradition and the Poem* (Baltimore, 1947), pp. 21-4.

[2] Sewell, *op. cit.*, p. 193.

cannot pass off his responsibility by putting the blame on to some semi-divine figure of evil. Satan is no very central figure in the Old Testament and scarcely appears in the earlier traditions; when he appears in *Job* he is merely one of the Sons of God. His task seems to be to find out our unsuspected weaknesses and put temptation in our path. These are not kind things for an angel to be doing; but the angel of Death is just as respected a member of the Divine entourage, and his manners are, if anything, even worse. The angel who fights with Jacob at Peniel (*Genesis* xxxii, 25) or who affronts Moses on his way from Midian (*Exodus* iv, 24) is clearly a close relation of Satan, but in both episodes the author has no doubt that it is God himself who lies in wait to terrify and overthrow the hero. The Daemonic is part of the Divine: we are surrounded by love, but we are also surrounded by dangers and darkness which test our nerves and courage. There is obviously a great deal of this in Milton. We saw that in *Paradise Lost* he has difficulties with Satan who sometimes takes on an alarmingly positive character as a projection of Milton's own pride and audacity.[1] Milton also plays with conceptions of the origin of evil which would abolish the necessity for a separate and, as it were, independent Devil-figure: Adam tells Eve:

> Evil into the mind of God or Man
> May come and go, so unapprov'd, and leave
> No spot or blame behind.
>
> (*Paradise Lost*, V, 117-18)

In other words, every moment of Temptation, or every impulse of revolt, is not to be taken as a sign that we are under the dominion of the Devil. The mind of God also has room, it seems, for evil. It is only in *Samson Agonistes* that Milton comes to a satisfactory resolution of his difficulties about Evil and Temptation. There, there is virtually no Devil-figure, no 'Antagonist of Heaven's Almighty King'. Pride and rebellion are lodged—along with faith and righteous zeal—in the figure of the hero himself. Harapha is no successor of Comus or the Satan of *Paradise Regained* for unlike them he is outdone in active energy by the hero Samson himself. If Samson's sufferings

---

[1] Cf. Werblowsky, *Lucifer and Prometheus*, pp. 73 f.

issue from God, his sins issue from his own weakness and concupiscence: in either case there is no function left for a transcendent Devil. Human free-will unsubverted by any Calvinistic doctrine of predestination and uninfluenced by fallen angels (as in *Paradise Lost*) is the key to the moral order. If Samson dies like Oedipus, blind and in exile, he is not like Oedipus the victim of a malignant or thoughtless goddess of Fortune which will lead him to sin even against his will; Samson is by contrast a figure of unmitigated moral responsibility. 'Whom have I to complain of but myself.' Along these lines Milton finally resolves the questions of Sin and Evil, preserving as he does so, a morally unified pattern in which both the Love and Terrors of God, the evil and the good in man, find their proper integration.

Just as there is no transcendental division of Good and Evil, so there is no deep and permanent moral taint in human nature from which Sin inevitably flows. *Paradise Lost* describes the genesis of the 'Mortall sin originall' and yet if Milton's position on free-will is pressed to its logical extreme, it will be found to leave no room for a regular Augustinian conception of Original Sin. If man is always free to choose good instead of evil—and Milton seems to agree with the prophet Ezekiel that this is so—it argues that he is decidedly not subject to congenital depravity. In this respect Milton is as far from the orthodox point of view as was his contemporary Jeremy Taylor. For them both, will, instinct, and emotion are free from *essential* corruption. Milton's positive outlook on this question is nowhere clearer than in his teaching on sexual matters. Just as Augustine's sense of Original Sin is nourished above all by an overwhelming consciousness of the burning fires of sex—the unextinguished embers of his preregenerate days—so Milton's non-Augustinian position on Original Sin is most evident in his frank acceptance of the sexual instinct as capable indeed of being perverted but as, in itself, essentially pure and healthy. The Hebraic nature of this 'heresy' scarcely needs to be pointed out.

In general, Milton's heresies with regard to the married state which he announces in the *De Doctrina*[1] specifically, freedom for divorce and polygamy—have an obvious and acknowledged link with the Old Testament legislation on both points. Against

[1] Book I, ch. 10 (*Works*, XV, 121-79).

the background of the sober exposition of his views in this and other theological tracts, the affirmative sexuality of *Paradise Lost* takes on a more serious doctrinal character:

> Hail wedded Love, mysterious Law, true sourse
> Of human offspring, sole proprietie,
> In Paradise of all things common else.
> By thee adulterous lust was driv'n from men
> Among the bestial herds to raunge, by thee
> Founded in Reason, Loyal, Just, and Pure,
> Relations dear, and all the Charities
> Of Father, Son, and Brother first were known.
> Farr be it, that I should write thee sin or blame,
> Or think thee unbefitting holiest place,
> Perpetual fountain of Domestic sweets,
> Whose Bed is undefil'd and chast pronounc't,
> Present, or past, as Saints and Patriarchs us'd.
>
> (*Paradise Lost*, IV, 750-62)

There is here the Protestant glorification of marriage of which Mr. C. S. Lewis has written so persuasively and which is so fully exemplified in Spenser earlier on, but there is something more too. Milton's drift is not towards that poetry of Platonic aspiration, that exalted but rarefied idealism of Spenser's *Hymns*; the Garden of Eden is not like the House of Temperance —in a way, it is more like the Bowre of Blisse. His is a franker sexuality than Spenser's. It slightly embarrasses Mr. Lewis himself, for example, who stated his wish that Milton could have 'treated the loves of Adam and Eve as remotely as those of Angels'.[1] He did not do so because he was operating with the categories of sexual realism that he had found in the Hebrew Scriptures. There the sexual relation was so little thought of as indelicate that it was used (with its fullest and frankest associations) as the normal analogy expressive of the Covenant-love of God for Israel. The word *be'ulah*, used in *Isaiah* lxii in connexion with Israel redeemed and restored to her heavenly Lord, means undoubtedly 'physically possessed as a wife'. The word 'know' *yada'* in *Hosea* ii in the passage, 'I will even betroth thee unto me in faithfulness, and thou shalt know the Lord' carries, as an undertone, the notion of carnal knowledge as in the phrase 'And Adam knew Eve his wife'.

[1] *Op. cit.*, p. 120.

Undoubtedly the sexual union in which the two partners mysteriously become one flesh (*Genesis* ii, 24) and no less mysteriously preserve their essential and separate identity in a fundamentally I/Thou complex, is a *unique* example of the Covenant-bond and an indispensable symbol of the Covenant in its larger sense of partnership between God and Man. No wonder then that Milton with his strong heterosexual instincts should have declared 'Farr be it, that I should write thee sin or blame.' Above all, in the marriage contract we have the most precise example of that synthesis of Law and Liberty which Milton was always trying to define. Marriage guarantees the free expression of physical and emotional need but governs that expression and dedicates it to moral and social ends.

Nowhere in fact does Milton define more clearly his sense of the interdependence of Law and Liberty than in his writings on Marriage and Divorce. In the tract entitled *The Doctrine and Discipline of Divorce*, he defends the principle of free sexual choice, i.e. the freedom to dissolve an unhappy marriage and start again, by arguing that if such freedom is not granted, Marriage is not the entrance into liberty but into slavery, slavery of the body and spirit. But Divorce is not to be confused with wantonness; it is itself a machinery of Law, and is like marriage itself to be controlled by Law.

> What though the brood of Belial, the draffe of men, to whom no liberty is pleasing, but unbridl'd and vagabond lust without pale or partition, will laugh broad perhaps, to see so great a strength of Scripture mustering up in favour, as they suppose, of their debausheries; they will know better, when they shall hence learne that honest liberty is the greatest foe to dishonest licence.[1]

In this tract, first published in 1643, Milton first seriously took issue with his Puritan compatriots on an important problem of civil and religious law. At a time when more pressing problems were exercising the minds of his lay and ecclesiastical fellow-Puritans, the work did not excite a major storm of protest, though more than one contemporary pronounced the author a heresiarch.[2] Yet he had done here in expositional form

[1] *Works*, III, 370.
[2] See D. Masson, *The Life of John Milton* (reprinted, New York, 1946), III, 155.

no more than he was to do in artistic terms later in *Samson Agonistes*, where Greek form was to be wedded to Scriptural content to produce a type of heroism based on active earth-bound Hebraic categories of righteousness. Here too he blends Renaissance and Reformation themes using Hebraism as a solvent. Specifically, he quotes (from Plato's *Symposium*) the prophetess Diotima relating the myth of the origin of Love in the Garden of Jupiter and blends it with the Biblical account of the origin of marriage in the Garden of Eden. But here are no old style harmonistics. He is not using Scripture and Pagan-ism to reinforce the accepted and time-honoured teaching of the Church on Marriage and Divorce, to bring (like Hooker) Reason to the aid of Faith. On the contrary, he is overthrowing the old rational structure of Christian compromise. He unites Christianity and Humanism, but what emerges is not 'Christian Humanism', but something new, electric, revolutionary—a plea for freedom to divorce! And what could be more audacious than a bid to extend the bounds of Christian liberty by an appeal from the New Testament to the Old? It is indeed revolutionary Hebraism.

Milton insists that the object of a religious system is not to 'root up our natural affections and disaffections'. Papistry had banned marriage for the clergy, so rooting up the natural instincts planted in humanity in the Garden of Eden. The Reformation had overthrown this regulation, but its continued ban on divorce, in Milton's view, equally violated human instinct. This reverence for the sacredness of the heart's affec-tions as well as its disaffections is typical of the Humanism of the 'Counter-Renaissance' whose child Milton was (we remember the extravagant cult of honour and individual rights) but it is just as typical—in a different way—of the Old Testa-ment. In that Scripture, Milton's humanistic instincts received the confirmation of a manifest and revealed ordinance, binding in the first instance on Israel, but no less binding, he would here maintain, on the New Israel after it had received the charter of gospel liberty.

We may suppose that following his hasty marriage to Mary Powell in June, 1642, Milton's desire to rid himself of an intoler-able burden in the form of an uncompliant and unsympathetic spouse was only exceeded by his desire not to contravene what he could be assured was the Divine Law, the will of God, on this particular question of divorce. In seeking relief he found that, according to the law of the Church as derived from the teachings of Paul and the record of the gospels themselves, divorce was, for practical purposes, forbidden. Confronted by such a directive as 'whosoever shall put away his wife, and marry another, committeth adultery against her' (*Mark*, x, 11), the canon-lawers had judged (quite rightly, one would suppose) that freedom to dissolve an unhappy marriage could not normally be justified in a Christian society, and the Reformed Churches had not sought to change this position.

Milton could not remain satisfied with this and so he undertook an independent examination of the Bible, beginning with the first chapter of *Genesis* so as to find 'those ordinances which were allotted to our solace and reviving'. The result was this eloquent, and in the circumstances in which it was written, deeply moving, appeal to the conscience of his countrymen.

> While we literally superstitious through customary faintnesse of heart, not venturing to pierce with our free thoughts into the full latitude of nature and religion, abandon our selves to serve under the tyranny of usurpt opinions, suffering those ordinances which were allotted to our solace and reviving, to trample over us and hale us into a multitude of sorrowes which God never meant us. And where he set us in a fair allowance of way, with honest liberty and prudence to our guard, we never leave subtilizing and casuisting till we have straitn'd and par'd that liberal path into a razors edge to walk on, between a precipice of unnecessary mischief on either side; and starting at every false Alarum, we doe not know which way to set a foot forward with manly confidence and Christian resolution, through the confused ringing in our ears of *panick* scruples and amazements.[1]

How different this is in tone and imagery from the normal run of Puritan prose! Milton succeeded in instilling as much through the clarity and fervour of his eloquence, indeed, as through the precise, legal formulae that he adopts, a concept of righteousness, more liberal, more practicable, and more exalted, than was to be found in England in his time, or perhaps in any other time. It would be irrelevant here to trace in detail the course of Milton's exegesis. But it may be said that, basically,

---

[1] *Works*, III, 496-7.

Milton's concept of marriage goes back to the second chapter of *Genesis*, 'It is not good that the man should be alone; I will make him an help meet for him.' His teaching with regard to divorce derives its authority from *Deut.* xxiv, 1-3:

> When a man taketh a wife, and marrieth her, then it shall be, if she find no favour in his eyes, because he hath found some unseemly thing in her, that he shall write her a bill of divorcement, and give it in her hand, and send her out of his house.

Some critics have failed to understand the nature of Milton's approach to the Scripture but if we follow Milton's argument and sources carefully both in the Tract of 1643 and, more particularly, in *Tetrachordon: Expositions upon the Four Chief Places in Scripture which treat of Marriage, or Nullities in Marriage* (1645), we shall see that what Milton is consistently trying to do is to adjust the teachings of the New Testament to those of the Old. What Milton says about marriage and divorce bringing in his hands, 'an ancient and most necessary, most charitable, and yet most injured statute of Moses', is in fact authentic Hebrew doctrine, attested by the numerous authorities he quotes, ranging from the first chapters of *Genesis*, to Maimonides, as translated by Buxtorf.[1]

II

So much then for Milton's heresies—heresies arising in a very special degree from the strong compulsion of his Hebraism and from his standing on the ground of the Covenant of Works. At this point this Chapter might properly come to an end, the case for Milton (or some might think, against Milton) having been duly proved: but such a conclusion would hardly do justice to Milton's many-sidedness or, put it more brutally, his truly heroic capacity for inconsistency. Milton was in fact no more consistent with regard to his Hebraism than he was in anything else. There were Judaizers among the Protestant sects

---

[1] Cf. H. F. Fletcher, *Milton's Semitic Studies* (Chicago, 1926), pp. 68, 73-8; and *Milton's Rabbinical Readings* (Urbana, 1930), pp. 41-3. Fletcher's books give a fair impression of the range of Milton's Hebrew studies, but no adequate conclusions are drawn.

from the sixteenth century onwards who wanted to bring in the whole Mosaic legislation for Christians, but Milton would have scorned the attribution of such notions to himself. *The Reason of Church Government* is a sort of seventeenth-century Ode to Duty, a gesture of profound respect for the notion of Law and Discipline: in this respect it suits well with his position on the Law and the Commandments as giving to human life purpose and direction. We noted his tendency to evoke in this connexion the very Hebraic image of Samson's locks, symbol of the *Torah* of the Nazirite, and, by wider inference, symbol of the righteous laws of a nation. Yet in the third chapter of this very treatise, Milton carries out a fierce attack in evangelical manner upon the Anglican (and ultimately Catholic) tendency to derive the bases of Church Government from the Old Testament! He speaks in an almost antinomian strain and quite unlike Hooker, of 'our liberty from the bondage of the Law'. And he goes on:

> How then the ripe age of the Gospell should be put to schoole againe, and learn to governe her selfe from the infancy of the Law, the stronger to imitate the weaker, the freeman to follow the captive, the learned to be lesson'd by the rude, will be a hard undertaking to evince from any of those principles which either art or inspiration hath written.

If it should be thought that he intends these strictures for the ceremonial or priestly code and not for the whole Old Testament Covenant as such, he expresses himself in a later Chapter even more unequivocally—

> For who gave the autority to fetch more from the patterne of the law then what the Apostles had already fetcht, if they fetcht anything at all, *as hath beene prov'd they did not* . . .?[1]

This insistence on the most radical application of the principle of Christian liberty, provoked at this point by his dislike of prelacy, is to become more systematically and clearly defined later on as a general principle in the *De Doctrina Christiana*, where he points out that the whole Mosaic law, moral, ceremonial, and religious is utterly abolished for Christians.[2]

How are we to account for this concurrence of powerful judaistic motifs with equally powerful anti-judaistic motifs the

[1] *Works*, III, 196-7, and 207 (my italics).
[2] Book I, ch. 27, in *Works*, XVI, 112-63.

latter expressed with something of the contemptuous violence of Luther himself? 'For that which was to the Jew but Jewish, is to the Christian no better than Canaanitish,' he remarks sweetly in one place. It is not sufficient to say that Milton was simply a Puritan at the last, and that such contradictions belong to Puritanism as we have described it. Milton was too independent in his attitude to be carried along simply by the tide of Calvinistic or Lutheran orthodoxy. Less courageous schismatics than Milton were in his day prepared to ignore both. Clearly, there was some personal motive operating with him to bring about these deviations from Hebraism—a personal motive, moreover, as powerful as that which in so many other instances led him to base his whole humanistic position on an appeal to the Old Testament Covenant.[1]

The question is made more piquant when we consider that whilst contending here against the judaic priestly code, he was not in his deepest nature the enemy of ceremonial. He was no iconoclast like Luther. We need only think of his festive and ceremonious style, so different from the austerities of typical Puritan writing. This, to the literary analyst at least, bespeaks a certain devotion to the ritualistic principle. Nor is it at all clear that Milton had always disliked bishops: he was himself designed for the Church and probably only turned against the ecclesiastical hierarchy at the time of the Laudian persecutions. In *Of Prelatical Episcopacy* (1641), we find him saying, 'No man will gainsay the constitution of bishops,' and he indicates that his objection is to 'the raising of them to a superior order above presbyters'. We note here the typical Miltonic conjunction of the idea of authority (Bishops) and freedom (Presbyters). In *Lycidas* we find Peter—surely the archetypal symbol of episcopacy—with his 'Miter'd locks' (an image collateral with

---

[1] On the contradictions in Milton's attitude towards the question of Law *versus* Gospel, see B. Rajan, *op. cit.*, pp. 90-1, 159-60 (commenting on *Paradise Lost*, XII, 299 f.). Rajan approximates Milton's attitude altogether too closely to that of Calvin and presents him as subordinating the Law to the Gospel; but this is to ignore Milton's constant use of the England-Israel analogy and his appeal to the Law as representing an ideal form of government for England. This type of argument is still very prominent in *The Tenure of Kings and Magistrates*, where it is clear that the old Covenant is in Milton's mind and not the 'better Cov'nant' of *Paradise Lost*, XII, 301. For a more balanced treatment see Kelley, *op. cit.*, pp. 56-57.

Milton's very central and very positive image of Samson's locks) bewailing the untimely loss of Edward King.

If Milton was in principle no enemy of the bishops, we may add that he was equally no enemy of Kings! He argued (quoting the Talmud) that the King was subject to the Law; his objection to Charles was that he had violated the law and must therefore suffer due punishment. But in *The Reason of Church Government* the king is compared—in a passage already quoted—to 'that mighty Nazirite Samson', 'his illustrious and sunny locks, the laws, waving and curling about his godlike shoulders'—a truly courtier-like and not inaccurate pen-portrait of the royal martyr. Had the king not betrayed as he did the integrity of the nation as a sacred community, we may suppose that Milton would have remained a royalist to the end. For unconscious evidence we may note—as so many critics have noted—the strong royalist features of the heavenly government in *Paradise Lost* and for more conscious testimony we have the elaborate compliments to the Queen of Sweden which Milton introduces into his *Second Defence of the People of England*. He calls her 'a particle of celestial flame so resplendently pure'. Burke in his praise of Marie Antoinette was not a more devoted and gracious courtier; and Milton, for his part, takes this opportunity of assuring us that 'I have spoken not a syllable against kings, but against the underminers and pests of kings, against tyrants only.'[1]

It would not be too much to suggest that Milton was drawn in his deepest nature to that integration of Power and Goodness which in political terms would be represented by an active combination of the forces of Church and State, not a theocracy on Genevan lines but one which allowed for a greater expression of national culture and tradition and a more festively royal and religious ceremonial. In Milton's theocracy there would have been not sumptuary laws and censorship of the Press, but music and poetry, Theatres and Masques, freedom for divorce, and above all a national church expressing through its form and spirit his sense of his country as a messiah-nation. Far from urging the separation of Church, State, and Crown, we would suppose him fighting for their unification as a necessary pre-requisite for that complete religious life which includes the whole

[1] *Works*, VIII, 105.

Man, his body and soul, his political as well as his ecclesiastical affiliations. His whole renaissance emphasis on the *patria* as well as his Hebraic stress on the nation as essentially coextensive with the sacred community would surely have led him in this direction. What then made him veer farther and farther away to the left, abandoning Presbyterianism for Independence, and then abandoning Independence in the attempt to realize an ever more radical separation of the religious life from State authority, a more and more complete decentralization of the ecclesiastical order? Does this movement for decentralization, for separation and Church and State, which is the great political theme of Milton's later tracts not inevitably imply that no national religious programme acceptable to all, no sacral community in fact coextensive with the nation, can ever arise? We have claimed Milton as the great integrator trying to bring together the fragments of a shattered world-order and doing so under the stress of his Hebraic Covenant-faith. Why then does he then appear in this critical instance as the apostle of division and dissociation?

Milton's tendency here may be explained along the lines of the difficulty which Protestant Christianity has experienced with regard to the priestly cult of the Old Testament. The priests, we know, were committed to the preservation of the cult, to ceremonial and tradition, whilst the prophets expressed the more dynamic side of the religious life, the moral challenge of the Covenant. The Protestants—and in particular the Puritans—felt themselves to be in the revolutionary tradition of the prophets, and saw in their Anglican and Catholic opponents the heirs of the priestly code of Judaism. From this developed a tendency to regard Priest and Prophet as somehow in principle opposed to one another.

This, however, may be nothing more than the projection into the Hebrew Scriptures of an internal Christian problem, with little relevance to Biblical Judaism. There is, after all, room in the Biblical Covenant for both Priest and Prophet; for the Covenant embraces in its parallelogram of forces, history and geography, change and inertia. Moses, the ideal leader, is simultaneously, king, priest, and prophet[1]—his demand for

[1] Buber almost makes this point (*Moses*, London, 1946) when he speaks of the union of functions in Moses which will later be distributed between

total moral renovation ('Be ye holy for I, the Lord your God am holy') proceeds side by side with a meticulous concern for the detail of the cult. The later prophets, it is true, were often opposed to the Establishment, but this was because the Establishment seemed to them not in conformity with the moral demands of the Covenant; in actual fact, they never lost their sense of a religious order in which there would be true priests and righteous kings, in place of false priests and unrighteous kings (*Malachi* iii, 3-4; *Isaiah* ix, 7). They never really despaired of the integration of Goodness and Power so essential for the complete realization of the sacred community as required by the Covenant. Biblical critics in the nineteenth century (issuing on the whole from a Protestant environment) were fond of portraying a basic antagonism of Priest and Prophet as typical of the whole Old Testament pattern, as though that literature was the creation of two opposed religious systems, some parts of it emanating from 'priestly' circles, and other parts from 'prophetic' circles. This view is still canvassed nowadays, but more recent scholarship (especially that coming from Scandinavia) has with a sounder instinct insisted on the existence of an intimate relationship between the two groups or forces, finding 'cultic' motifs and ritualistic fragments in the work of the writing prophets from the eighth century onwards whose original oracles are said to have been preserved actually in priestly circles.[1] In so far as later Jewish history may be regarded as a sort of existential gloss upon the Biblical Covenant and its various components, it might be taken as resolving the

[1] Cf. H. H. Rowley, *The Old Testament and Modern Study* (Oxford, 1951), ed. of 1961, pp. 300-2.

Priest and Judge (i.e., Joshua and Eleazar). 'Those functions which were united in him, in Moses, namely the sacral utterance of oracles, the direction of communal offerings and the political organization and leadership of the people's life, must be divided between two men, two kinds of men, two series of men . . . the division would of necessity have its effect in splitting what was marked for unity' (pp. 198-9). But Buber with a certain 'protestant' tendency to undervalue the ceremonial sacral side of the religion of Israel, denies that Moses is a genuinely priestly personality (p. 114). Moreover he fails to do justice to the constant tendency in later Jewish history to reassert the theme of unity. (David and Solomon are both seen as exercising priestly functions, and the later Maccabeans are both priests and political leaders).

supposed Priest/Prophet antithesis, for the Jew in history has always accommodated a profound traditionalism (involving ceremonies and ritual and an unyielding attachment to precedent) side by side with revolutionary ardour (we recall the Maccabeans—who were incidentally priests—and Bar Cochba). The Jew is often fanatical in his attachment to the past, but he is at the same time everlastingly discontented with the present. He is both Catholic and Protestant; both Disraeli and Karl Marx.

Now I think it can be justly urged without any distortion of the literary evidence that Milton was working on the lines of a true interdependence of Priest and Prophet—a very non-Protestant point of view. Without needing to analyse its sources in the way that these paragraphs attempt to do, he had arrived at a way of thinking which demonstrates a certain Hebraic co-ordination of Law and Freedom, a feeling for a theo-political order excluding neither Bishops nor Kings. But when the Bishops stood in the way of the creation of a sacred community on biblical lines by lending themselves to be the political instruments of a corrupt régime what was to be done—when History—contemporary History that is—forced itself upon him by contradicting the theo-political ideal? Milton suffered a series of traumatic shocks of this kind, beginning perhaps as early as 1640. First, the Priesthood, then the King, then the Presbyters, and finally all organized religion and politics whatsoever revealed themselves as failing to match the standards of a messiah-nation. Here is the danger of that over-exact indentification of Israel and England—of Albion and Jerusalem if you like—of which Milton was guilty. When the Israelite prophet such as Amos or Hosea found a corrupt régime and a sycophantic priesthood he was not obliged to resort to mythology in order to assert his faith in a true priesthood of the order of Melchizedek or a true monarchy of the Davidic type. History was fundamentally on his side. As the substratum of all Israelite historical thinking, and more fundamental than the passing political and priestly constellations, was the memory of the sacerdotal 'amphictyony' in the wilderness, of the royal Covenant sealed in blood (*Exodus* xxiv), of the exchange of solemn oaths at the foot of Mount Sinai.[1] In Milton's case

[1] Cf. Buber, *Moses*, section entitled 'The Covenant', pp. 110-18.

history was all too obviously *not* on his side, and Milton was much too realistic, much too down-to-earth to ignore completely the harsh pressures of history. Perhaps there was never a major English poet more history-conscious than Milton. He could in his imagination embrace the Israelite covenant, its ideal unity of royal and priestly symbols, but he could not (like Blake) take refuge in myths by persuading himself of some Druid or pre-Druid origin for the Hebrew and English nations alike: he was all too conscious of the lack, in the case of Albion, of historical precedent or promise. There was no certain reference point indigenous to English history which could serve to reassure the poet of the Covenant during a phase in which contemporary politics failed to measure up to his ideal. And therefore, as all around him the Commonwealth was visibly failing to realize his dream of a sacred community, he came to feel that only in the complete separation of Church and State—with complete religious freedom as its corollary—would room be found for the development of that distinctive religious culture of which he dreamed. In one sense, this is a positive drive in so far as it aims at some new, unhampered, humanistic formulation of protestantism; but in another sense, it is a negative and funda-mentally despairing movement of the spirit, for it involves giving up the State to its own unredeemed devices, it involves rendering to Caesar that which is Caesar's, and is thus the denial of Milton's instinctive holism. Now, it is in this despairing counter-theme in Milton's thinking, in this increasing disjunc-tion of the spheres of God and Man, Church and State, that Milton's anti-judaic evangelical theology with its stress on Salvation through faith alone is to be located. This is 'the better Cov'nant, disciplin'd From shadowie Types to Truth, from Flesh to Spirit' of which he speaks in the twelfth book of *Paradise Lost*.

Such is the psychological background against which we should judge Milton's demand for a more and more complete separation of Church and State. And by a process of guilt trans-ference which no psychologist (and no lay-student of human nature for that matter) would find any difficulty in understand-ing, his discontent with false priesthood and false state power in the England of his day is translated into a radical attack on the Hebraic doctrine of State and Community, the union of King,

Priest, and Prophet ideally posited by Hebraism. History had forced him to reject this side of Hebraism as inapplicable to the situation of England in 1650, and so his objections to it clothe themselves with the typical evangelical, Lutheran attitude of scorn for the judaic priestly ceremonial as such, for the judaic combination of political and ecclesiastical authority; thus he comes to affirm that 'that which is to the Jew but Jewish, is to the Christian no better than Canaanitish'. He had given up his reliance on authority because the established authority had failed to satisfy his sense of what authority ought to be. He yearned to see something like the Mosaic Covenant established in England both as a moral discipline and as a national cult, but the national traditions of Albion were too different from those of Jerusalem; and at the same time his use of the analogy between the two was too rigid to permit him to consider a more general application of the Covenant-theology to England. The result was that he reached a psychological and theological impasse which is reflected in those striking inconsistencies with regard to Hebraism to be found in the *De Doctrina Christiana.*

Here in the *De Doctrina Christiana* he maintains in the manner of the passage quoted earlier from *Paradise Lost* that Christians are delivered from the whole law of Moses, but he also maintains at the same time that not only divorce, but polygamy as well, might be sanctioned for Christians on the basis of the law and usage of the Old Testament![1] He declares that even the moral table of the Decalogue has no binding character for everything is to be finally referred to the spirit and unwritten word,[2] yet in his anti-Trinitarian Chapter he appeals to the first of the Commandments (viz. *Deut.* vi, 4) as his proof for the indivisible unity of the Godhead. It is here in the *De Doctrina* that his evangelical repudiation of the Law of Works is most earnestly proclaimed, and here also that all the most characteristic elements of his Hebraism receive their final formulation—his Materialism, his Mortalism, his Arianism, his Arminianism, and his unshakeable faith, in spite of the Christian doctrine of the Fall, in what he elsewhere calls 'the blameless nature of Man'.

This curious complex of Hebraic optimism and evangelical

[1] Book I, ch. 10.   [2] *Ibid.*, ch. 27.

pessimism is what marks Milton's psychological state at the close of the Commonwealth; it is a faith in Man but a despair of human history and institutions, or, to put it another way, it is a hope which springs out of his organic centre of being, but which, failing to find any satisfactory object in the world outside, turns back upon itself and condemns its author to 'a fugitive and cloister'd vertue, unexercis'd and unbreath'd'.

PART FOUR

Characterisms of Virtue

XI

JEREMY TAYLOR

I

IT WAS Milton's Hebraic committal to History which led him into difficulties and into conflicts with his environment, and which also paradoxically, by way of adjustment to these difficulties, brought about his striking deviations from Hebraism. It may be said that Milton was, in Biblical terms, right in giving to history this decisive role in his religious life, but he overlooked the fact that the Bible recognizes meaningful histories other than the history of Israel (see *Amos* ix, 7). The identification of the Christian Community as the New Israel (expressed so strongly by Milton in his repeated use of the England-Israel analogy) could only lead to a distortion of English (or gentile) history, and thus make impossible that marriage of Albion and Jerusalem which Milton was inwardly seeking.

Now what was called for here was not only spiritual vision and tenacity—Milton had those—but a spirit of compromise (which Milton lacked) and, above all, a standpoint located more centrally in the English cultural and religious tradition itself. We have spoken above of Milton's patriotism and his awareness of the English tradition. But the intensity with which these aims and affiliations are clothed is itself not especially English! His messianic ardours are easily explicable in terms of the particular environment of his generation and the atmosphere of Puritan spirituality then prevalent, but they are out of place against the broader background of an English heritage stretching back from the Middle Ages to modern times, and this was no doubt sensed by many of his contemporaries. Disraeli's messianic ardours were similarly felt as misplaced at a later day. Both of them (the latter in such a novel as *Tancred*) were in effect singing the songs of Zion in a strange land.

Now, a more balanced sense of tradition, a more relaxed and less problematical (if less intense and dynamic) understanding of Hebraism was achieved by the moderate Anglicans, the exponents in theology of the *via media*. Some of these, such as Hall, leaned towards the Calvinist side; others, such as Taylor, Herbert, and Boyle, leaned towards the Arminians. But they were all making for a temperate region of compromise; that was the special characteristic of the Anglican *via media*. Above all, whilst lacking the patriotic ardours of Milton or the ecstasies of Blake, they had a sense of the continuity and worth-whileness of the English tradition as such. They were Anglican not only in that they adhered to certain ecclesiastical forms laid down by the English Church, but also in their sense of an organic culture, a native soil in which the English religion had grown and from which it was not to be uprooted, however much it might need to be reformed and purified. In this respect their sense of history was as strong as that of Milton and the Puritans, but it was a sense of history which stressed the inheritance of the past rather than the supposed extraordinary opportunities of the present.

One could put it in another way: the Covenant-pattern which determines and underlies the Biblical conception of history involves the dialectic of Exile and Return.[1] And the rhythm of Exile and Return is the rhythm of universal history no less than that of the history of Israel. Now, if a clear distinction is at all possible between the historical outlook of the Anglicans and that of the apocalyptic and messianic sects in Puritanism including Milton, one can perhaps employ these Biblical categories and say that Milton and his like—the Fifth Monarchy Men, the Antinomians, the Levellers and the rest—stressed the aspect of Return: they thought Salvation was round the corner or had already come; whilst the Anglican pietists were more impressed by the relevance of the aspect of Exile. They were soberly conscious of the long journey which men still had to make before all could be well. They were tutored by the past to recognize the limitations and difficulties which beset their nation in its religious concerns. And perhaps theirs was the truer instinct. After the destruction of the Temple, the great founder of post-

---

[1] What for Christian theology is the primeval fall is for Jewish theology the primeval exile. The exile of Adam from the Garden parallels later events. Many traces of this link between the Eden story and the later record of Jewish History are to be found in the Bible itself, e.g., *Ezekiel* xxxvi, 35. It is a commonplace of Rabbinic homily.

exiliᴄ Judaism, Rabbi Jokhanan ben Zakkai said, 'Give me Jabneh and its Sages'; thither he retired from the struggle to concentrate upon the erection of a 'holy community' organized upon more limited, domestic lines. This does not mean that his sense of history was less acute than that of (say) Bar Cochba: on the contrary it was, in the long-term, more acute and more soundly based. Similarly, the tendency of the Anglican mode-rates was to retire from the pressures of contemporary history (to Bemerton or Little Gidding, or Norwich or Golden Grove) and organize themselves in circles for study and devotion (we think of the circle centering on Susanna Hopton at Kington to which Traherne belonged); they sought to cultivate their gardens and achieve useful and pious lives; they stressed the virtue of silent meditation.[1] These men were parish-priests, not because they could not have done better for themselves in Church and State but because the holy community had become for them, in an important sense, co-extensive with the parish, coloured by its domestic concerns, and environed by its natural beauty. Nor should it be thought that in this retirement from the world they had need to set up Puritan barriers to protect the spiritual order from being infringed by the breath of the world's mutability and the carnal reason of Man. They were very far from evangelical narrowness, and indeed they sought, no less insistently than Milton, an integration of their strong humanis-tic concerns with their equally strong sense of an otherworldly destiny. Here as in every other department of their life and thought the spirit of compromise ruled. They were seeking a formulation of the religious life in which there would be room for seriousness and strenuousness, but room also for the daily life of Man and Nature. For this purpose they had recourse, in an interesting and surprising degree, to the this-worldly pattern of righteousness laid down in the Hebrew Bible. Here they and Milton with certain of the left-wing sects in Puritanism were on fundamentally common ground, however divided they may have been in other important respects.

We may start with a right-wing Anglican, Jeremy Taylor, whose theological position and temper coincide remarkably

---

[1] For a balanced account of the place of meditation and devotion in moderate Anglicanism, see H. R. McAdoo, *The Structure of Caroline Moral Theology* (London, 1949), pp. 138 f.

with those of Milton. Both are children of the Renaissance, stirred by the poetry of antiquity, and the Renaissance call for liberty. But above all both are heirs of the Reformation, putting the Bible as word and life before all dogmas and doctrines whatsoever. We have adverted earlier to the Hebraic undertones and rhythms of Taylor's prose, to his combination of Elizabethan amplitude and Hebraic directness and urgency. In respect of his style he is as much, and as little, a Puritan as Milton. Both of them have command of the elaborate classical manner of the High Renaissance, and enjoy the luxury of a poetical phrase, but the deeper rhythm in both cases is one expressive of moral earnestness and power. In the quotations from Taylor embodied in the following paragraphs, the reader will discover a style of exposition which is both practical and glowing. There is eloquence but it is subordinated after the Hebrew fashion to the moral business.

To begin with his vision of Man, here Taylor developed a positive attitude which involved him—much to the embarrassment of his Anglican colleagues—in the Pelagian heresy, the denial of the doctrine of Original Sin. The offending document was his *Unum Necessarium* (1655) in which he questioned whether 'the depravation of Man's nature after the fall was so total as had been generally apprehended'. A dangerous heresy, indeed, but one which was implicit in the whole humanist tradition, and which had, in addition, long English antecedents. Pelagius was, after all, an English monk. There is an irony, amounting to scorn, in Taylor's account of current left-wing theological opinion and its result in terms of moral conduct. He expressed his impatience of these dogmas with a certain self-consciously 'English' robustness:

> For besides that I am told that a man hath no liberty, but a liberty to sin, and this definite liberty is *in plain English* a very necessity, we see it by a daily experience that those who call themselves good men, are such who do what they would not, and cannot do what they would; and if it be so, it is better to do what I have a mind to quietly, than to vex myself, and yet do it nevertheless, and that it is so, I am taught in almost all the discourses I have read or heard upon the seventh chapter to the Romans.[1]

[1] *The Preface to the Clergy of England*, in *Works* (London, 1837), II, 422-3.

He goes on to explain that, according to these standard views, the regenerate will always have to succumb—in spite of all their efforts—to the power of sin which has dominion over them.[1] Nor is it only among the Presbyterians that he found this tendency; he also attacked the system of pardons and indulgences whereby the Catholic Church administered salvation and thus provided cover for habitual sins. His sharpest attack, however, was levelled against the belief almost universally held as to the efficacy of death-bed repentance. As one modern student of Caroline theology has put it, 'If a man may defer his repentance until he finds himself in danger of death then the necessity for leading a good life disappears.'[2] If a proper state of grace could be achieved in time—righteousness would be imputed at the last moment. (The last-minute repentance of Edmund in the final Act of *King Lear* would be an example and the sensational repentance of some of Webster's characters at the end of their lives.) No satisfactory denial of this doctrine was forthcoming from either the left or right-wing of the Church, in spite of the fact that the most notorious profligates (such as Rochester later on) took advantage of it to lead vicious lives and die exemplary deaths. It was against this and similar evils that Jeremy Taylor's treatise was directed. It was also intended to serve as a Preface to a manual of casuistry—his *Ductor Dubitantium* (1660) which he was planning as a guide to the good life, but which he thought would be rendered null and void in advance by the prevailing climate of dogma, according to which either a Man will be damned in spite of his good deeds or he will be saved without regard to them. In either event, they mattered little:

> what is there left to discourage the evil lives of men, or to lessen a full iniquity, since upon the account of the premises, either we may do what we list without sin, or sin without punishment, or go on without fear, or repent without danger, and without scruple be confident of heaven?[3]

Taylor could not remain satisfied with such a state of affairs and his consequent stress upon moral liberty and responsibility linked him inevitably to the Arminians.

[1] *Ibid.*, p. 423. [2] McAdoo, *op. cit.*, p. 132.
[3] *Works*, II, 424.

Taylor is like Milton in his practical emphasis and his impatience of dogma. In his *Liberty of Prophecying* (1647), he asks,

> Why are we so zealous against those we call heretics, and yet great friends with drunkards, fornicators, and swearers, and intemperate and idle persons?[1]

There is an obvious parallel between this treatise and Milton's *Areopagitica*. Like Milton, Taylor complains of the cramping effect of dogma; it is only when dogma takes the place of right reason and the good life, that the Church will seek to control the thoughts of its members. As in Judaism, Taylor places his emphasis on right-doing rather than right-thinking. If men are to be killed for heresy, says Taylor, 'we are not sure we do not fight against God'.[2] It is notable that Taylor has the same difficulty as Milton with the Trinitarian dogmas—he does not carry it to the same Arian conclusions as Milton in the *De Doctrina*, but he objects to the censorious tone of the Athanasian Creed and remarks 'how contrary to natural reason it seems, how little the Scripture says of those curiosities of explication. . . .'[3] Taylor has nothing of Milton's Puritan revolutionary spirit but he makes the same essentially Protestant appeal to Scripture, right reason, and individual judgement.

If we look into Taylor's works, we shall find that he shares (in a somewhat less obtrusive manner) nearly all Milton's heresies, and that they spring like Milton's out of a positive and essentially Hebraic conviction as to the goodness of Man. In Taylor's version of the Fall, Man is not impaired either in his liberty or his natural goodness—he is simply thrown on his natural resources. Even death did not come into the world because of Adam's sin; imperfection, concupiscence, and death —all belonged to Adam before the Fall as part of the *normal* condition of human nature.[4] As a means of meeting the difficulty presented by the stress upon the doctrine of the Fall in the Christian tradition, Taylor maintains that Adam lost for himself and his heirs certain special advantages connected with residence in the Garden of Eden; 'if Adam had not sinned he should have been immortal by grace, that is by the use of the

[1] *Works*, II, 300. [2] *Works*, II, 376.
[3] *Works*, II, 323. [4] *Works*, II, 535.

tree of life. . . .'[1] What the children of Adam inherit, according to Taylor, is not congenital depravity but the full natural endowment of Adam as a child of God, and what they lack, is the promise of a 'preternatural immortality.' Death is therefore neither an evil, nor essentially, a punishment, but simply a part of human nature. This again is not unlike Milton's view and it is not surprising that Taylor here and elsewhere subscribes to the mortalist heresy, claiming that death is not a translation to some unearthly state but a natural dissolution of body and soul. He postpones the future life which seems to be demanded by Christian doctrine to a distant Resurrection.[2]

Taylor's criticism of orthodox beliefs is indeed far-reaching and fundamental. To take one further example, as part of his reformulation of the doctrine of the Fall, he considers the status of new-born children, condemned to damnation through the guilt of Original Sin (a notion explicitly maintained by Augustine). Taylor passionately rejects this belief and argues—

> that because God is true, and just, and wise, and good and merciful, it is not to be supposed that he will snatch infants from their mother's breasts, and throw them into the everlasting flames of hell for the sin of Adam, that is, as to them for their mere natural state, of which himself was Author and Creator; that is, he will not damn them for being good. For 'God saw everything that he had made, and behold it was very good.'[3]

In opposing the notion of inherited guilt, Taylor thus invokes the Old Testament doctrine as to the goodness of Man and his moral freedom; but it is not merely the goodness of Man, but the justice of God which is at stake. In his simple faith, he is at one with Milton who declares to the end, 'Just are the ways of

---

[1] *Works*, II, 534. In the Hebrew text, it is not at all clear that Adam was originally immortal, and that Death came into the world as a result of Adam's sin. The announced penalty for eating of the fruit was immediate death (*Genesis* ii, 17) which did not take place; the story is thus not one of crime and punishment, but of crime and forgiveness, or at least, commutation of sentence (from death to exile). Read in this way it is parallel to the story of Cain and Abel which follows, and indeed, in some Jewish sources the two are linked as patterns of successful repentance (for instance, in the hymn composed by Binyamin ben Zerach for the penitential prayers on the Fast of Gedaliah).

[2] Cf. *The Great Exemplar* (1649), Part III, sect. xvi, 15.

[3] *Works*, II, 537.

God and justifiable to man'—here the high-churchman and the
Puritan radical speak with the same voice because they share
the same blend of Renaissance humanism and Hebraic Reformation earnestness, and it yields in either case the same positive ideal of human freedom and responsibility.

We may remind ourselves of an equally unorthodox attitude
to the matter of the guilt or innocence of new-born children
which is to be found in Traherne's poem, 'Innocence' and in
Henry Vaughan's famous poem 'The Retreate',

> Happy those early dayes! when I
> Shin'd in my Angell-infancy.

Professor L. C. Martin[1] makes the point that Vaughan's attitude is not, as commonly supposed, Platonic. The idea of pre-
existence in Plato confers no special majesty upon the child, and
the technique of *anamnesis* is a matter of intellect and intuition—
of *logos* in short—achieved by a sort of retrospective effort on
the part of the adult philosopher. But in Vaughan's poem the
child's whole organic personality is seen to be irradiated with
purity and innocence:

> But felt through all this fleshly dresse
> Bright shootes of everlastingnesse.

Martin finds a truer source for his notion in the Hermetic
literature and in the literature of Rabbinic Judaism, which
insists strongly, in the quotations adduced by Professor Martin,
on the essential innocence of children.

> Understand that the Almighty is pure, His messengers are pure;
> and the soul which He has placed within thee is pure.

And elsewhere, the Rabbis declare,

> Happy is the man whose hour of death is like the hour of his birth;
> as at his birth he is free of sin, so at his death may he be free of
> sin. . . .[2]

[1] 'Henry Vaughan and the Theme of Infancy', *Seventeenth Century Studies*.
Presented to Sir Herbert Grierson (Oxford, 1938), pp. 243-55.
[2] Cited by Martin, *ibid.*, 249, 248. As Martin points out there were
differing views among the Rabbis; some held that the evil instinct (*yeser
hara*) is inborn, whilst others held that it only made its appearance at the
age of puberty. It should be noted however that even on the first view the
evil *yeser* is a very different thing from what in Christianity is termed
Original Sin. It is rather the potentiality for sin, and is thus an aspect of

This is hardly compatible with any orthodox formulation of Original Sin and Professor Martin remarks that Christians who entertained such Jewish notions 'would risk the charge that they were straying from the paths of orthodox belief in the direction of the Pelagian heresy'. This was in fact the charge directed against Jeremy Taylor and it might equally well have been directed against Henry Vaughan if he had worked out systematically the ideas implied in his poem.[1]

What Jeremy Taylor, Traherne, and Vaughan are doing, in effect, is to place a tremendous emphasis on Man's natural gifts and potentialities, so that Grace, as a gift distinct from Nature, becomes unnecessary. In fact the whole Augustinian position with its dualism of Nature/Grace is questioned in the writings of Taylor. He goes beyond the Pelagian heresy. He claims that the whole Decalogue exclusive only of the law of the Sabbath is 'moral and of the law of Nature' and even the evangelical laws of the gospel are equally part of natural law and reason. He will not allow that faith is 'a grace above the greatest reason'.[2] The gospel is for him not a new dispensation, but a continuation of the Old Testament Scripture 'intending glory to the same God by the same principles of prime reason'.[3] Both are products of the same developing process of natural religion.

II

Taylor's originality in regard to the idea of natural law can only be fully grasped if we consider how differently this idea had

[1] The differences between Judaism and Christianity on the matter of Original Sin had been a major topic in the medieval debates between Jewish Rabbis and Christian doctors, for instance in that between Nahmanides and Fra Paulo in 1263 (cf. O. S. Rankin, *Jewish Religious Polemic*, Edinburgh, 1956, p. 170). Had Taylor been present, he would have had to vote for the Jew.

[2] *The Great Exemplar*, Preface.

[3] *Ductor Dubitantium*, in *Works* III, 244.

---

human freedom; without it, the victories of the good *yeser* are meaningless. The Rabbinic gloss on *Deut.* vi, 5, is interesting. They explain that 'Thou shalt love the Lord thy God with all thy heart,' means 'Love him with both the good *yeser* and the bad *yeser*' (Babylonian Talmud, *Berakhot, fol.* 54a).

been employed traditionally by Christian thinkers. Aquinas gave due prominence to it as the source of a human 'positive' law, but the naturalization of religion could not be carried out completely in reference to the New Testament and its miracles; he therefore distinguished between the human positive law and the divine positive law of the gospel. The commandment 'love your enemies', however imperative in religion, is scarcely explicable in terms of the Law of Nature. In maintaining this distinction between the region of Nature and that of Grace, Aquinas was undoubtedly expressing the sense of Pauline Christianity according to which salvation is not offered to man as he is *made* in Nature but as he is *remade* through Grace. The region of Grace was the special region of the gospel and the life of Christ. This same distinction between Nature and Grace was fundamental also to Puritanism in Taylor's day; many of the Puritan social writers and moralists expounded a version of the Law of Nature as constituting that part of our duty which belonged to the 'universal and normal' as against the 'supernatural' aspect of our inheritance.[1] Now Jeremy Taylor, in effect, casts this whole distinction on one side. As one would expect, a certain degree of reinterpretation of the gospel record and doctrine is necessary in order to establish this position; in order to achieve a presentation of Christianity as entirely in accord with natural law, the divinity of Christ, for instance, has to be considerably muted: he is for Taylor the 'Great Exemplar' rather than the visible godhead. 'The Cross of Christ,' said Coleridge, 'is dimly seen in Taylor's works.'[2] Faith, Hope and Charity remain, but the emphasis in Taylor's works of casuistry is clearly on the more 'natural' Law of Works, on the Law addressed, that is, to mortal and fleshly man. Here again his likeness to Milton in the Divorce tracts, unintentionally rewriting the gospel to make it compatible with the earthly and practical legislation of the Old Testament, is evident. Taylor adheres, more than Milton, to the vocabulary of Christian belief, but he fails to convince us that he is operating, any more than Milton is, with the real categories of Christian

[1] Cf. Perry Miller, *The New England Mind*, I, 273-6; A. S. P. Woodhouse, *Puritanism and Liberty* (London, 1938), Introduction, p. 94.

[2] *Table Talk*, entry of June 4, 1830 (ed. of H. Morley, London, 1884, p. 96).

theology. In spite of a furious and skilful use of defensive logic, the basic unorthodoxy of his position is clearly apparent.

Taylor has evidently a good deal in common with the Deists. With them too 'natural law' takes on an all-embracing character and the boundary previously dividing it from Grace is abolished. They were too, like Taylor, in sharp reaction against contemporary Puritanism with its harsh reaffirmation of the Augustinian antithesis of Nature and Grace. Lord Herbert's 'common notions' include the notion that God exists and that virtue and piety are the proper mode of worship due to him. There was no need to have recourse to a separate system of Revelation as to the nature of God or his demands upon men: Reason and Nature are a sufficient guide. But here we must insist on the real and fundamental novelty of Taylor's treatment of natural law in comparison with the Deists. For Aquinas, and the Schoolmen, natural law or *jus naturale*, strong though its religious overtones might be, was a Stoic notion which could be usefully imported into, and harmonized with, Christianity. But its logistic character was never lost; it expressed a static, Pagan conception of human nature as automatically obedient to certain immanent patterns; it was essentially non-dramatic. And this is even more true of the new deistic presentation of natural law which takes its rise from the Stoicism of Cicero and his elaborate handling of the theme of law in the *De Legibus*. For the Deist, Reason, Nature, and Morality coincide: Man is blended with the *mundus*—his ethical rhythm is patterned upon the physical rhythm of the outer world. It is not surprising that later Deism should have made use of the image of the clock and of God as a clockmaker. What above all impresses the Deist is the regularity of the mechanism which determines both the physical and moral action of the universe. Nothing beyond this mechanical ordering of the world is required, for God's laws are perfectly unarbitrary and perfectly adapted to our needs. Now here, Taylor parts company with the Deists, because for him the key to natural law is no longer Reason, but Revelation. He has abolished, as they have, the distinction between Nature and Grace but he has carried out this simplification under entirely different, non-secular auspices.

According to Taylor, the law of nature by which we are governed is not itself co-terminous with our natural instinct nor is it an automatic product of it—it is, he says, 'superinduced' upon it. It was 'written with the finger of God, first in the tables of our hearts. But these tables, we, like Moses, brake with letting them fall out of our hands, upon occasion of the evil manners of the world; *but God wrought them again for us, as he did Moses, by his spirit*'. One is struck also by the pregnant phrase of Joseph Hall when he speaks of the ancients as receiving an 'inbred law in the Sinai of Nature'. Natural Law is thus, itself, an act of Grace. Paradoxically, we may say, that it is itself *supernatural* law. Man is summoned to fulfil it not because it is already a part of his human nature, but because it is a categorical demand made on him by God. This doctrine is essentially not Greek, but Hebraic. For the Greek, natural law is a reflection in a mirror; for the Hebrew it is (if it means anything) a challenge, a path to salvation. To quote Taylor again, the law of nature is 'given to mankind for the conservation of his nature, and *the promotion of his perfective end*'.[1] There is expressed the true historical orientation of the Hebrew religion.

What gives coherence and clarity to this whole idea is the Talmudic doctrine regarding the 'Seven Commandments of the Sons of Noah.'[2] This doctrine, based upon the rabbinic reading of the ninth chapter of *Genesis*, is invoked by Taylor at the beginning of his consideration of the laws of nature. Moreover, it is a doctrine which was becoming widely known in Christian theological circles during the seventeenth century. It was made by Selden the basis for his discussion of the Law of Nations. No doubt there was much confusion about the exact import of this rabbinic idea, but to Jeremy Taylor, at all events, it was clear that it meant a Covenant of Works embracing the human race, a Revelation imparted to mankind and consisting of concrete ethical and religious laws. The Commandments,

---

[1] *Ductor Dubitantium*, II, 1, in *Works*, III, 190-1 (my italics).

[2] The chief source for this is in the Babylonian Talmud, *Sanhedrin*, 56a. The contents of this tractate were well known at this period through the work of Selden, especially his *De Jure Naturali et Gentium Juxta Disciplinam Ebraeorum* (1640), and his *De Synedriis veterum Ebraeorum* (1650-53). The Rabbis who discuss this topic in the Talmud are not agreed on the precise number of the commandments given to the gentiles or on their precise contents, but all are agreed that the 'Sons of Noah' are, like the Children of Israel, held to obligations which regulate their behaviour to one another, their relationship to God, and also (strikingly enough) to the brute Creation.

moreover, are *given to* the Sons of Noah; they are not immanent laws *flowing from* their essential nature. Here is the break with Paganism; it is a crucial turning-point. For the Noahide Covenant implied a dynamic creative purpose for the human race, no longer carrying out the unvarying law of their nature in accordance with the rhythm of an eternally changeless universe, no longer obedient to an Unmoved First Mover, but commanded by a Creator God to participate with him in an historical enterprise. The Sons of Noah are felt to be subject not to Law in the Greek or Roman sense but to *Torah*, and this term presupposes a calling God who challenges Man to perform his bidding.

The Hebrew concept of *Torah*, too readily and inaccurately translated as Law, is not to be identified either with the concept of Law in the natural sphere to which we have become accustomed in Newtonian physics, nor with the Stoic concept of natural law in the human sphere which has found its way into Western legal thought and into Deism. In the nineteenth Psalm, for instance, the very physical laws of nature are seen to be no mere mechanical process, but rather an inaudible song of praise ('The heavens declare the glory of the Lord'); a testimony, and an act of renewal. Nature in fact responds joyfully to the divine creative bidding as Man does to the revealed Word. Nature is bound to God as Man is, by means of a Covenant (cf. *Jeremiah* xxxiii, 20, 25), which likewise implies that she willingly responds to a *command* rather than mechanically obeys a fixed *law*. All this suggests that there is no chasm between Nature and Revelation—but that Nature is at all points caught up into the sphere of Revelation. Both in the microcosm and the macrocosm we observe the same creative will at work, and the same lively and conscious response on the part of the creatures called into obedience to it.

Puritanism in laying its stress upon the particular Israelite Covenant as that which was to be appropriated by the faithful, had obscured this larger and more universal Covenant which forms the groundwork and context of the special Covenant with Israel. The result was that in his reaction against the imposition of an intolerable 'Puritan' privilege in the form of the Calvinist doctrine of election, Western Man (as represented by the Deists for example) has tended to overthrow the Hebraic categories as a whole and has lapsed into a Pagan impassivity. He has failed to see that it was not only the Chosen People who were chosen. The Covenant of the Sons of Noah (which embraced according to the ninth chapter of *Genesis* the whole animate and inanimate Creation) brings the Hebraic categories of Election, of Revelation, and Salvation back into the sphere of universal history. It is indeed the Biblical Covenant in its universal aspect and no whit different in its imperative character from the particular Covenant entered into with the Patriarchs and the Children of Israel. But unlike the special Covenant with Israel, the Noahide Covenant—which is its true ancestor and permanent corollary—is aimed at mankind as a whole; its commands are not the special laws of a priestly nation but the basic laws of human society, aimed, as Taylor would say, at 'the promotion of our perfective end'. They point to our ultimate return to Eden.

Here then was a formulation of Hebraism which involved no break with gentile history and tradition, no over-rigid equation of England and Israel. Taylor and other positive religious humanists like him, especially among the Cambridge Platonists,[1] were trying to save the Biblical doctrine of Revelation, Salvation, and Creation for their generation by freeing it from the narrow limits of Puritanism. In the idea of the Law of Nature, conceived not in Pagan, but in Hebraic terms as the 'Seven Commandments of the Sons of Noah', could be found a sanction and a system entirely suited to this purpose. On this healthier Biblical ground of righteousness, the wedding of Albion and Jerusalem could be truly enacted, for now the partners could address one another in the full awareness of their common and reciprocal destiny. Seen in this light, Hebraism was not only a message for the 'elect people of God' but a message for labouring mankind, and a working alternative to all the secular philosophies of the Renaissance.

[1] See Chapter following.

XII

THE CAMBRIDGE PLATONISTS

IN ARRIVING at his Arminian position and his rational account of divinity, Taylor makes particular mention of the twelfth-century Jewish doctor, Moses Maimonides,[1] whom likewise Milton had drawn upon in his Divorce Tract.[2] It may be even that the title of Taylor's casuistical work, *Ductor Dubitantium* was suggested by that of Maimonides' great philosophical treatise translated by the younger Buxtorf in 1629 as *Doctor Perplexorum*. What had impressed Taylor was Maimonides' firm stand on the question of human free-will, a position which is of course not peculiar to Maimonides but belongs to Jewish theology in general. The Arminians in their rational account of religion were extremely hospitable to the writings of the Jewish doctors, who were in many ways more welcome allies to Protestantism than were the Church Fathers, and who presented a Biblical faith which did not necessitate a rupture between Grace and Nature; at the same time they were to be preferred to the Pagan authorities such as Cicero and the Stoics because with the Jews, however rational and practical they might become, the light of Revelation never burned dim. It is a personal God with whom they ultimately had to do.

The possible part played by Menasseh ben Israel, the seventeenth-century spokesman of Jewish philosophy, in helping his Christian friends in Amsterdam to formulate the Arminian position, has never been fully explored. But it is known that he was a close friend of Episcopius and the other members of the group,[3] and he is referred to widely by the Arminians and

---

[1] In *Unum Necessarium*, ch. 6; *Works*, II, 548.

[2] On the wide dissemination of Maimonides' teachings in England, see (for a brief account), J. L. Teicher, 'Maimonides and England', in *Transactions of the Jewish Historical Society*, XVI, 98-100.

[3] Cf. C. Roth, *A Life of Menasseh ben Israel* (Philadelphia, printing of 1945), pp. 156-7.

their sympathizers (by Robert Boyle for instance) as the Jewish spokesman on the question of free-will. His own writings show many close affinities with their doctrines. In England, Menasseh was of course well known through the part he had played in the negotiations for the Jewish resettlement during the early years of the Commonwealth, and English Protestants would naturally turn to his philosophical works for guidance on the Jewish attitude to this or that question. Whilst the influence of Renaissance Humanism with its cry for freedom has long been recognized as fundamental for the understanding of the Arminian deviation from Calvinism, the influence of Hebraism both in its ancient and contemporary presentations, has not been generally taken into account.

But post-biblical Judaism with its emphasis on Works had an important shaping influence on the left-wing also. Joseph Hall had helped to defeat the Remonstrants, i.e. the Arminians, at the Synod of Dort, in 1619. He had complained of the 'odious composition of Judaism, Arianism, and Anabaptism' that he had found in Amsterdam. Nevertheless, he had himself a strong sympathy with the Jewish doctrine of Works as is evident from the first of his printed Sermons, entitled 'Pharisaisme and Christianity' (1608). In it, he calls upon Christians to emulate the Pharisees in their practical piety, and in their zealous and unremitting use of prayer; he calls them 'a fraternity or college of extraordinary devotion', drawing attention especially to their scrupulous fulfilment of the Law. The Pharisees had to wait another three centuries for a genuinely unprejudiced appreciation from Anglican quarters, but here in this sermon by a seventeenth-century Bishop not especially marked for his Judaic sympathies, we have an intimation of a positive evaluation of the Hebraic type of sainthood so different in its practical emphasis from the traditional patterns of Catholic or Puritan sainthood. Towards the end of his life, Hall proposed the formation of what he called 'The Holy Order of the Mourners in Sion' which would be a voluntary association of Englishmen ready to take it upon themselves by devotional exercises and austere living to avert the evil which threatened the country during the hard years of civil strife. Possibly he had in mind something similar to the Pharisaic type of college (Rabbi Jokhanan's school at Jabneh would do as an example) about

which he had spoken at the beginning of his ecclesiastical
career in such unmistakeable, albeit qualified, terms of praise.

Apart from particular Judaic positions in theology which
influenced the minds of Anglican moderates both on the right
and left-wing of the Church, there was also in general a disposition to think better of Jews—even post-Biblical Jews—and treat
them as living witnesses to the true faith. George Herbert's
poem, 'The Jews' with its extremely cordial opening lines.

> Poor nation, whose sweet sap and juice
> Our scions have purloin'd, and left you dry . . .

is to my knowledge the first clearly sympathetic reference to
post-biblical Jews in the annals of English Literature. It is
followed by the even more cordial poem of the same title by
Herbert's imitator, Henry Vaughan. Neither Herbert nor
Vaughan abandons any important Christian qualification or
reservation in regard to the shortcomings of Israel as the people
which so dismally failed to recognize their Saviour when he
appeared, but nevertheless these two poems, employing Paul's
image of Israel as the good olive tree whose branches, or scions,
will one day be restored to it (*Romans* ix), breathe a strain of
true charity and concern for the exiled people of God.

In this Chapter it is proposed to deal with the important
Jewish elements in the thought of that group of philosophically
minded Anglicans, the Cambridge Platonists. Close in spirit to
Jeremy Taylor, Milton, and other authors discussed above,
they are surely a crucial example of that constellation of feelings
and ideas presented here under the title of 'Jerusalem'—for
seventeenth-century Hebraism, we have maintained, whilst
unthinkable except in the context of Puritanism, is nevertheless
to be correctly understood as a reaction against it. Now this
exactly fits the situation of the Cambridge Platonists. They had
all passed through the Puritan experience; indeed, with only
one exception, they had all been nurtured in the Puritan
foundation of Emmanuel College at Cambridge.[1] If these men,

---

[1] The exception was Henry More who was at Christ's College, Cambridge, from 1631—beginning just as Milton's residence at the same college
was coming to an end. They evidently both came under the influence of
that remarkable Platonist scholar, Joseph Mede. More's parents were strict
Calvinists, but he found at an early age that (like Milton) he 'could never
swallow the hard doctrine concerning fate'.

Whichcot, More, John Smith, Cudworth, and Culverwel returned, by way of reaction against the stern, fideistic doctrines of the Puritans, to a more rational type of theology, we may well suspect that what they ultimately attained was not a simple restatement of High Renaissance orderliness and right reason such as might be found in Hooker, but something more strenuous and more paradoxical. And it would be surprising if, in their search for a new rational principle of order and integration, they had not stumbled upon certain important features of Judaism.

It has been remarked by one careful student that for these Cambridge men, as for Grotius and Selden, 'Judaism seemed to enter into a kind of prestabilized harmony with Natural Law and Natural Religion.'[1] In an age, which was seeking, above all things, a rational theology, it provided an impressive and comprehensive account of the place of right reason in religion. With Maimonides, for instance, right reason enters into all aspects of religious experience, and the following three aphorisms of Whichcot might be paralleled with very slight verbal alteration in Maimonides' *Guide for the Perplexed*—

> Reason discovers what is Natural; and Reason *receives* what is supernatural.
> Religion doth not *destroy* Nature; but is built upon it. Nothing *without* Reason is to be proposed; nothing *against* Reason is to be *believed*: Scripture is to be taken in a rational sense.[2]

The last phrase reminds us strongly of Maimonides' theory of homonyms and his rationalizing treatment of miracles and angelic visitations as described in Scripture. On the other hand, Maimonides' synthesis of Religion and Philosophy had not been achieved by sacrificing the concept of Revelation. He teaches a genuinely Biblical religion, anchored at all points to Old Testament categories. This was the difference between the natural religion offered by him, and that offered by the Pagan philosophy of the Renaissance, in particular that of Cicero; and it was this aspect of his teaching that rendered his work particularly valuable to the Cambridge men.

[1] A. Altmann, 'William Wollaston, English Deist and Rabbinic Scholar', *Transactions of the Jewish Historical Society*, XVI (London, 1952), 207.

[2] *The Cambridge Platonists*, ed. E. T. Campagnac (Oxford, 1901), pp. 67, 68, 70.

Perhaps the most characteristic example of Maimonides' rational treatment of mysteries of Revelation occurs in his section on Prophecy. The qualifications for a prophet are three: reason, imagination, and moral integrity; those who have developed these qualities to the uttermost assume the nature of prophets. The actual gift of prophecy may be withheld, so that fully qualified people do not in fact always prophesy (*Guide*, Part II, ch. 32), but the whole phenomenon is rooted in a normal human psychology and belongs to a normal process of development. There is an unbroken connexion between the humblest exercises of human intellect and imagination by poet and philosopher and the most comprehensive insights achieved by the great prophets—they are received through essentially the same media of sensibility.

This stress on the normality of the prophetic experience was eagerly taken up by the Cambridge Platonists. We find Whichcot referring to the view of the sages of the *Talmud* (which he may have derived intermediately from Maimonides) that the prophet cannot prophesy unless his mind is rationally composed[1] (the exact opposite, incidentally, of the modern view of Mowinckel and others as to the 'ecstatic' nature of prophecy). Then again John Smith—another Platonist—points out in his Discourse, 'Of Prophecy', very much in the manner of Maimonides (and with explicit reference to him) that

> the true prophetical spirit seats itself as well in the rational as in the sensitive powers, and that it never alienates the mind, but informs and enlightens it.[2]

Perhaps the most important Jewish doctrine that Smith makes use of in this Discourse—it is found not only in Maimonides, but also in Albo and among the talmudic Rabbis—is that of inspirational 'grades'. According to this conception, not all of Scripture was equally inspired; there were numerous grades ascending from the humbler manifestations of the Holy Spirit among the authors of the *Hagiographa* to the heights of inspira-

[1] *Ibid.*, p. 21.
[2] *Select Discourses of John Smith*, ed. H. G. Williams (Cambridge, 1859), p. 193 (from this Discourse 'Of Prophecy', ch. 6). The link with Maimonides is discussed by B. Willey, *The Seventeenth Century Background* (London, 1934), pp. 145-51.

tion to be found among the later Prophets, and ultimately in Moses himself.[1] This suggests a certain relativism within the sphere of Revelation itself and was thus highly congenial to the Cambridge Platonists since it provided a basis for a normal literary and intellectual response to Scripture. The same perception of the human element in Scripture, and particularly in prophecy, had been achieved in the early Middle Ages by Jerome. Later, Andrew of St. Victor,[2] under the influence of the same kind of Jewish exegesis that became popular later among the English Platonists of the seventeenth century, had emphasized the distinctive personality of each prophet as an ingredient in his work, giving preference at the same time to natural or common-sense explanations. Through such Hebraic modes of thought infiltrating also into the writings of seventeenth-century divines and philosophers, an attitude to Scripture, quite the reverse of Puritan inflexibility was facilitated. It became possible to apply normal categories of appreciation to the Bible; reason had access there, as well as imagination. The Bible became, more than anything else, an inspired literature, rather than a peculiar brand of automatic writing. All this is especially characteristic of the work of the Cambridge Platonists.

It should not be thought that the Cambridge Platonists wanted a levelling-down of Scripture, so as to render it an ordinary book. It is rather the human faculties that were to be levelled up! They were fond of quoting *Proverbs* xx, 27; and Whichcot remarks on the verse,

> *The Spirit of Man is the Candle of the Lord;* Lighted *by* God, and lighting us *to* God.[3]

Reason was for them the divine spark in man enabling him to rise from sense-perceptions to a knowledge of the truths of Revelation. Their rationalism was interwoven with a certain mystic attitude giving to their conception of the human mind a decidedly ambiguous character. They were unlike all other rational theologians. Like the Deists and like Hooker, they

---

[1] *Select Discourses, ed. cit.,* pp. 178-93.

[2] See Beryl Smalley, *The Study of the Bible in the Middle Ages* (Second edition, Oxford, 1952), pp. 136-8.

[3] Campagnac, p. 70.

were aware of God as the end-term of a logical argument, but quite unlike the Deists, they were also aware of Him as an immanent reality, shining, by means of love, through the life of man and nature. Says John Smith,

> We should love all things in God, and God in all things, because He is all in all, the beginning and original of being, the perfect idea of their goodness and the end of their motion.[1]

Hooker would not have expressed himself in quite this way, nor would Tillotson later on. There are undeniable links here with the sixteenth-century Platonists, with Ficino and Bruno, and earlier with Nicholas of Cusa, but there is also the influence of the *Kabbalah* and the medieval Jewish mystics. It was this kind of authority which served to anchor their mystical speculations to the Scriptures thus preventing their pantheism from taking charge and overclouding the transcendent otherness of their God; on the other hand, it was their earthbound Hebraism which prevented their Platonic eros-worship from soaring beyond the bounds of flesh and blood. Henry More, perhaps the most mystical of the Cambridge men—he was capable of a real mystical transport and also capable of communicating something of it to the readers of his poetry and prose—was nevertheless as conscious as Milton of the inexorability of our fleshly nature and the holiness of the heart's very carnal affections. This is the burden of much of his Hebraically coloured *Defense of the Threefold Cabbala*. In his positive attitude to Flesh, Matter, and Woman, he is, we are told, 'like the cabbalists, and unlike the orthodox Platonists'.[2] This does not mean that More really understood or read the *Kabbalah*, a privilege denied to many more skilful Hebraists than the Cambridge men could claim to be; but what he meant by 'Kabbalah' and what most of his contemporaries understood by it was a mode of free exegesis which could make Scripture meaningful at a literal level as well as at a philosophical and mystical level.[3] It presupposed also a certain freedom from dogma and an openness to new thought.

---

[1] *Select Discourses*, p. 440.

[2] M. Nicolson, 'Milton and the *Conjectura Cabbalistica*', *P.Q.*, VI (1927), 13.

[3] On the title page of *The Defense of the Threefold Cabbala* Philo and Maimonides are quoted; neither of them is in the least 'kabbalistic'.

In this respect, 'Kabbalah' was more dynamic and exciting than medieval Christian exegesis, and what was more, it was not tainted with Catholicism. Under its broad umbrella, could be comprehended the allegorical interpretations of Philo (from whom More took a great deal) and the philosophical rationalizing of Maimonides. But whichever element or phase of Hebraism might be referred to under the term 'Kabbalah', its enormous advantage to the Cambridge men was that by its means, they were able to seize hold of the rich experience of Platonism with its doctrine of *eros*, in the confidence that they could keep it attached to the norms of revealed Religion. It enabled them to satisfy the urgent demands of the Renaissance as well as those of the Reformation, whilst at the same time affording them a freedom in either sphere which Christian scholasticism had denied.

II

Since Philo's name has been mentioned, it is perhaps as well to be quite clear about the exact nature of his influence on Henry More. It has been well said that he

> proved of peculiar interest [to More] by reason of his allegorical interpretation of Scripture, his use of the analogy between microcosm in proving the existence of intellectual causality in the universe, but above all by his reconciliation of Platonism with Judaism.[1]

These were all useful procedures for the construction of a religious philosophy attached to Biblical sources which is what More was seeking to formulate. One could add that More found in Philo a confirmation for his view of the Mind. To Philo there was both an intellectual and intuitive path to God; he declared that Moses' laws are perfect reason, but also that Scripture can afford a direct apprehension of Divine Truth. To More, in a similar fashion, Reason itself was of mysterious origin and belonged (as he tells us in *The Grand Mystery of Godliness*) to the 'middle life' of the soul 'betwixt the Divine and Animal'.

[1] G. Bullough, *The Philosophical Poems of Henry More* (Manchester, 1931), Introduction, p. xxii.

Now when all this has been said and acknowledged we are left with a feeling that though this represents a genuine account of Revelation in terms of our earthbound human nature and, as such, marks a true feature of the new Hebraic climate of the seventeenth century, it does not represent quite that specific rendering of the Hebrew Covenant-religion which we found in other writers. Philo was, after all, the great spokesman of the *logos*-philosophy, and his presentation of Judaism was attached at all points to basic Hellenic thought-forms. The analogy of microcosm and macrocosm is a *logos*-formulation and More's picture of Reason as poised 'betwixt the Divine and Animal',—possibly drawn from Philo—is the old Platonic image of the Great Chain of Being once again. There is nothing here evidently of the Hebrew stress on History, on the mighty task and adventure which the Covenant imposes. It is a contemplative and static world rather than an active and dynamic one that the Cambridge men seem to be fashioning. One should not overlook the moral earnestness of the Cambridge philosophers, an earnestness derived from their Puritan antecedents and environment—this is an aspect of Hebraism important in forming a total picture; but it must be admitted that in the main they seek *gnosis*, the ideal of contemplative knowledge, and that what is often missing from their work and religious activities (as Cassirer noted) is 'the energy of action'. The spirit of industry and progress so noteworthy in Bacon and the Puritans, and in Milton too, is somehow absent, from the writings of the Cambridge Platonists.[1] They were of course in reaction, as has been said, against Puritanism, and perhaps because of their distrust of the narrow intensities of the Covenant-idea as found in Puritanism, they took refuge in less demanding and less strenuous forms of religion. Certainly, the Cambridge men did not take part in revolutionary movements; they did not interest themselves in schemes of reform, and in a century of action, they retired into philosophical and academic seclusion. In this sense they were more contemplative and retired than men like Taylor, Hall, or Herbert who were parish priests, or bishops actively engaged in the affairs of a busy diocese. Henry More and his friends were more radically disengaged. This is the

[1] E. Cassirer, *The Platonic Renaissance in England* (Trans. J. P. Pettegrove, London, 1953), pp. 70-1.

limitation of their Hebraism. One could say that they were inhabitants of Athens rather than Jerusalem, but it would be perhaps truer to say that they were seeking the peace of Jerusalem without its strength and active virtues; they had forgotten that, authentically, the two go together (as in *Psalm* xxix, 11). It should also be noted in this connexion that the medieval exponents of Hebraism to whom they generally turned, namely Maimonides and Philo, were characteristically those Jewish philosophers who, through the influence of Greek thought, stressed least the dynamic covenant side of Israel's religion as a special task and responsibility, with messianic objectives to be realized as a result of historical effort.[1]

III

This is, however, not quite the last word. True, the Covenant-idea, in so far as it concerned Man in Society, was of little interest to the Cambridge Platonists: their religion had become too placidly philosophical for that; but in their Natural Philosophy it seems that they departed in a significant way from the Hellenic teleology as well as from the various mechanical world-views that were becoming fashionable in their day, and tried to define something more purposeful and alive. To them, the world was not a clock which God had one day wound up, but a Divine Creation. More tells us in 1668, 'There is no Phaenomenon in Nature purely mechanicall.' After embracing

---

[1] There is, for instance, in *The Guide for the Perplexed* (cf. Trans. M. Friedlander, 2nd ed., London, 1904, *passim*), practically no treatment of such topics as the Messianic Age; the special virtues of the Land of Israel; the election and special tasks of Israel. It speaks much of God's design in Nature, but says little or nothing of His design in History. The place of History and Geography, so vital in Judaism, is taken by Physics and Metaphysics. This becomes easier to understand when we consider the dominion exercised over Maimonides in this treatise by the philosophy of Aristotle— a system which inevitably lacks the historical dimension. On the other hand, in a work like the *Iggeret Teman*—a letter to his fellow-Jews in Yemen —in which Maimonides expresses his Jewish instincts directly without any attempt to formulate his thoughts into a philosophical pattern, the historical theme is to the fore; the meaning of the Exile, the special historical destiny of Israel, and its hope of redemption, all receive their full emphasis. But it was the *Guide*, not the *Iggeret*, that the Cambridge philosophers read.

the Cartesian system with its mathematical account of the world of Nature as system of self-subsisting vortices, explicable simply in terms of Matter, extension, and local motion, More finally cast it aside and he came to identify such views with the 'atomic atheism' of Hobbes. It is true that Descartes in his system had left room for Spirit; in addition to the material reality, there was a non-spatial, and non-material reality which constituted an autonomous sector unsusceptible to mathematical laws. But Body and Soul, Matter and Spirit, are for Descartes inevitably separate. The principle of dissociation achieves its most solemn and formal confirmation in his philosophy. And it is against this dissociative principle that More rebelled; he was not prepared to accept a material universe that was quite life-less, nor a spiritual universe that was quite immaterial and divorced from the World and the Flesh. His instinct demanded a unified and not a bisected account of human nature and of the outward Creation. And this search for unity, for integration, involved ultimately a break not only with Descartes, but with Plato also in whom likewise there is no real escape from dual-ism.[1] More cannot rest content with this.

It is true that both More and Cudworth, the former in his *Conjectura Cabbalistica* and the latter in his *Intellectual System of the Universe*, sought to harmonize the Book of *Genesis* with the cosmogony of Plato, but they were well aware also of the differences between a doctrine of impersonal emanation, and one which presupposed will, activity, and purpose. Cudworth's theory of a Plastic Nature is, it seems to me, of extraordinary interest and originality. As will be shown in the next Chapter it anticipates the theories of evolution which were to rock the foundations of the biological sciences in the nineteenth century. He brought History into the domain of Nature. He was com-mitted to a view of the *cosmos* which saw it as being in progress from created beginnings to foreseen ends and objectives, and

---

[1] For a good discussion of More's rejection of Cartesian dualism, see Willey, *op. cit.*, pp. 162-9. 'More's arguments can best be viewed', says Willey, 'as an endeavour to reunite matter and spirit, which the rigid logic of Descartes had left in unbridgeable opposition.' Willey, however, fails to observe that this pre-occupation is part of that Hebraic impulse which More shared with the other Cambridge philosophers, Smith and Cud-worth.

this is at bottom Hebrew rather than Greek.[1] Now More had grasped this same principle more clearly than anyone else in his generation, for although he had discovered Hebraism in its quieter and more tranquil forms, eschewing the dangerous intensities of Puritanism which he so much feared and distrusted, even in those quieter formulations, Hebraism does not abandon this basic principle of historical Creation and of a Creation informed with dynamic purpose. It was precisely on this point, for instance, that Maimonides had broken away from Aristotle.[2] He had recognized the appeal of Aristotle's account of a universe based on changeless self-subsisting laws, but if this could only be achieved by sacrificing the concept of Creation, then not Creation but Aristotle must be abandoned; for from Creation, and from Creation only, flow the possibilities of election, revelation, and miracle. And in the last analysis, the universe we inhabit is not one of eternal sameness but of change and miracle.

It is in Henry More's beautifully conceived and written *Divine Dialogues* of 1668 that he achieves his clearest intuition of this non-hellenic *Cosmos* in which the covenantal drama, presupposed by the Hebrew Bible, can take place. In fact, it is the image of Drama which he uses in the second of these Dialogues to describe God's Providence as manifested in the world around us. He may have left behind the particularistic Covenant-formulae of the Puritans, but in his picture of the universe, no longer a *cosmos*, but a vital Creation, we sense the reinstatement of the Covenant-idea in a broader and more majestic form. He comes to speak of Nature, not as a machine, nor as law, nor as a work of art, nor as a system of Cartesian vortices but as a Drama proceeding from a divine Dramatist who has shaped it according to his Will.[3] We are, he says, 'the spectators of this terrestrial stage-play' and we are called upon to observe 'the

---

[1] On Cudworth's doctrine of Plastic Nature and its links with the ideas of More, Boyle, and the alchemists, see by the present author, 'The Scientist as Priest', *Isis*, XLIV (Cambridge, Mass., 1953), 262-4

[2] *The Guide for the Perplexed*, Part II, ch. 25.

[3] The idea of a world-theatre goes back to Plato and is echoed by Clement of Alexandria, John of Salisbury, Shakespeare, Sir Thomas Browne, and hosts of others (see E. R. Curtius, *European Literature and the Latin Middle Ages* [London, ed. of 1953], pp. 138-44). It would be true to say, however, that up to the time of Henry More, this *topos* had expressed basically the feeling of the limitations of human life, and of a repeated,

admirable windings of Providence in her Dramatick Plot which has been acting on this Stage of the Earth from the beginning of the World'. Nor is it a 'languid or flat thing', but a Drama, exciting, complex, and all-important to the spectator who is called upon to seize its meaning and intention. Moreover, we have our own part to play in it, and exercise our own free will, subject to the broad limits of the plot. There is in fact (as in the Drama proper) a dialectical relation, a tension, between the Creator and his materials; the *dramatis personae* have their own quasi-independence.

If we are wise, we consider Drama as a constantly unfolding revelation of the mind of the Dramatist, a revelation through his characters and the happenings that befall them. Seen in this way, every event in this 'terrestrial stage-play' becomes dramatic and every trivial natural phenomenon becomes a symbol or poetic image related to the intention of the whole Drama as well as a manifestation to be considered in terms of 'local motion'—i.e. in terms of the logic of the particular scene or episode.

We may see a good deal of the Divine plan as it reveals itself in that small scene or act in which we are called upon to play our part. Only prophets can expect to see more. But if, as More says, 'we cannot judge of the tendency of what is past or acting or present', we may nevertheless attend patiently and with faith for 'the entrance of the last Act, which shall bring in righteousness in triumph'.[1]

[1] *Divine Dialogues*, ed. of 1713, p. 172. The idea of the Natural History of the earth as a play or opera is later on taken up in a more secular fashion and appears in the writings of Fontenelle, Burnet, Whiston, and Pope. See G. Sherburn, 'Pope and "The Great Shew of Nature" ', in *The Seventeenth Century, Studies by R. F. Jones and others writing in his Honor* (Stanford, 1951), pp. 306-15. To my knowledge, More's contribution to this *topos* has not been noted hitherto.

---

meaningless cycle of events. The speech of Jacques in *As You Like It*:

> All the world's a stage
> And all the men and women *merely* players—

suggests the eternal sameness of the play. It suggests the Pagan view of an eternally repeated world-cycle. But for More, the Drama of Nature is a unique and unrepeatable performance; it is in fact historical time from Creation to its cosmic *dénouement* at the end of days, conceived as a dramatic plot of immense significance for everyone concerned. That is why I think we are justified in linking it here with the Covenant-idea.

XIII

THE PIOUS NATURALISTS

A good man finds every place he treads upon holy ground; to him
the world is God's temple; he is ready to say with Jacob, 'How
dreadful is this place! this is none other but the house of God.'

I

THE ABOVE quotation from the *Discourses* of the Cambridge
Platonist, John Smith, expresses one of the central images in
what might be termed the Hebraic reaction against the secular
developments in Science during the period reviewed in this
study; it is the image of the World as Temple and Man as
Priest.[1] According to this *topos*, the outer world is not the
Baconian universe stripped of its divine penumbra, nor is Man
the unlicensed conquistador of Nature's secrets obedient only to
his own will and desires. The world is seen instead to be itself
radiant with divinity, and Man to whose rule indeed the
material universe is given over, undertakes this task in a spirit
of humility and reverence. He is not the 'Final Cause' of the
Creation, but the servant and steward of the Creator.

The *topos* carries, of course, strong traditional overtones and

[1] The idea has been attributed to various sources, among them Seneca
and the Persian *magi*. In a paganized form it was a favourite image later on
of the poet Keats (especially in *Endymion*). In the sixteenth century it is a
major *topos* in Ficino, and in the fifteenth in Nicholas of Cusa; see E.
Cassirer, *Individuum und Kosmos in der Philosophie des Renaissance* (Leipzig,
1927). In our period, its provenance is to be traced chiefly to the *Hermetica*
where it is pervasive, and to the writings of Philo (cf., for instance, *Vita
Mosis*, Bk. II). See also H. A. Wolfson, *Philo* (Cambridge, Mass., 1947),
II, 247. But its direct Biblical inspiration should not be ignored. Seventeenth-century religious writers were fond of quoting the twenty-fourth
Psalm for its 'Natural Philosophy'. 'The earth is the Lord's, and the fullness
thereof; the world and they that dwell therein. For he hath founded it upon
the seas, and established it upon the floods. Who shall ascend into the hill
of the Lord? or shall stand in his holy place? He that hath clean hands
and a pure heart. . . .' Sanctuary and Priest are here pictured in clear association with the vastness of the universe 'established upon the floods'.

may be thought to express a medieval view of the world in which divinity and natural philosophy are still fairly enfolded with one another. This, however, would not be quite correct; the priesthood of Nature is not a theme for scholasticism, and it is found in the sixteenth and seventeenth centuries often in alliance with new and revolutionary ideas in Science. Copernicus, for instance, sets the sun in the centre of the world, telling us that in that way he has unveiled a new wonder in the *Temple* of Nature:

> Then in the middle of all stands the sun. For who in our most beautiful temple, could set this light in another or better place, than that from which it can at once illuminate the whole? Not to speak of the fact that not unfittingly do some call it the light of the world, others the soul, still others the governor. Trismegistus calls it the visible God. . . .[1]

Milton too embraces the new notion of a heliocentric universe which for him fits in well with his sense of the spirituality of light. If the universe is a Temple, the habitation of God, then it is fitting that the light of the Sun should occupy a central place in it,

> since God is light
> And never but in unapproached light
> Dwelt from Eternitie, dwelt then in thee,
> Bright effluence of bright essence increate.
> *(Paradise Lost*, III, 3-6)

It is evident from an echo further on that he is thinking of the hundred and fourth Psalm, 'He covereth himself with light as with a garment.' Thomas Browne similarly maintains (citing Hermes, as Copernicus does in the passage earlier on) that, 'Lux est umbra dei.'

The most effective and consistent use of this image is to be found among the later alchemical writers. They are strongly in opposition to Aristotle and the schoolmen and believe in an empirical rather than a theoretical and abstract science of Nature. To them the idea of Nature as a Temple and man as the active priest engaged in his priestly tasks, exactly conveyed the impression of the devout naturalist bent over the fire with

[1] Quoted by H. Haydn, *Counter-Renaissance*, p. 339.

his metals and oxides like the ancient priest in the Temple attending to the sacrifices. Says Thomas Vaughan,

> The Peripateticks [i.e. the Aristotelians] look on God as they do on Carpenters, who build with stone and timber, without any infusion of life. But the world *which is God's building*—is full of spirit, quick and living.[1] (My italics.)

And elsewhere, he says of Aristotle, 'Observe then that this Stagyrite and Nature are at a great distance: the one ends in works, the other in words.'[2]

The general philosophical position of the alchemists is worth noting. Thomas Vaughan was perhaps (apart from the Cambridge Platonists) the most eloquent opponent of the dualism both of Bacon and Descartes, who, in their different ways, sought to banish religion from the sphere of natural science believing that 'from this unwholesome mixture of things there arises not only a fantastic philosophy but also an heretical religion'. He expresses the opposite view:

> we see that God in His work hath united spirit and matter, visibles and invisibles; and out of the union of spiritual and natural substances riseth a perfect compound, whose very nature and being consists in that union. How then is it possible to demonstrate the nature of that compound by a divided theory of spirit by itself and matter by itself? . . . Besides, who hath ever seen a spirit without matter or matter without spirit, that he should be able to give us a true theory of both principles in their simplicity?[3]

His brother, Henry Vaughan, the metaphysical poet, drew on the same fund of vitalistic ideas as did Thomas Vaughan, for we have here a type of Natural Philosophy which might form the basis for poetry as well as science. The philosopher took in the ideal world in his vision of Nature, and the poet took in Nature in his vision of the ideal world:

> O thou! whose spirit did at first inflame
> And warm the dead,

[1] *Anthroposophia Theomagica, Works of Thomas Vaughan*, ed. A. E. Waite (London, 1919), p. 8.
[2] *Anima Magica Abscondita, Works*, p. 75.
[3] *Euphrates, Works*, p. 394.

And by a sacred Incubation fed[1]
  With life this frame
Which once had neither being, forme, nor name,
  Grant I may so
Thy steps track here below.

That in these Masques and shadows I may see
  Thy sacred way;
And by those hid ascents climb to that day,
  Which breaks from thee,
Who art in all things, though invisibly.[2]

The natural order is paralleled in the human or moral order. Man, too, has his *Archeus* or indwelling spirit: for him, it is his immortal Soul whereby his Creator has stamped upon him His own express Image, so that Man may know and love Him. Thus the terms used in relation to the moral and spiritual life and the terms of alchemy become, to a large extent, interchangeable: to the alchemists, Mercury is Spirit, Sulphur is Soul, and Salt is Body; in fact, they frequently use the language of chemical operations as a kind of parable, for describing spiritual states.

The spiritual order is not confined to the inner life of the soul, as Descartes thought, but is a universal influence linking Man with the order of Nature and linking the whole order of Nature to the Divine Creator and Nourisher of all things. A great part of the speculative activity of the alchemists was concerned with tracing the analogy between the material and the human order. The mystic hints with which their works abound, are thus not so much scientific observations, as metaphors, expressing this absolute conviction. The main type of phenomena in which they saw this law of analogy operating was the transmutation of metals. In the 'mortification' of

---

[1] This is the idea of the Divine Incubation of the world, popularized in the century through Tremellius's version of *Genesis* i, 2, which he renders, 'Spiritus dei incubabat superficiei aquarum.' (Found also in Milton, *P.L.*, I, 20, *P.L.*, VII, 235 f., in Browne, *Religio Medici*, I, sect. xxxii; in Ralegh, *History of the World*, Book I, ch. 1, sect. vi.)

[2] From 'Man'. Henry Vaughan's alchemical images and ideas have been studied by many writers, including Elizabeth Holmes, *Henry Vaughan and the Hermetic Philosophy* (Oxford, 1932); the most recent contribution to this discussion is by E. C. Pettet, *Of Paradise and Light* (Cambridge, 1960).

metals (through oxidization, etc.) and its subsequent recon-
stitution by the chemist to its original state, they found a potent
symbol expressing for them the experience of Sin and Regeneration. They dreamed of amazing transmutations whereby all
metals might be converted to gold or mercury, but at the centre
of their wild speculations, there was a core of genuine scientific
observation, observation moreover, which held a symbolism of
eternal significance.

This symbolism is naturally a feature of alchemy as a neo-
Platonic system; but we should note that the internal unity of
Man, God, and Nature was not something to be simply contemplated after the neo-Platonic fashion. It was to be regarded
as a stimulus for *work* and discovery, and under the stress of
the Scriptural religion of the Reformation, it takes on a strongly
moral character. From this point of view, alchemy at the period
at which we are concerned with it, is almost invariably tinged
with Hebraism. Thus the younger van Helmont discussing the
analogy of the Law of Nature and the moral law turns to the
Rabbis of the Talmud for an apt illustration. They maintain, he
tells us, that the six hundred and thirteen positive and negative
precepts, which are comprised in the law of Moses, correspond
to the number of Veins, Nerves, Sinews, and Bones 'which are
within the Flesh of Man'.[1] We note in van Helmont at all times
this strongly Biblical emphasis, supported with appropriate
rabbinic, kabbalistic, and pseudo-kabbalistic glosses.

Likewise, the works of Thomas Vaughan, in particular his
Magia Adamica (1650) and *Lumen de Lumine* (1651), have a
noticeable kabbalistic colouring. In the latter text, he makes
use of kabbalistic terms to define his conception of the First
Matter.[2] He felt that the alchemist, like the kabbalist, had the
active task of healing the metaphysical splits which prevented
the divine influence from flowing freely into the world.[3] In his
Coelum Terrae (1650), he finds encouragement for his spiritual
view of Nature in the rabbinic saying, 'The building of the
Sanctuary which is here below is framed according to that of
the Sanctuary which is above.'[4] In such ways, the alchemists
were enabled to give their speculations a genuinely religious,

---

[1] *Paradoxal Discourses*, trans. J. B. (London, 1685), p. 85.
[2] See *Works*, pp. 269-70.
[3] *Works*, p. 139.   [4] *Works*, p. 192.

indeed, Biblical character. The *cosmos* was not merely a temple; it was the outer court of the Temple which had been erected in Jerusalem in honour of the God of Israel.

The notion of the *cosmos* as Temple appears again prominently in the writings of that thorough-going English alchemist, Elias Ashmole. He gives to the idea of a priesthood of Nature a rather exclusive character. They are the elect few,

> For as amongst the people of the *Jews*, there was but one that might enter into the *Holy of Holies*, (and that but once a year) so there is seldom more in a *Nation*, whom God lets into this *Sanctum Sanctorum* of *Philosophy*; but some there are.[1]

We note the insistence on the peculiar privileges of the *adepti* who have been admitted into the alchemical mysteries; they alone are entitled to enter the Sanctum of Nature. They form a body of the elect rather after the manner of the predestined few in Calvinism and perhaps the same false and narrow application of the Hebraic Covenant-doctrine is here at work. The idea of the naturalists as an elect and exclusive priesthood had been powerfully expressed by Paracelsus in the sixteenth century; he had thought of himself especially as having been divinely elected to bring to light the great *arcana* of Nature,[2] and from this brooding illusion of special tasks and exclusive revelations, issued many of the eccentric aspects, the strange obsessions of alchemy and iatrochemistry in the period we are considering.

II

We saw in relation to the Covenant-religion of the Puritans, that side by side with it, and partly in reaction against it, grew up a more 'latitudinarian' Covenant-faith. In Jeremy Taylor and the moderate Anglicans, we sensed a less exclusive form of Hebraism in which the doctrine of Revelation was seen to have reference to mankind as a whole rather than to the elect. Now this liberal alternative was achieved also in the field of Natural

---

[1] From the *Prolegomenon* to Arthur Dee's *Fasciculus Chemicus* (1650).

[2] He says in one place (*Works*, ed. A. E. Waite, London, 1894, I, 19): 'I have been chosen of God to extinguish and blot out all the phantasies of elaborate and false works, of delusive and presumptuous words, be they the words of Aristotle, Galen, Avicenna, Mesva. . . .'

Characterisms of Virtue

Philosophy. Thomas Browne and Robert Boyle were in many ways close in spirit to the alchemists; they both manifested that blend of Greek, Jewish, and Hermetical philosophies which characterized the Paracelsan writers. Boyle indeed was much nearer both in spirit and laboratory practice to the alchemists than is commonly recognized.[1] But both of them, Browne and Boyle, whilst adopting the conceptions of a divinely impregnated world, of a world-temple, and of the practitioner as a devout acolyte, widen the field of reference. Instead of pointing to the *arcana* of Nature, to its occult secrets, they think of it—in Browne's fine phrase—as a 'universal and public manuscript'.[2] Instead of a closed and exclusive priesthood, they think of a broad, indeed universal priesthood, the only limiting qualifications for which are Reason and Knowledge. For, says, Boyle, 'Knowledge is a prerogative, that can confer a priesthood without unction or imposition of hands.'[3] The world is a Temple, but contrary to what Ashmole had supposed, it has no Holy of Holies in which it is dangerous for all except the privileged few to enter. 'There is no danger to profound these mysteries,' says Browne, 'no *sanctum sanctorum* in philosophy.'[4]

Thomas Browne is a man who had reached a happy integration of Reason and Religion without reconstructing the logistic pattern of pre-renaissance scholasticism. He knew and quoted Aristotle, but did not subscribe to his system of entelechies. He enjoyed, with Plato, to lose himself in an 'O altitudo' but he was no systematic Platonist; in respect of sources and authorities, he was thoroughly eclectic. He came nearest in his outlook on science to the new experimental philosophers, for he had been trained at the famous medical school in Padua where Vesalius had earlier on overthrown the authority of Galen and founded

---

[1] See, for a fuller treatment of Boyle's alchemical affiliations, H. Fisch, 'The Scientist as Priest: A Note on Robert Boyle's Natural Theology', *Isis*, XLIV (1953), 252-65. And see, L. T. More, *Life and Works of the Hon. Robert Boyle* (Oxford, 1944), ch. 11.

[2] *Religio Medici*, Part I, sect. xvi.

[3] Essay I, *The Usefulness of Natural Philosophy*, 1663.

[4] *Religio Medici*, Part I, sect. xiii. There are many echoes of Browne's *Religio Medici* to be noted in Boyle's *Essays* of 1663. The two naturalists thought alike on all fundamentals and Boyle was happy to make use of the metaphors and phrases of his older contemporary, a less systematic and enlightened scientist than himself but a more eloquent writer.

the modern science of anatomy. He insisted on the priority of experiment and condemned as 'the mortallest enemy unto Knowledge . . . a peremptory adhesion unto Authority, and more especially, the establishing of our belief upon the dictates of Antiquity'.[1] So far this is very much like Bacon, and indeed the treatise from which this quotation is taken, Browne's *Vulgar Errors* of 1646, is throughout a kind of extension of Bacon's attack in the *Novum Organum* on the Idols of the Tribe, those false assertions which achieve popular currency and have their root in fallible human nature. He is also like Bacon in his insistence on a fittingly controlled language for the transmission of scientific knowledge. 'Strict and definitive expressions are always required in philosophy' he says.[2] Yet how vastly does he in fact differ in his own writing from this Baconian ideal! As we have already seen, he allows his imagination to express itself in glowing images, to take wing from some observed fact, first judiciously noted with a certain Baconian sobriety, but afterwards seen in a more poetically significant way. When he comes to 'suck divinity from the flowers of nature'[3] he cannot confine himself to the Baconian style of report but resorts instead to simile and metaphor and to a certain emphatically patterned rhetoric. But there is a principle of unity in Browne's style; it is, as we have insisted in an earlier Chapter, the Hebraic principle. And similarly there is a Hebraic principle of integration in his thinking; though this does not render it into an organized and consistent philosophy, for philosopher Browne was none.

The key to the unity of Browne's mind—in spite of his dilettantism and inconsistencies—could be expressed in the Hebrew word *Hokhmah*. It is reason, but it is also even more importantly, 'the fear of God'. Reason is not simply the 'lumen siccum' that it was for Bacon. To Browne, Eve's error in reporting the Divine prohibition when she spoke to the serpent (*Genesis* iii, 3) and the error of Franciscus Sanctius in supposing that nightingales had no tongues are both offences against Reason. Truth is wide and rich enough to include moral and religious matters as well as the truths of scientific observation. There are no strict barriers—as in Bacon—dividing Divinity

---

[1] *Vulgar Errors*, Book I, ch. 6; *Works*, I, 152.
[2] *Ibid.*, ch. 9; *Works*, I, 1, 179.
[3] *Religio Medici*, Part I, sect. xvi.

from Natural Philosophy, for once Nature is seen as a Temple and the scientist as a Priest, the religious attitude may coincide with the most scrupulous attention to the tasks of observation and research. We should not suppose that Browne, in his quaint way, joined theological and scientific matters together, because he had not yet learned the new scientific approach of his generation. The fact is that he had learned it well, and had understood its limitations. Browne is in full possession of the new and emancipating discoveries of the Reformation and the New Philosophy, as well as of the characteristic new Humanism of Montaigne (which accounts for his easy introspective manner). He is as modern a man, against the background of the seventeenth-century world, as Bacon was,[1] but Bacon had divided the world and bisected the human intelligence which contemplated it, allowing no contact between reason and imagination, analysis and synthesis, fact and symbol. Browne on the other hand had sought unity and integration; he had climbed (to use his own incomparable phrase) 'the hill and asperous way which leadeth unto the house of sanity'.

If we consider his position in divinity as set out in his familiar theological tract, *Religio Medici*, we shall realize how close in spirit he was to the divines of the *via media* (such as Taylor and the Cambridge men) whom we have considered earlier. He adopts or at least savours the same opinions as they held; the same compromises and heresies peep forth in his writing. He cannot admit the harsh doctrine of eternal damnation; he believes that 'many are saved who to man seem reprobated; and many are reprobated, who in the opinion and sentence of man, stand elected'. And in the spirit of practical Christianity,

---

[1] An objection must be stated here to W. P. Dunn's otherwise excellent book on Browne (*Sir Thomas Browne, A Study in Religious Philosophy*, Minneapolis, 1950). Dunn whilst appreciating the many novelties in Browne's thinking, argues that his philosophy 'lies within the framework of knowledge and beliefs that was inherited from the Middle Ages and carried down through the Renaissance in the long tradition of Christian humanism' (p. 77). Browne was certainly more catholic (in all senses) than the other writers dealt with in this Chapter, and more hospitable to the remnants of medievalism. He reminds us of Meister Eckhart, of Roger Bacon, and his writings betray not a few affinities with the *De Docta Ignorantia* of Nicholas of Cusa. But the total effect of his work is modern, and in his firm attachment to experiment he is a post-Baconian.

he condemns those 'insolent zeals that do decry good Works, and rely onely upon Faith'.[1] Here is again the reaction against the harshness of Calvinism; here is the insistence on the Covenant of Works which we have discerned among the liberal theologians of the seventeenth century and in Milton among the left-wing Arminians. Indeed, Browne has much in common with Milton. In his earlier days he tells us he had strayed in the paths of the 'Mortalist' heresy (*R.M.*, Part I, sect. vii) but he did not pursue his 'singular' ideas to the extreme, believing that there should be enough tolerance in the national Church to allow of singularity without necessitating the proliferation of sects and schisms. His temper was undogmatic, and the toleration he expects for himself, he is prepared to give to others.

Above all what justifies us in regarding Browne as a writer of Hebraic temper is his optimistic attitude, his thoroughly positive attitude to the World and Flesh. There is no transcendent evil in Browne's world; there is even no transcendent ugliness. All that God made is good he insists, 'conformable to his Will, which abhors deformity, [and] that is the rule of order and beauty'.[2] He attempts no systematic account of Sin and Evil, not even so full a treatment as Milton in his poetry and his theological writing, but his dislike of moral dualism springs like Milton's from the same biblical, Hebraic origins. As in Milton so in Browne, Original Sin, fades into a rather dim uncertainty; the world itself is too radiant, and Man's nature too richly endowed to allow of so dark a judgement. And without having to look outside the limits of his own personality, Browne is too entirely convinced of life as a moral adventure, of its gaiety and promise, to permit him to embrace the more pessimistic philosophies and religions of the Renaissance. No one has written with a more vigorous rapture on the subject of death, and yet it is entirely characteristic of him that he should, nevertheless, have embraced life and questioned whether un-

[1] *Religio Medici*, Part I, sect. lvii, lx.

[2] *Ibid.*, Part I, sect. xvi; for an interesting and perceptive discussion of Browne's views in this section, see Dunn, *op. cit.*, pp. 101-5. Dunn points out that in saying this, Browne is 'parting company with the ugly dualism of the day'. He shares with the Cambridge philosophers their sense of the unity of the world, though 'Browne is too close to the scriptural view, *too Hebraic* to go far with the Cabbalists or the Platonists' (my italics).

necessary martyrdom was really acceptable to God. With a truly enlightened common sense he speaks of 'the moral duty I owe to the commandment of God, and the natural respects that I tender unto the conservation of my essence and being'.[1] The attitude that holds that God is served by life and activity, that in our flesh we may see God, is part of the religious realism that we have associated with Hebraism. This is that prudence of the wise king who had said (*Ecclesiastes* ix, 4), 'For to him that is joined to the living there is hope: for a living dog is better than a dead lion.' It is that wisdom which does not have to abandon prudence for the fear of heaven. Here there is no division between the religious and secular which would necessitate a double standard of morality; *Hokhmah* legislates for both:

> The leaven therefore and ferment of all, not only Civil, but Religious actions, is Wisdom; without which, to commit ourselves to the flames is Homicide, and (I fear) but to pass through one fire into another.
>
> (*R.M.*, sect. xxvi)

It is indeed a religion for men of flesh and blood.[2]

III

Robert Boyle was a devout naturalist whose proximity to Hebraism, both in its Biblical and post-Biblical manifestations, has never been fully appreciated. His opinions on free-will—on which he was radical Arminian—had been formed by the Jewish doctors, in particular Maimonides ('their great Rabbi') and by his friend and contemporary, Menasseh ben Israel. But he perceived that the Jewish stress on free-will does not mean a denial of the grace of God, of *hesed*. He claims that a closer attention to their teaching shows them to have a true conception of the relation between Divine Grace and human liberty,

> To which purpose I remember that a Jewish professor of Hebrew (who assisted me in my studies of that mysterious tongue) being,

[1] *Religio Medici*, Part I, sect. xxvi.

[2] It may be remarked that though Browne is a truly Hebraic writer in most of the senses in which the term is employed in this study, he had no overt sympathy for Jews or Judaism. Cf. *Religio Medici*, Part I, sect. xxv. In this he differs from Robert Boyle.

as the rest of his nation, an eager and peremptory champion of free-will, conceived, that even that liberty, which to us seems least to indebt men to their Creator, did transcendently oblige him unto God. . . .[1]

The point was that the gift of human freedom was itself an unmerited and inexplicable gift of Divine Grace. The very possibility of human effort is itself miraculous. Nature, whether we speak of human nature or of the physical world which surrounds us, is the sphere of Revelation.

Boyle was of course one of the prominent exponents of the New Science. He applied the new mechanical principle to the field of chemistry achieving thereby astonishing results. He was to that extent a Baconian. In fact, his work as a whole may be regarded as the continuation (and for the seventeenth century, almost the completion) of the task Bacon set himself in the *Sylva Sylvarum*—the task, that is, of recording a complete Natural History.[2] And yet we should remember that (as he tells us in his autobiography) his religious sensibilities had been thoroughly awakened even before he came across the 'paradoxes of the great star-gazer Galileo' and so became converted to the New Philosophy, and that his earnest study of the Biblical texts *in their original languages* began at about the same time as he was enrolled a member of the Invisible College. The fact that Boyle did not find any opposition developing between his scientific and his religious interests is to be explained by his stress on the Hebraic rather than the evangelical elements in his religious tradition. He is fond of quoting the Psalmist who says, 'I will praise thee, because I am fearfully and wonderfully made' and he remarks that many of David's songs of praise were such 'as the naturalist may best give'. In this very definite turning to the Old Testament Scripture, he was very like his friends, the Cambridge philosophers. But of course he was more directly concerned with practical scientific matters than they were, and when he affirms, as he so often does in his Essays, *Of the Usefulness of Natural Philosophy* (1663), that Nature and Divinity are

---

[1] *Works* (1744), I, 178.

[2] Cf. Marie Boas, 'Boyle as a Theoretical Scientist', *Isis*, XLI (1950), 267: 'What Bacon had hoped for was exactly what Boyle undertook: a thorough, detailed, experimental survey of the whole realm of chemical and physical properties.'

intimately to be related to one another, we may be sure that he is not just making a philosophical gesture but is expressing rather a pragmatic truth, valid for his own experience. His physico-theology was applied, and in a way discovered, in the laboratory.

One of his problems—equally scientific and theological— was to discern a unity in the Democritan race of atoms. Browne, like Whichcot, had entertained a belief in the *anima mundi*. The alchemists, among whom was Boyle's friend George Starkey, believed in an *archeus* or quintessence which acted as the agent to carry the spiritual principle into the world of matter. Boyle avoids such esoteric speculations, but speaks nevertheless of an 'Incorporeal and Intelligent Being' working upon Matter,[1] and elsewhere of an 'architectonick principle or power' which organizes and conducts the race of atoms so as to produce an orderly and beautiful world.[2] At all events, the entry of a divine shaping principle into the material world—in whichever way conceived—was for Boyle a scientific necessity. 'There is incomparably more art expressed in the structure of a dog's foot, than in that famous clock at Strasbourg.' And from a consideration of any animal as 'an entire and distinct system of organized parts', the truly enlightened scientist will naturally proceed to 'the cosmical, and therefore primary and over-ruling ends, that may have been designed by nature in the construction of the whole animal'.[3] Like Cudworth and More he protests against the Cartesian exclusion of 'Final Causes' from the realm of Physics. For Physics no less than for Biology the question 'Why' cannot be ignored, for the true scientist is concerned not with mere 'local motion', with the mechanics of independent and discrete manifestations, but with objects linked purposefully together. They have ends which transcend their individuality; and though the naturalist is bound to consider each factor in isolation, he must also consider it in its wider context, or to put it in theological terms, its place in the Creation.

In his third Essay on *The Usefulness of Natural Philosophy*, Boyle presents at considerable length the idea that 'the whole world is to be accounted the chiefest temple of God', deriving

[1] *Of the Usefulness of Natural Philosophy*, Essay IV.
[2] *The Sceptical Chymist* (1661).
[3] *Works*, IV, 549.

the notion, as he tells us, from Seneca and Philo, but chiefly from Philo. The great advantage of the Philonic handling of the *topos* (which is found repeatedly in Philo's writings on the *Pentateuch*) was that here the *cosmos* was not only sanctified in a general way but in a particular way related by analogy to the Temple at Jerusalem (or the Sanctuary in the Wilderness) with its priests and Levites. The Temple of Nature was thus given a Biblical basis—a fact of inestimable value in enabling Boyle, an earnest student of Jewish antiquities, to construct his physico-theological position. His use of the *topos* takes on an inevitably Biblical, Hebraic colour:

> It is an act of piety to offer up for the creatures the sacrifice of praise to the creator; for as anciently among the Jews, by virtue of an Aaronical extraction, men were born with a right to priest-hood; so reason is a natural dignity, and knowledge a prerogative, that can confer a priesthood without unction or imposition of hands.

> (Essay I)

But the priest of Nature was required to do more than labour at the furnace, serving God by the honest and scrupulous pursuit of scientific research. He had an additional duty. 'The thanks and praises of men, are the noblest incense that can be offered up to God,' says Boyle elsewhere (Essay V). He was not exempted from acts of devotion which, whilst not aimed at furthering a particular experiment, nevertheless took their rise from some concrete observation or experience of God's working in the field of Nature. At this level of activity the work of the scientist is conceived as providing the materials, the images and symbols, for acts of devotion and meditation. And this devotional side of his doctrine brings Boyle again into close proximity with those moderate Anglican divines as well as with the poets such as Herbert and Vaughan who applied themselves systematically to literary meditations based on the Scriptures or on the phenomena of Nature.[1] Boyle wrote a whole collection of such Meditations under the title of *Occasional Reflections* (published 1660); he even coins a new word, 'Meleteticks' to denote the art of writing Meditations. Like Thomas Browne, he believed in pursuing a scientific truth until he had extracted from it some

---

[1] See Chapters III and IV above.

moral or spiritual profit. 'Beasts inhabit and enjoy the World; Man if he will do more must study and . . . Spiritualize it.'[1] The Magnetic Needle forms the starting-point for one of his Meditations; other titles are, 'Upon the Quenching of quick-lime', and 'Upon his distilling spirit of roses in a limbick'. He composed a long series of Meditations (sect. ii) during a fever, finding in the ills of the flesh a potent symbol for the sick soul. In this way, he felt able to gain a perception of moral and spiritual truths without ever relaxing his hold on those material and physical factors which, as a scientist, he felt bound to stress. Swift may have later on made fun—in his 'Meditation on a Broomstick'— of the good man's literary efforts, but it seems men will always turn to the world of Nature for solace and enlightenment in this fashion—witness the American Jonathan Edwards's *Images or Shadows of Divine Things* in Swift's own day, and witness also Wordsworth's many nature-emblems and homilies later on. And perhaps it would have been better for us all if modern science had pursued the line set down by Boyle and Browne; we would have lost nothing in the way of knowledge or curiosity, but our power-drives would perhaps have been curbed by a reverent admiration for the divine infinitude.

Boyle himself was a competent and sometimes eloquent writer and in pursuit of his moral and religious symbolism, he was prepared to leave behind the dry Baconian style of report (adopted in his more practical writings). He defends his use of 'analogous instances' in his Preface to *The Christian Virtuoso* claiming that a freer, more imaginative style is appropriate to the discursive essay even though its subject may belong to the exact sciences:

> Apposite comparisons do not only give light, but strength, to the passages they belong to, since they are not always bare pictures and resemblances, but a kind of arguments; being often, if I may so call them, analogous instances, which do declare the nature, or way of operating, of the thing they relate to.[2]

And he speaks elsewhere in commendation of 'that noble figure of rhetorick called hyperbole'. All this would not have recom-

---

[1] Essay V.

[2] *Works*, V, 39. For Boyle's views on the dryer style required for experimental essays, see *Works*, I, 195.

mended him much to Bacon, although it undoubtedly did win
him the sympathy and commendation of other contemporaries
such as Thomas Browne and the Cambridge Platonists. Boyle
was especially interested in the style and rhetoric of the Bible,
and in his tract entitled 'Some Considerations touching the
Style of the Holy Scriptures' (1653), he tries to present an
argument for the Bible as a rhetorical model—especially for
men of science—equal in value to the Ciceronian, classical
style.[1] He declares himself unsatisfied with the existing English
translations which, he says, fail to do justice to the 'significant
and sinewy' quality of the original. There can be no doubt that
for Boyle himself (as for Traherne and Herbert) the decisive,
and stylistically normative text in the Bible is the Book of
Psalms. Its literary character had been obscured, he tells us, by
the crude rhyming version of Sternhold and Hopkins, but its
true beauty in the original is warranted by the fact that it was
surely 'written by a person, who (setting aside his inspiration)
was both a traveller, a courtier, and a poet'.[2] The parenthesis
is noteworthy. He aimed in this tract to make his readers
appreciate the Bible as literature, telling them that 'the king's
daughter is all glorious within, and her clothing is of wrought
gold'.

Boyle in short was a man of literary sensibility, whose imagination had been kindled by the poetry of the Holy Scriptures,
especially by the *Psalter* with its picture of nature sanctified and
of man thanking God because he is wonderfully made. His
literary imagination—thus nurtured—is then summoned to
the support of his own scientific work and by the use of 'analogous instances' and biblical quotations, he finds he can suck
the honey of divinity out of the flowers of Nature. There is
no need at this practical, devotional, level, to erect artificial
philosophical barriers between Divinity and Natural Philosophy—both lead to the praise of the same Creator God and
both employ the same literary means. It is only the abstract,
non-practical philosopher who never handles the materials of
Nature, or else the literalist who fails to allow his imagination
to respond to the living vibrations of the sacred text who will
find an opposition developing between the Bible and the world

---

[1] *Ibid.* II, 120 f.   [2] *Ibid.* II, 121.

surveyed by Natural Philosophy. That pragmatic faith in the possibility of integrating the two—as his own experience had led him to do—is the ground of Boyle's physico-theological position.

IV

The Biblical image of the World as a Temple (and the allied image of the world as God's book) undoubtedly expressed important Hebraic contents and tended for the men who had faith in them to confirm them in a positive this-worldly programme of religious belief and practice which in no way came into conflict with the new science. For men who had no vested interest in scholasticism, the New Philosophy did not put all in doubt, and if their Biblical faith was pitched in a more rational key than that of the Calvinists or Jansenists, the silence of the infinite spaces did not terrify them. The new knowledge could abet that faith in the Creator God which the reader of the Bible, responsive to the poetry of the *Psalms*, already felt. The telescope and the microscope alike declared the glory of God, for the Grace of God was not merely extended to the elect through the secret passages of the soul; it was displayed at large in the world around. The divine penetration into the world of matter was comprehensive, pervasive and unlimited. As Blake was to say later on:

> He who doubts from what he sees
> Will ne'er believe, do what you please.
> If the sun and moon should doubt,
> They'd immediately go out.
>
> *(Auguries of Innocence)*

The priest of Nature (or the devout student of Nature's book—'God's epistle to mankind, written in mathematical letters'[1] as

---

[1] In Essay V he speaks of Nature (here echoing Browne, *R.M.*, Part I, sect. xii) as 'the stenography of God's omniscient hand'. The image of the world as a Book is discussed by Curtius, *op. cit.*, pp. 319 f. In the seventeenth century in England it is pervasive; examples are Bacon, *Advancement of Learning*, I, 1; Hall, Sermon xxx 'the vast volume of the world . . . that huge folio'; Browne, *R.M.*, Part I, sect. xvi. The *topos* has, so far as I know, no special Hebraic authority: it is a typical *logos* formula going back to Plato;

Boyle styled it) was thus in a position to express the sense of a sanctified world-order and to comport himself, by an attitude of humility and reverence, as though he was indeed a worshipper and priest standing in awe before the author of all things.

Here was something other than the old time-honoured mould of Christian humanism, for the keynote of this form of natural piety was *work*. For the devout naturalists of the type of Browne and Boyle, the religious life meant the vigorous pursuit of the daily task, not the contemplation of Nature's order. They were in this respect more industrious, and more essentially Hebraic, than even the Cambridge Platonists, for the spirit of work and industry is the true inheritance of Hebraism in the post-reformation world. One day is given for recollection, but six days for work.

But when all this has been said, we are bound to recognize the essential limitation of the form of natural piety which can be discovered in Boyle and Browne, marked though it be by the active spirit that we associate with Hebraism. Here again we may invoke the classical antithesis of Priest and Prophet, for the priesthood of Nature by itself, whilst it presumes a sense of moral obligation, an earnestness, and piety, nevertheless presumes no revolutionary call, no summons to participate in a world-transforming adventure. The realm of Nature which these men seek to sanctify by work and devotion is a static realm; for Boyle it is marked essentially by design, by the perfection and wisdom of its contrivance. It is, he says, a 'pregnant automaton'. For Browne similarly, Nature was, above all 'the Art of God'.[1] The idea of the universe as itself in the process of change, of Man as called to assist and collaborate in a great historical drama which has been playing out, as Henry More taught, from the Creation of the World, and which will proceed to its majestic conclusion in the last Act destined to

---

[1] *Religio Medici*, Part I, sect. xvi.

the *cosmos* is visualized as a written, rationally comprehensible document. But in our century it gets involved with Hebraic motifs, and the 'Book of Nature' is often thought of as a Hebrew book and as somehow interchangeable with the Bible itself. For further discussion of the symbolic use of the 'Book of the Creatures' in seventeenth-century poetry and of its patristic sources, see also, Ruth C. Wallerstein, *Studies in Seventeenth Century Poetic* (University of Wisconsin, 1950).

'bring in righteousness in triumph'—all this is scarcely sensed in the writings of Browne and Boyle with their more quietistic notion of the priesthood of Nature. They were not prophets, prophesying the end of days or urging men forward to great enterprises; they were indeed priests, devoted to the daily round of practical piety. Bacon had more of the prophetic zeal of Hebraism—albeit secularized and perverted—in his sense of an approaching millennium of scientific advancement, and in his confidence of his own messianic call to lead the army of progress and open up (like Columbus) a New World of discovery and enlightenment.

A less secularized system of Natural Magic had remained alive among the alchemists of the seventeenth century, and if we can detach the symbolism used by Thomas Vaughan, the younger van Helmont, and Elias Ashmole from their various fantasies we shall be able to discern certain important features of Hebraism, of a more dynamic 'prophetic' kind than those discernible in Browne or in Boyle, the 'sceptical chymist'. An unsceptical chemist (and Hebraist) such as Robert Fludd thinks of Creation itself as the great alchemical experiment which the alchemists in their smaller way were trying to reproduce; he speaks of God's 'spagyrick operation' at the division of the lower waters. The alchemist's task is to seize and possess something of this creative principle in order to promote the ends of creation and salvation. In Paracelsus himself we have a powerfully expressed notion of a kind of creative evolution of the natural world which was to be promoted essentially through the co-operation of the elect:

> All things on earth have been given into the hands of man. And they are given into his hands in order that he may bring them to the highest development, just as the earth does with all that it brings forth.[1]

This might easily have been written by Bacon, but between this expression of millennial hope in Paracelsus and that in Bacon lies all the difference between a poetically rich and religiously meaningful universe, and one almost entirely

[1] *Selected Writings of Paracelsus*, ed. J. Jacobi (Trans. N. Guterman, London, 1951), p. 182. The whole section, entitled, 'School of Nature' (pp. 182-93) is relevant here.

destitute of both poetry and divine glory.[1] The alchemists for all their fantasies and obsessions preserved the Hebraic sense of a miraculous world-destiny, of a new heaven and a new earth to be filled with the glory of God 'as the waters cover the sea'.

It was not by chance that Browning in his poem on the theme of Paracelsus (1835) actually anticipated the evolutionary hypothesis which was later to upset the more narrow-minded theological writers of the nineteenth century.[2] For to his hero, Paracelsus, Nature implied above all dynamic change, not, as in the Aristotelian, non-created universe, the sameness of eternal forms. And this attitude towards the world of Nature preserved by the alchemists and later to appear in a secularized form in nineteenth-century science, is not only the decisive determinant of modern scientific thought, it is also a primary tenet of Hebraism which sees all things, including the natural order, in terms of History. And History, let us remember, is not neutral 'linear' History; it is not a meaningless series of accidents but the History of promise and fulfilment, exile and return, trial and punishment. Behind its pattern there is a God who *wills*, and in whose Will our destiny is ultimately held in control.

Apart from the alchemists, it is I think with the Cambridge philosopher, Ralph Cudworth, author of *The True Intellectual System of the Universe* (1678), that we find the clearest intimation of such a non-hellenic world-view in the seventeenth century. He attacks the mechanists (including Hobbes and Descartes) for having made 'a kind of dead and wooden world as it were a carved statue, that hath nothing neither vital nor magical at

[1] Cf. by the present author, 'Bacon and Paracelsus', *The Cambridge Journal* (Cambridge, 1952) vol. 5.

[2] It has been suggested that Browning's source for his evolutionary ideas expressed in *Paracelsus* (Part V) is the *Zohar*. See Edward Berdoe, *The Browning Cyclopaedia* (London, ed. of 1949), p. 326. It is always as well to be wary about ideas connected with Natural Science and Natural Philosophy which are said to have their origin in the Kabbalah. But the theme of 'the worlds that were built and destroyed' prior to the final production of the present world is found in the classical Jewish rabbinic literature before the period of the *Kabbalah* proper. (Cf. *Midrash Bereshit Rabbah*, iii, 9; ix, 2). Such 'Evolutionism', if that is the word for it, is built into orthodox Jewish thinking from very early times.

all in it'.[1] He is opposed to such a mechanical world as we discern even in the writings of Boyle with his favourite image of the universe as a kind of elaborate Strasbourg clock, and he opposes this not only because it is static, but also—and here a very interesting intuition on the part of Cudworth—because such a universe is too perfect! Both Browne and Boyle were impressed by the entire perfection of Nature's design. For Boyle, the world is a pregnant automaton with every part ideally contrived; for Browne it is a perfect work of art. Whilst this agrees with the positive appreciation of the goodness of the created universe which is to be attributed to Hebraism, it also implies that schematic ideality of the Stoic world-picture in which every part is ideally adapted to its end, or the aetiological refinement of Aristotle with his four perfectly interlocking causes. Now, whilst it may please the aesthetic faculty to conceive the universe as operating according to perfect circles (and the Greek world-view is above all aesthetic) it surely does not always accord with the phenomena. We have to reckon not only with 'Nature red in tooth and claw' but also—in the organic realm—with occasional deformity and inconsistency, 'those errors and bungles', which, says Cudworth, 'are committed when the matter is inept and contumacious'.[2] There is, as Boyle noted with admiration, the 'melodious music of singing birds' and the beauty of the peacock's train; but, then, what about rudimentary tails in tailless sheep and wings on birds that cannot fly? Cudworth's notion of a Plastic Nature, from this point of view, saves the phenomena in a way that the aesthetically contrived and perfect world of Boyle and Browne does not. It supposes nature to have a certain autonomy. If the world of Nature is given this quasi-independence (such as is assumed in the Hebrew Covenant-view) and if it is seen as not static but in growth and change, then it is possible to imagine that for any one scene of the play, it will not display an ideal order in the interdependence and contrivance of its parts. We must not suppose God to be so 'operose, solicitous, and distractious' says Cudworth, to imagine him to be directly concerned with every trivial manifestation. Nature, whilst ultimately under divine control, has its own 'archeus' (here an

[1] Edition of Mosheim, London, 1845 (Trans. J. Harrison), I, 221.
[2] *Ibid.*, I, 223.

alchemical term), its own interior principle of government.[1] And
he goes on to speak with remarkable intuition of 'the slow and
gradual process that is in the generation of things'. Free-will,
it seems, may be predicated of Nature as well as of Man.

Here is indeed a deviation from the whole world-machine
school of theism represented by Boyle, Derham, and Paley,
and from the later school of Deism. It leaves behind the
seventeenth-century dispute on the subject of Final Causes
which Boyle wished to include in Physics whilst Bacon and
Descartes wished to omit them. Here Cudworth opens up an
exciting new prospect, for he is concerned, not with a static
principle of design but with a creative principle of growth; not
the adaptability of means to ends, but the gradual achievement
through a long process of development, through trial and
error, of desired and foreseen objectives. Cudworth is in fact
turning aside here (as More had done using different metaphors)
from a purely Hellenic teleology, towards something like a
doctrine of evolution, which presupposes a willing and creating
God, who operates through dynamic change.

This study will not follow up the transmigration of the theory
of evolution into the nineteenth century, when there was little
left of its Hebraic colour; as in so many other manifestations
of Hebraism the progress of secularization had isolated the
historical driving-force from its moral and religious context.
The same was to happen in Marxism which is indeed a messianic
religion but entirely lacking the dimension of the sacred. It is
the pursuit of a fragmented righteousness, but the abandonment
of the indispensable basis of that righteousness, 'Be ye holy,
for I the Lord your God am holy.'

How was it possible in nineteenth-century theories of Nature
and Society to achieve this neat dismemberment of the totality
Hebraism, to lay hold of its divine imperative, of its sense of
historical meaning and promise, and yet to turn out the lights
of heaven, to deny that we are inhabitants of the Kingdom of
God, that the World is a Temple and Man its Priest? The next
Chapter will attempt to trace the beginning of this process of
exfoliation. For like so many other vital ingredients of the modern world, this fundamentally secularized Hebraism likewise
has its genesis in the world of the seventeenth century.

[1] *Ibid.*, II, 594.

PART FIVE

Albion Disrobed

XIV

THE INFERNAL COVENANT

Ye have said, we have made a covenant with death, and with
Sheol are we at agreement.

(Isaiah xxviii, 15)

I

THE KEY to the special secular mutation which Hebraism as
doctrine and life underwent in the latter half of the seventeenth
century is that strange and obsessive writer, Thomas Hobbes.
Obsessed to an incredible degree by the Baconian plan of
making prose discourse approximate to geometrical theorems,
he deliberately cut out from his writing all imaginative suggestiveness, all emotional colour. Metaphors, he says, are to be
'utterly excluded. For seeing they openly professe deceipt; to
admit them into Councell, or Reasoning, were manifest folly'.[1]
And yet, we may ask, what is his *Leviathan* but one extended
and fantastic metaphor? Whilst he has excluded imagery from
the texture of his writing in his endeavour to be rational and
objective, a vast, monstrous image has crept in, as it were,
through the back-door. Hobbes's whole conception of human
society under its absolute monarch as 'Leviathan' and of the
State as 'the mortall God' is surely the vision of a perverted
poetic imagination. What he has created is ultimately as
grotesque as the final Book of Swift's *Gulliver's Travels* or the
nightmarish Utopias of an Orwell or a Huxley. And it is no
accident that the image he has chosen to project upon the world
of humanity is an Hebraic image. To express his notion of a
this-worldly power, dynamic, insulting, and trampling upon
traditional forms and loyalties, he chooses the dread beast
with which God challenges Job out of the whirlwind, taking as
his text the following verses:

> There is nothing on earth to be compared with him. He is made
> so as not to be afraid.

[1] *Leviathan,* ch. 8 (ed. of A. R. Waller, Cambridge, 1935, p. 43).

225

He seeth every high thing below him: and is King of all the children of pride.[1]

Leviathan is the symbol of stupendous and all-but-unconditioned power. It is true that he is ultimately the creature of God and subject to his will and arbitrament; but Hobbes omits the theological dimension; power is what he wants, for power is the new ingredient which Hobbes wishes to inject into Philosophy. 'The end of Knowledge is Power.'[2] The human will is now supreme over the realms of Man and Nature, for Bacon's dream of world-conquest and human self-conquest has now achieved the status of philosophical axiom.

Hobbes has in him a great deal of Bacon, also of Machiavelli, of the Puritans and the Stoics, yet he differs from them in his capacity to overcome the dualistic tendencies in their systems. Like the Hebraic writers considered in the previous three Chapters, he is a holist; as with Jeremy Taylor so with Hobbes, there is no Augustinian boundary separating the earthly City from the heavenly City, separating natural from supernatural; there is no fatal decree of predestination ultimately nullifying human effort; there is no hellenistic division of soul and body. And above all, as with the Hebraic writers, so with Hobbes, there is no retreat from History. As Strauss has remarked, he 'does not follow Aristotle, but opens up the way to Hegel'.[3]

We shall see that Hobbes's system as finally expounded in the *Leviathan*, bears a strange, and one might almost say, lunatic resemblance to the Hebraic doctrine of Revelation, of Covenant. For it is the Covenant (by which he understands the Social Contract) which, for Hobbes, creates Society and makes all progress and morality possible. Hobbes uses the grammar, and to some extent also, the vocabulary of Hebraism whilst ignoring its real meaning and discarding its syntax. The State (or Sovereign) takes the place of God; and human Reason takes the place of Divine Revelation. Hobbes is indeed the extreme image presented to us by Albion when he has fallen away most completely from Jerusalem and when he at the same time reveals most clearly his kinship with her.

[1] This is the version of *Job* xli, 33-4, quoted by Hobbes. *Leviathan*, ch. 28.
[2] *Elements of Philosophy*, ch. 1. English Works, ed. W. Molesworth (London, 1839), I, 7.
[3] Leo Strauss, *The Political Philosophy of Hobbes* (Oxford, 1936), p. 105.

II

It is not difficult to see Hobbes's affiliation to those disruptive, anti-traditional forces in the Renaissance defined earlier in our discussion of Bacon, the Puritans, and the Stoics. If not the heir of the Counter-Renaissance, then he is certainly its bastard child. To take Bacon first, we recall that Hobbes had acted for some time as his Secretary. He occasionally echoes his words and sentiments. Bacon too had harboured few idealistic illusions about human nature. If, says Bacon, 'there were taken out of Mens mindes, Vaine Opinions, Flattering Hopes, false Valuations . . . it would leave the Mindes of a number of Men, poore shrunken things'.[1] Hobbes pursues such notions to a much more relentlessly logical extreme, and the wise and practical courtier of Bacon's Essays, systematically pursuing his own interests but also paying lip-service to truth and godliness, is far outstripped by the strange creatures who inhabit Hobbes's world. The break with tradition is much more complete. Also, there is a difference in the form in which he casts his thoughts. Where Bacon had looked to Aristotle, Hobbes looks to Galileo. Above all, there is a narrowing of the scope of Philosophy, for Bacon, whilst proposing (like Hobbes) as the chief end of Philosophy the propagation of man's empire over the universe, had retained in his scheme a consideration of Divine Philosophy as the third great constituent of all knowledge. However separated from one another they might be, the three realities of Man, God, and Nature, remained, for Bacon, intact. Hobbes goes further and introduces a more radical simplification; theology is excluded, and the province of the Philosopher is limited to 'bodies naturall', 'dispositions and manners of men', and the 'civil duties of subjects'.

Again his link with the Puritans hardly needs to be argued. They share the same notion of the essential depravity of human nature. For Hobbes, as for the Calvinists, Man in his natural state lives a life 'solitary, poore, nasty, brutish and short'. As in Calvinism he can only be redeemed from this state of depravity by entering into a Covenant—not indeed now the Covenant of Grace but rather a political parody of it. In Hobbes's doctrine of Social Contract, human reason takes the place of divine grace.

[1] *Of Truth.*

227

Like the Puritans he directs his onslaught against the chimaeras of the medieval church and the Aristotelian metaphysics which supported them; but he goes further than the Puritans for he overthrows all 'abstract essences' whatever, and indeed abolishes the soul, substituting for it a sort of mechanical engine. 'Soul' is for Hobbes no more than a word coined to distinguish a living body from a dead one. Now here Hobbes has against him not only all Christians whatsoever (whether Catholic or Reformed) but also Descartes and the Cartesians. This is indeed the pith of his *Objections* to the *Meditations* of Descartes (1641). Hobbes had objected to the entire spiritual side of Descartes's system with its affirmation of the existence of an 'immaterial substance'. For Hobbes this is a pure contradiction in terms; all bodies are material and everything in the universe is body. 'That which is not body is not part of the universe.'[1] Thus the dualism of Descartes (and of the Puritans) is abandoned. Instead of presenting side by side a material and a non-material reality, with the soul anomalously located in the pineal gland, Hobbes gives us a unified world-picture explicable throughout in terms of Matter and Motion.

In casting out the logical anomalies of others, Hobbes, did not fail, of course, to incur even mightier anomalies and self-contradictions himself. And the psychic branch of his own philosophy is surely the *reductio ad absurdum* of his entire system. The soul is for him like the rest of the universe. It is a highly sensitive machine capable of registering vibrations from the organs of sense and storing them in the Memory like so many gramophone records. The soul which he displays to our view is like something which has emerged from the laboratory of a Frankenstein. That which thinks, he declares, is material. He has plucked out the heart of the mystery, only to discover that there is no mystery there. But assuming with Hobbes that the highest function of the mind is its power of Reason, we may ask how does the soul which is merely mechanical become capable of independent reasoning? If it is a corporeal substance whirled about by the motion of its own laws, how does it achieve a philosophical comprehension of those laws? This, it has been

[1] See 'Objections to Descartes' in *Works of Descartes*, trans. Haldane and Ross (Cambridge, 1912), II, 62. 'That which thinks is material rather than immaterial,' he adds.

pointed out, is the paradox of all his thinking. To the mind of man are attributed transcendent powers of mastery; from it salvation comes; and yet it is no whit different in its nature or operations from the phenomena which it transcends and over which it exercises its mastery. This paradox he overcomes by a steam-roller process of assertion: the soul simply has no powers which do not belong to the world of sense and motion.

Like other late Renaissance humanists, Hobbes employs the Stoic style of aphorism, earlier considered, but he refines it into a kind of ethical calculus. He displays the Senecan economy which we detected in Bacon and even Browne, but he employs it in a dryer, more geometrical fashion, urging his ideas in the form of tight aphorisms and antitheses. How do we distinguish between dreams and waking thoughts? He explains as follows:

> And because waking I often observe the absurdity of Dreames, but never dream of the absurdities of my waking Thoughts; I am well satisfied, that being awake, I know I dreame not; though when I dreame, I think my selfe awake.[1]

Here is the same art of introspection as practised by the Renaissance neo-stoics; but Hobbes exercises himself in it with a more calculated zeal than Lipsius or Montaigne. For him, the I/Myself relation has blotted out any possibility of an I/Thou tremor of sympathetic consciousness. Being awake he is never likely to dream of things beyond sense or motion, of confrontations with any transcendent otherness such as was affirmed for instance in the *Meditations* of Descartes. In the I/Myself correlation there is also, strictly speaking, no room for human love. Iago—a sort of pre-Hobbesian Hobbist—had remarked that love was 'merely a lust of the blood and a permission of the will' (*Othello*, Act I, scene iii): likewise, for Hobbes, family affection 'dependeth on naturall lust'.[2] Honour and Virtue (mocked also by Iago) take on a form determined by the primary impulses of Fear and Vanity (motion from and towards). Fear is essentially fear of Death, and Vanity is essentially self-interest. Both are self-regarding motives. The soul, never galvanized into activity outside the circumference of its

[1] *Leviathan*, ch. 2, *ed. cit.*, p. 5.
[2] *Ibid.*, ch. 13, *ed. cit.*, p. 85. Iago is something Hobbes is not, namely a cynic. Cf. also J. F. Danby, *Shakespeare's Doctrine of Nature* (London, 1949).

own self-consciousness, remains confined to predictable and observable motions about its axis. There is no transforming encounter, no new experience outside the confining pale of selfhood. Henry More, expressing the Judaeo-Christian objection to stoicism, had said:

> For this Kingdome of the *Stoicks* is the Kingdome of *Selfishness*, and *Self-love* sways the Sceptre there and wears the Diademe: but in the Kingdome of God, God himself, who is that pure, free, and perfectly *unselfed love*, has the full dominion of the soul, and the ordering and rule of all the Passions.[1]

It was the same stoical self-sufficiency that Milton also had finally, in *Paradise Regained* found so obnoxious. In Hobbes it achieves its most extreme form; and it should be added that he omits the mystical pantheism, the blending of the self with the *mundus* which ultimately provided the Stoic with an escape from selfhood. Again, Hobbes simplifies, restoring unity to a world fragmented and divided by the operation of dualistic categories.

Finally, in placing Hobbes among his Renaissance antecedents, we are not to ignore the obvious link with Machiavelli in his moral and political philosophy. Hobbes certainly agreed with Machiavelli's statement in *The Prince* that 'men will always prove bad, unless by necessity they are compelled to be good' (ch. 23). Machiavelli's account of the rise of Justice in the *Discorsi* resembles Hobbism. Justice arose, according to Machiavelli, when men were forced to recognize that the injuries done to others might one day, if unchecked, be done to themselves. Laws were thus a self-protecting device; they were

---

[1] Dialogue IV, in *Divine Dialogues* (1668). The traditional, medieval debate between the Christian Fathers and the Stoics is not always strictly relevant to the situation we are discussing in the post-Reformation and post-Renaissance era. Augustine's complaint that the Stoics placed Man's beatitude in this life rather than in the life to come would still be voiced by the pietists, but for most writers who had been impressed by the new humanism (Milton and Jeremy Taylor for instance) this would be a strength of stoicism. The problem of such men, and we may include such a Christian Stoic as Joseph Hall, was to adapt the sense of the values inherent *in this life* to the Christian scheme of salvation. Here a rather non-medieval note tends to be struck. The objection of Lactantius (*De Ira Dei*) that the Stoic God is remote and impersonal, whereas in the light of biblical revelation, he is seen to be a 'living God' showing both love and anger, would be more relevant for our period in its reaction to the challenge of a revived stoicism.

not an acknowledgement of some obligation to an entity which transcended the individual members of society but merely a collective reaction to injuries which men were not prepared to tolerate:

> It was thus that men learned how to distinguish what is honest and good from what is pernicious and wicked, for the sight of someone injuring his benefactor evoked in them hatred and sympathy and they blamed the ungrateful and respected those who showed gratitude, *well aware that the same injuries might have been done to themselves*. Hence to prevent evil of this kind they took to making laws and to assigning punishments to those who contravened them. The notion of justice thus came into being. . . .[1]

Now the pragmatic tone of this, the scientific objectivity, and the appeal to a purely secular system of sanctions, are exactly matched in Hobbes's handling of the same subject in the fourteenth and fifteenth chapters of *Leviathan*. But again there is a difference which one may suspect to be a decisive one between the two sets of moral and political doctrine. It may be put as follows: for Machiavelli, Man in Society was no whit different from Man as he was found originally scattered over the face of the earth. Nothing had *happened* to moderate his egoism. No new purpose had been injected into his life by the discovery of the laws of Justice. To put it a different way, one could say that according to the Machiavellian realism, society is little more than the sum-total of the individuals composing it, and laws are merely the reflection of the individual's demands on, or resentment of, his neighbour. In this he carries Renaissance individualism to its furthest point.[2] But Hobbes has a new reference point beyond the individual. He does not see civil society as a mere continuation of the State of Nature, nor does

---

[1] *The Discourses of Niccolo Machiavelli*, ed. L. J. Walker (London, 1950), I, 212-13.

[2] In the rather special political society that he outlines in *The Prince*, we may suppose that he has abolished individual self-expression and supplanted it by tyranny. But surely from another angle, individuality here finds its intensest expression. Concentrated in the single unique ruler, it has triumphed over every other consideration. Hobbes avoids these contradictions. True he proposes an absolute ruler, but the basis for his authority is not to be found in his own boundless individuality, but rather in the existence of civil society, as a unity transcending individual interests.

he think of it as the sum-total of the individuals who compose it. A new thing comes into existence when men begin to apply their reasons and determine to put an end to the State of Nature. There is a transforming moment, a moment which changes the mutual relations of men and gives reality to law and justice, making them something other than an expression of individual resentment and desire. That moment is the entry into the compact, or Covenant. The social contract is the decisive step for Hobbes in the creation of a true community bound by mutual obligation. From this henceforward there will be no return. After this, there can be no resumption of the State of mere Nature.

III

No student of Hobbes can fail to be impressed by the gravity of his moral doctrine. He may have given philosophical comfort to the libertines of the reign of Charles II, but he himself was no libertine. The state of lawlessness in which Man lived as a child of Nature, was a state of war, and the whole strength of Hobbes's political theory is directed at the ending of such a state. It is easy for us to supply the psychological background of his passionate plea for peace when we consider the struggles of the mid-century and the confusion of parties in the Commonwealth era. Rather than this, he seems to say, let us have peace at any price. To Hobbes, the appointment of an absolute ruler seemed a reasonable price to pay for law and order. But it is not the Sovereign who imposes law—he merely secures and preserves it. Justice as such has its fountain and origin in the Law of Nature (*Leviathan*, ch. 15) and is implicit in the covenantal promises which men take upon themselves when they abandon the State of War and enter upon the State of Peace. The earnestness with which Hobbes urges the absolute validity of the moral law is to be weighed as a major feature of his teaching:

> The Lawes of Nature are Immutable and Eternall; For Injustice, Ingratitude, Arrogance, Pride, Iniquity, Acception of persons, and the rest, can never be made lawfull. For it can never be that Warre shall preserve life, and Peace destroy it.
>
> (ch. 15)

Although Hobbes claimed that it is Reason which discovered these 'Laws of Nature' and that they are linked together as logically and rationally as a theorem in geometry, this is not the aspect which strikes a reader who is sensitive to the emotional charge of his paragraphs on this theme. He does not seem to be demonstrating interesting scientific theories. His anthropology may borrow a mathematical form, but neither Machiavellian pragmatism nor Euclidian geometry provide the ground for its peculiar dogmatic intensity. We do not feel that theorems command, and above all Hobbes rests his view of civil society upon a sense of imperative and inescapable duty. The primary discovery of his brutish *anthropos* as he emerges from the 'meer state of nature' is not geometry; it is *obligation*.

The dynamic character of Hobbes's moral philosophy, we need not doubt, is owing to the transfer into the secular sphere of the moral intensities of Puritanism,[1] and as in Puritanism, so in Hobbes, the Covenant-principle is the source of ethical obligation. What then is the meaning of 'Covenant' for Hobbes, and (closely related to this question) what is the meaning of those 'Laws of Nature' which mark the end of the State of War and inaugurate the Peace of a tolerable order? And to what extent may these concepts of Hobbes be related to what we have discovered earlier regarding the Hebrew doctrine of Law and Covenant?

The solemnity with which the Covenant or Social Contract is invested in Hobbes's political theory suggests that he is not working with a mere legal fiction, a convenient metaphor enabling him to construct his totalitarian state upon some sort of theoretical foundation. The fact is that the Covenant for Hobbes, is the foundation of all human society; it is that which makes a real community possible in place of a mere collection of separate individuals. The Puritans thought of the Covenant of Grace as the origin of the sacred community; Hobbes thought of the primordial contract as the origin of all community whatever, the source of unity among men:

> This is more than Consent, or Concord; it is a reall Unitie of them all, in one and the same Person, made by Covenant of every man

[1] This has been noted by several students, including Cassirer, *The Platonic Renaissance in England* (Trans. Pettegrove, London, 1953), p. 78.

with every man, in such manner, as if every man should say to every man, *I Authorise and give up my Right of Governing my selfe, to this Man, or to this Assembly of men, on this condition, that thou give up thy Right to him, and Authorise all his Actions in like manner.* This done, the Multitude so united in one Person, is called a Commonwealth, in latine Civitas.[1]

It would hardly be an exaggeration to say that for Hobbes this primordial Compact by which civil society is created is invested with the solemnity and awe which in Hebraism belongs to the exchange of covenantal promises at Mount Sinai. It is for Hobbes the act from which the whole possibility of a moral order for the human race takes its rise.

Of course, the transfer of the Covenant-idea from the religious to the secular sphere had already taken place in Puritanism itself, and in this respect Hobbes is not a complete innovator.[2] We have seen that Milton's conception of civil society in his political tracts is based on the Israel-England parallelism, with explicit reference to the various public acts of solemn promise-making between King and subject mentioned in the Old Testament.[3] The Levellers, the first of modern revolutionary democrats, appealed to the Biblical Covenants for their sanction in drawing up their proposed *Agreements of the People*. The Mayflower Contract of 1620 is an example of the application of common law conceptions to a new political enterprise, but the traditional aspect is outweighed by the dynamic force of a freely undertaken mutual contract. There is a sense of new commitment; there is a personal call felt to be as momentous as that which in the case of Abraham summoned him from his birthplace and his father's house to depart for a new, strange land. It is a truism that English Puritanism achieved its ultimate political expression in the Bill of Rights of 1689, the first contractual instrument in the history of parliamentary democracy in England. In a somewhat less sensational way than the French revolutionaries a century later, the Whigs who instituted

---

[1] *Leviathan*, ch. 17, *ed. cit.*, pp. 118-19.

[2] Cf. Samuel Rutherford, *Lex Rex* (1644), and Richard Mather, *An Apology for Church Covenant* (1643), reprinted by A. S. P. Woodhouse, *Puritanism and Liberty*, pp. 207, 299. See also J. W. Gough, *The Social Contract* (Oxford, second ed., 1957), pp. 84 f.

[3] *The Tenure of Kings and Magistrates*, in *Works*, V, 14-15.

the Bill and Declaration of Rights were conscious of inaugurating by a deliberate and solemn act of mutual promise-making, a new Revolution which it has been said was 'cradled in contract'.[1] Behind that too lurks the Puritan tradition of Covenant and League.

Hobbes's use of the Covenant-idea as the basis for an absolute monarchy in which God would have little or no place, was naturally calculated to horrify the Puritans of his day, and indeed all religious theorists whatever, but nevertheless Puritanism had given him the dynamic form of his idea, and had also in a way given the whole impetus to Hobbism through its tendency to see everything outside the inward life of the spirit as given to Caesar. A new secularization of the State had been authorized in contrast to the hierarchical sanctified order of the Middle Ages, and this radical re-examination of the State in secular terms produced, on the right wing of the Puritan party in England, a climate not essentially unfavourable to a system of political absolutism such as that of Hobbes.[2] Hobbes simplified by doing away with the division of human loyalties into that which belonged to God and that which belonged to Caesar. Under the pressure of his monistic thinking, everything is seen as belonging to Caesar. Again, unity instead of duality.

It is a little difficult for us perhaps to reconcile Hobbes's use of Puritan political terms and categories to the notion, especially current in the United States, that Puritanism inevitably yielded a democratic pattern when applied to the problems of civil society. Certainly, for the Levellers, and for the majority of American Puritans, the Social Contract spelled Democracy. In Milton and Locke too the theory of political contract which both employ in more or less open allusion to Biblical precedent, is the guarantee of religious liberty and also the justification for resistance against tyranny. For Locke, such resistance, was merely theoretical, but Milton actually invoked the sanction on the joint basis of the Law of Nature and Holy Scripture, and proceeded to urge the overthrow of King and Government in the

[1] Sir Ernest Barker (ed.) *Social Contract, Essays by Locke, Hume and Rousseau* (Oxford, 1947), Introduction, p. lx.

[2] Cf. A. S. P. Woodhouse, *op. cit.*, Introduction, p. 85. For the analogy between Puritanism and Hobbism, cf. also, E. Cassirer, *The Platonic Renaissance in England*, p. 78.

interests of those rights secured by primordial contract. How is it possible then that for Hobbes it was precisely the primordial contract which for all time outlawed resistance to tyranny and gave to King and Government their unquestionable and unsubvertible authority? It would appear that the Social Covenant is a two-edged weapon; it can take a Whig or Tory form. It can beget the democratic Agreements of the People when handled by the Levellers, but it can also beget the repressive Solemn League and Covenant when employed by the right-wing Presbyterians. It can give us Rousseau fighting for the self-governing community, but it can also perversely yield a Napoleon, or a Robespierre.

We may attempt to resolve the difficulty by differentiating, as some have done, between the contract of Government, the *Herrschaftsvertrag* (which is in a way the theme of Hobbes),[1] and the contract of Society, the *Gesellschaftsvertrag* (which is the theme of Rousseau and the Whigs). One tends to lead in the direction of a strong central authority, in the direction briefly of Totalitarianism; the other leads in the direction of a sort of ideal Society ruled, if at all, by a General Will which makes State interference and control practically unnecessary. And paradoxical though it may seem, both these forms of Social Contract have an Hebraic origin, or at least a partially Hebraic origin, in so far as they both originate in the intellectual climate of post-Reformation biblical spirituality. And it is easy to see why such opposed systems should both have their ground in Hebraism, for in Hebraism *Herrschaftsvertrag* and *Gesellschaftsvertrag* are originally part of the same act: they are not opposed to one another. The Holy Community is created at exactly the same moment as the Divine Kingship is announced. Man surrenders his rights ('devesting himself' of them, as Hobbes says in his extraordinarily significant phrase) at precisely the same moment that he also breaks free from slavery and affirms his inalienable 'democratic' privileges. 'I am the

---

[1] It has been argued that Hobbes really repudiates the contract of Government because 'the Sovereign was no party to Hobbes's contract, but simply the recipient of powers conferred on him by a contract of all with all' (Gough, *op. cit.*, p. 108). Cf. also E. Barker, *op. cit.*, pp. xii f. On the other hand, Hobbes's whole theory was designed to make room for a powerful monarchy to which the people are, by the terms of *their* contract, bound to submit. The *Herrschaftsvertag* is, in that sense, very much his theme.

Lord thy God which brought thee out of the land of Egypt out of the house of bondage. Thou shalt have no other gods before me.' It is a crucial juxtaposition: maximal authority goes hand in hand with maximal personal responsibility and freedom. Here is indeed a paradox, but it is a theological paradox, a mystery which finds its solution in the fact that God is both Creator and Lawgiver. As Creator he bestows on Man his privilege of freedom, and as Lawgiver he reveals to Man his imperative and inescapable burden of obligation. In the life-experience of the Covenant, it is the tension between the two which gives meaning to the dialogue between God and Man. Far from implying contradiction or inconsistency, the setting over against one another of a morally free agent and an omnipotent divine sovereignty is that which makes the Covenant into a real Covenant. The Kingdom of God is a real Kingdom, a monarchy, with all the exactions and demands which that could imply; but it is also a free republic in which ideally no human king could rise to assert himself and tyrannize over his fellow-men. It is only when the Covenant is secularized and the Kingdom of God, so to say, abrogated, that difficulties and inconsistencies arise. Then political societies split into Right and Left, authority and freedom are divided from one another, and the Great Powers (as at the present day) confront one another across a seemingly unbridgeable gulf. A little history would show them that they had each laid hold of a fragmented portion of Hebraism and seized upon it as the whole of truth and the whole of salvation for humanity.

In insisting upon the Hebraic sources of Hobbes's Covenant-thinking (and that of his contemporaries and successors in the history of the Social Contract) there is no intention of losing sight of the classical and medieval sanctions which were often invoked. The Law of Nature as generally understood from Aquinas onwards was a Pagan Stoic concept, as we have noted several times already, and the Social Contract was felt to be rooted, to some extent at least, in the Law of Nature. This is strongly felt in Hooker, and later in Locke and the English Liberals for all of whom the Social Contract was a kind of ratification of the immanent laws of Nature. But it is hardly the case with Hobbes or Rousseau, for whom surely the Social Contract was a dynamic, rather than a static political theory.

237

It spelled revolutionary change, rather than order and traditional privilege. And to that extent it represented the predominance of the Biblical Covenant pattern over the Stoic and medieval natural law pattern.

There can be no doubt, as far as Hobbes is concerned, that in visualizing his Covenant as the precondition of all human progress, he has come much nearer than even the Puritans to the Hebraic notion of Covenant as expressed in the formula already considered in an earlier Chapter: 'The Seven Commandments of the Sons of Noah.' To Hobbes it is clear also that the laws of Nature are no automatic property of Man. Man has natural *right*; but natural *law*—in the sense in which Hobbes employs that term—is something that he voluntarily undertakes as a creative complement to his Nature. Hobbes is in fact opposed to the medieval Thomist (and ultimately Hellenic) conception of natural law,[1] a notion dear in our period to the Cambridge Platonists. Culverwel, for instance, speaks of 'the *eternal law*, that fountain of Law, out of which you may see the *Law of Nature* bubbling out and flowing forth to the sons of men'. But Hobbes will have none of this; by rooting natural law in Covenant, it becomes dynamic; it becomes part of the history of salvation—albeit a purely secular salvation—and not a description of Man's native state as such.

Hobbes has, in fact, more in common with Jeremy Taylor than any of the Platonists here. There are some passages on 'The Law of Nature' in Taylor's *Ductor Dubitantium* which bear a striking resemblance to Hobbes's formulations in *Leviathan*. Taylor denies, for instance, the Roman idea of a universal instinctive law or *Jus Gentium* to which nations were automatically subject. This idea was going to be revived in a more philosophical form by the Deists in Taylor's day and later; but for Taylor such conceptions made nonsense of the term 'Law'. Law is enacted; it does not arise spontaneously. Further down, he makes a distinction between natural right and natural law:

> When God made man a free agent, he by nature gave him power to do all that he could desire; and all that is 'jus

---

[1] Cf. Strauss, *op. cit.*, Introduction, pp. xii-xiii.

naturale', a 'natural right or power:' and it needs no instances; for it is every thing he could in eating and drinking, and pleasures, and rule, and possession; *but the law was superinduced upon this.*[1]

This is exactly the distinction Hobbes makes in Chapter 14 between *Jus Naturale* and *Lex Naturalis*:

> The RIGHT OF NATURE, which Writers commonly call *Jus Naturale*, is the Liberty each man hath, to use his own power, as he will himselfe, for the preservation of his own Nature; that is to say, of his own Life; and consequently, of doing anything, which in his own Judgement, and Reason, hee shall conceive to be the aptest means thereunto. . . . For though they that speak on this subject, use to confound *Jus* and *Lex*, *Right* and *Law*; yet they ought to be distinguished; because RIGHT, consisteth in liberty to do, or to forbeare; Whereas LAW, determineth, and bindeth to one of them: so that Law, and Right, differ as much, as Obligation, and Liberty; which in one and the same matter are inconsistent.[2]

There can be little doubt that this represents, both for Hobbes and Taylor, an Hebraic approach to the concept of natural law. Moreover, Hobbes—to strengthen this impression—insists that the *Lex Naturalis* is the fruit of a Covenant or compact. Nor does Hobbes's 'Hebraism' stop here. It reveals itself in the way in which he visualizes his ethical system as essentially flowing out of History, and flowing back into History. This is something, as Leo Strauss has shown, which Hobbes shares with Bacon, and it can be illustrated from the very first term of Hobbes's political philosophy—viz., the primeval contract itself:

> he acknowledges that the subject of at least the fundamental part, and precisely of that fundamental part, of his political philosophy, is an history, a genesis, and not an order which is static and perfect.[3]

The emergence of Man from the State of Nature into the State of Civil Society represents in fact the beginning of an evolutionary process and points forward to a final state in which the full implications of that momentous step will have been

---

[1] Book II, ch. I, sect. xxviii, xxxiv. (*Works of Jeremy Taylor, ed. cit.*, III, 189, 190.) (My italics.)

[2] *Ed. cit.*, pp. 86-7.

[3] Strauss, p. 104.

realized in the life of men. Hobbes gives to all this, of course, an entirely secular colouring. It is not a Divine Covenant, but a human Covenant by which Man is saved. But its dynamic character is preserved. His philosophy is one of becoming rather than being; and is in that sense the rejection of the Hellenism of the Renaissance.

Hobbes's revolt against Aristotle is not (as with the naturalists) due to a desire for greater simplicity and freedom from dogma; indeed, his own system is, if anything, more rigidly dogmatic. It is due precisely to his wish to replace the static by the active, the contemplative ideal by the dynamic historical programme.[1] Significantly, when Hobbes enumerates the pleasant things in life, he omits those which Aristotle had listed, such as idleness and freedom from care. For him, the essentially pleasant things are work and progress. He maintains that 'there is no such thing as perpetuall Tranquillity of mind, while we live here; because Life it selfe is but Motion' (*Leviathan*, ch. 6). Delight, for him consists 'not in possession and enjoyment, but in successful striving and desiring'.[2] Strauss, who makes this point, surprisingly fails to point out the analogy with Hebraism, yet it is surely the Hebraic as against the Greek spirit which is at work in Hobbes. For him, as for the Jew, life is a task, not a holiday. He has no time for the cultivation of the 'beatifical vision'.[3]

At the same time, there is no intention of denying the Pagan sources of Hobbes's thinking. To attempt a balanced account of Hobbes without introducing him in the character of an 'epicurean atheist' would be to oppose the judgement of many of the wisest of his contemporaries. And in fact, there is more than a little truth in the view of Hobbes as an 'Epicurean' philosopher. The very usage of the term 'Covenant' in Hobbes has a certain Epicurean reference and basis, for the primordial compact of human society is a theme both for Epicurus and for his Roman successor, Lucretius. As for Hobbes, so for Lucretius, it is reason which suggests the *foedus* of social contract, and it is

---

[1] This makes Hobbes in a way the first of the Jacobins; he is the forerunner of the revolutionaries of the eighteenth century both in his ideal of action and in his dogmatic conception of a state made to measure. See below, p. 251, note 3.

[2] Strauss, p. 134.   [3] Cf. Basil Willey, *op. cit.*, p. 108.

the *foedus* which brings in its wake, justice, pity for the weak, and moral restraints generally. Nevertheless, the significance of the social contract for the Epicureans should not be over-stressed. It did not for them herald any marvellous transforma-tion of human affairs. It was essentially an invention for safe-guarding private interests; or perhaps, more correctly stated, it was a useful fiction for explaining the existence and necessity of civil society. With Epicurus, the basic utilitarianism, and the atomistic view of society as consisting of individuals pursuing private ends, are left intact. The compact does not create a genuine *community*. If men enter society, it is 'only for the sake of the goods which as individuals they could not obtain or could not protect'.[1] It would not be too much to say that for Epi-curus, Society is not a good in itself, so much as a necessary evil.

When we turn to Hobbes and his concept of 'Leviathan', we see that the creation of the State and of mutual obligations between men is now of immeasurably greater significance. Civil society is not merely a good in itself; it is a supreme good. The possibility which Reason affords through the drawing up of 'Articles of Peace' of an escape from the natural condition of mankind, is the precondition of all hope, all progress, and all order in human affairs. It is not merely a step forward, but the decisive step in human history. It marks the actual creation of Man as a moral being capable of undertaking social obliga-tions. Henceforward, as has been said, there can be no return to the moral chaos of the State of Nature. Nor is this obligation imposed against the will of men; were that so, human beings might one day hope to burst forth and renounce it in some catastrophic act of reversion. The marvellous part of the idea is that the Covenant is, like the Covenants in the Bible, rooted in freedom. Men freely 'devest themselves' of their hitherto guarded rights, by a mutual solemn exchange of promises. Thus, both in its moral climate and in the relation it bears to his total anthropology, the Covenant-idea in Hobbes differs from the *foedus* of Lucretius and the *syntheke* of Epicurus before him. The measure of the difference is the measure of Hobbes's debt to Hebraism.

[1] W. Windelband, *History of Philosophy* (Trans. Tufts, New York, 1931), p. 175.

IV

Hobbes is indeed a sort of apostate Jew. Ignoring the time-honoured Christian compromises, he has made his own audacious union of Hebraism and Paganism. He has used the structure of ideas, the dynamic forces latent in Hebraism to further ends which are decidedly unhebraic. His this-worldly emphasis rests on a theological foundation attributable to the Old Testament Scripture and the rediscovered Hebraism of his generation. Like Milton, he is a materialist, but the world of Matter which he reveals to us as the sole subject of our concern is not the divine world of Henry Vaughan or Jeremy Taylor in which eternity is visible in every grain of sand; it is one of *mere* corporeal substance and *mere* mathematical motion. It is a dead world from which both poetry and divinity have been banished.

The closeness of Hobbes's attachment to the other Hebraic thought-forms examined in this study may also be noted. He refuses to gloze over the absolute antithesis of life and death by introducing any Christian consolations beyond the grave. He is a mortalist—again like Milton. But of course he refuses the Hebraic 'consolations' as well, or rather the Hebraic sense of God's Providence as infinitely transcending the individual destiny of men, and of death as the final yielding up of the creature to the hand of God who made him and whose mercy embraces him in *Sheol* itself. That is to say that Hobbes lacks all the warmth and spiritual overtones of Hebraism; but he has, like Milton and Jeremy Taylor, this holistic demand for a conception of Man as a creature formed out of the dust, living and dying, and returning to the dust from which he came. In this connexion, his *Objections* to Descartes represent a Hebraic protest against the hellenistic Body/Soul dualism. Both his materialism and his mortalism thus have their affinities with similar views held by the theistic writers to whom we have pointed as examples of Hebraic thinking. He complains that the idea of necessary immortality for everyone (as distinct from a special act of grace whereby selected people are revived at the final resurrection) is an idea imported from Pagan Greek demonology according to which 'the Souls of men were substances distinct from their Bodies, and therefore that when the Body was dead, the Soule of every man, whether godly, or wicked, must subsist somewhere by vertue of its own nature' (*Leviathan*, ch. 44). His objection to this and his urgent demand for a simpler and more unified conception of human existence explains the length and detailed character of his attack on the Catholic doctrine of Purgatory—but of course his criticism has reference to reformed Christianity as well. Hobbes's account of the Fall (*ibid.*) is identical with that of Jeremy Taylor. He points out, after the manner of Taylor, that death was a necessary condition of human nature from the beginning and did not arise as a punishment for Adam's sin; the 'eternal life' offered to Adam, says Hobbes (again in exactly the same strain as Jeremy Taylor) 'was not essentiall to Humane Nature, but consequent to the vertue of the Tree of Life; whereof he had liberty to eat, as long as hee had not sinned'.

Hobbes is not unlike Milton in trying to re-interpret the New Testament in the light of the Old. Thus he points out that 'the *Soule* in Scripture, signifieth alwaies, either the Life, or the Living Creature; and the Body and Soule jointly, the *Body alive*' (*Leviathan*, ch. 44). He draws his examples from *Genesis* and *Deuteronomy*. For mortalism, he cites *Job* and *Ecclesiastes*. He then has the problem of explaining the New Testament references to everlasting Fire and the life beyond the Grave, which he does in a typically Protestant manner by asserting the right of every man to be the judge and interpreter of Scripture. 'There ought to be no Power over the consciences of men,' he declares, 'but of the word it selfe, working Faith in every one.' Following this principle, his judgement leads him to accept the texts of the Old Testament as normative on these points and those of the New as not bearing their literal or apparent meaning. So far, he does no more than Milton had done in his Divorce Tracts.

We see then that Hobbes not only derived certain basic attitudes from the prevailing climate of seventeenth-century Hebraism in England but that on important issues of doctrine, he turned for support directly and explicitly to the Hebrew Scriptures. The question that now arises is, how did he succeed in doing so whilst ignoring what to most readers of the Hebrew Scriptures would seem to be the irreducible core of Hebraism, viz., its teachings regarding the Divine Kingdom, Divine

Providence in History, and the nature and responsibilities of Man as a creature fashioned in the Divine Image? How did he leave out God? The special nature of Hobbes's use of Scripture is what we must now at once consider.

V

At this point, we should not fall into the error of supposing that Hobbes's use of Biblical evidence is mere hypocrisy and a way of throwing dust in the eyes of the theists. Edward Herbert, though a far less 'atheistic' writer than Hobbes, succeeded in presenting his views without recourse to Biblical evidence. Why did Hobbes devote such a large proportion of his book to the sifting of Biblical evidence? There can be no doubt, I feel, that for Hobbes Biblical exegesis (his own particular kind of Biblical exegesis of course) seemed to be of central significance and value. It is not to be explained simply as a convenient weapon for attacking natural theology,[1] or as a skilful and cynical way of defending a philosophical system drawn up in complete independence of Scripture. On the contrary, the Bible, *in the particular way that Hobbes read it*, provided him with a positive authority for many of the most characteristic teachings of the *Leviathan*, and indirectly, through the Covenant-religion of Puritanism, it provided, as we have seen, the dynamic background for Hobbes's concept of moral duty and of historical commitment.[2]

If Hobbes then was not simply a hypocrite, how did he succeed in ignoring what was to Milton and Jeremy Taylor so vivid a part of Hebraism, namely the sense of a pervasive Divine Justice, of an unlimited Divine Kingship which demands our first allegiance, and of the *imago dei* as the inalienable centre of the human personality? The answer to this, I feel, is that Hobbes had learned from the Puritans the trick of the disjunctive syllogism. He could dichotomize as well as any Puritan

---

[1] This is the view of Strauss, *op. cit.*, pp. 76-7. Willey goes further in denying that Hobbes's use of Scriptural proof has any real significance, *op. cit.*, p. 116.

[2] Cf. A. E. Taylor, 'An Apology for Mr. Hobbes', in *Seventeenth Century Studies Presented to Sir Herbert Grierson*, p. 141. He takes Hobbes's use of Scripture more seriously than either Strauss or Willey.

logic-chopper—hence the forensic quality of his style—and dismiss as *mere* allegory all that he could not treat baldly and simply at the literal level.[1] He employs the simplicity of the steam-roller; he irons out (in the Puritan-Ramist fashion) all the imaginative overtones of the text before him, all its spiritual suggestions, all its symbolism; and he is left with a bald, matter-of-fact statement which becomes at once amenable to the type of construction he wishes to impose upon it. His discussion, for instance, in Chapter 31 of 'The Kingdom of God by Nature' is essentially Ramist in form:—

> From the difference between the other two kinds of Gods Word, *Rationall*, and *Prophetique*, there may be attributed to God, a twofold Kingdome, *Naturall*, and *Prophetique*: Naturall, wherein he governeth as many of Mankind as acknowledge his Providence, by the naturall Dictates of Right Reason; And Prophetique, wherein having chosen out one peculiar Nation (the Jewes) for his Subjects, he governeth them, and none but them, not onely by naturall Reason, but by Positive Lawes, which he gave them by the mouths of his holy Prophets. Of the Naturall Kingdome of God I intend to speak in this Chapter.[2]

Here we observe the typical progression by means of dichotomies—in this case aimed at making a clear distinction between the special relation of God to Israel and that of God to Mankind in general. This leads up to the disjunctive, 'he governed them, and none but them'—thus enabling Hobbes to ignore the wider and more universal concept of a Divine Kingdom (as in *Psalm* cxlv, 13) or treat it as 'mere' metaphor. By another series of disjunctive arguments elsewhere, Hobbes shows that the 'Kingdom of God' even in the special sense in which this term applied to the People of Israel, came to an end in the Biblical period itself, in fact before the reign of Saul when the people refused to have 'God as King over them'. Hobbes understands this phrase in its most literal and legalistic sense and is able to conclude from it that any future resumption of the Divine Kingdom can safely be left out of account as belonging to some long-distant millennium (*Leviathan*, ch. 30).

[1] Mr. W. J. Ong argues convincingly that 'Hobbes is a Ramist at heart'. See 'Hobbes and Talon's Ramist Rhetoric in English' (*Transactions of the Cambridge Bibliographical Society*), III (1951), 260-9.

[2] *Ed. cit.*, p. 259.

He is left with the present and the foreseeable future when, for practical purposes, no Kingdom of God exists or is likely to come into existence (cf. ch. 44). This is the main point he is seeking to prove in the final Book of the *Leviathan* and in doing so, he makes use of the 'disjunctive' method of the New Testament itself. Jesus had, after all, declared, 'My Kingdom is not of this world.' This phrase might be taken (and indeed was so taken by Calvin and the Puritans) as proclaiming an otherworldly Kingship constituted by the communion of the faithful. Hobbes who operates with the material, concrete vocabulary of Hebraism, cannot accept such an otherworldly Kingdom which would be to him a nonentity, and so the phrase with its disjunctive force comes as an important reinforcement for his argument against the postulate of any Divine Kingdom whatsoever. In other words, he is using the vocabulary of Hebraism but the syntax of the Christian gospels. In this same way, he finds comfort in the Christian doctrine of the Second Coming,

> Which second coming not yet being, the Kingdome of God is not yet come, and wee are not now under any other Kings by Pact, but our Civill Sovereigns; saving onely, that Christian men are already in the Kingdome of Grace, in as much as they have already the Promise of being received at his comming againe.[1]

With the virtual suspension of the Kingdom of God, it follows logically that the system of moral law laid down in the Old Testament is no longer in force by virtue of its Divine sanction; morality and obligation have become a secular rather than a religious prerogative (see ch. 43). The State has become the 'mortall God'.

We see the same kind of procedure in Hobbes's treatment of prophecy. He shares with the Cambridge Platonist, John Smith, something of the latter's view (derived from Maimonides) of the essential normality of prophecy. Hobbes remarks,

> Neither did the other Prophets of the Old Testament pretend Enthusiasme; or, that God spake in them; but to them by Voyce, Vision, or Dream; and the *Burthen of the Lord* was not possession but Command . . .[2]

---

[1] *Ed. cit.*, p. 449 (ch. 44).
[2] *Ed. cit.*, p. 49 (ch. 8.)

But whereas John Smith can visualize human reason as a means
of revelation and the spirit of man as the candle of the Lord,
Hobbes argues in his disjunctive fashion that the 'Spirit of
God' in man means *no more than* 'a mans Spirit, enclined to
Godlinesse' (*ibid.*). He claims that prophecy does not mean
Divine Possession, but that it means either a direct message
like a telegram, literally communicated to the Prophet, or
something very ordinary, very every-day and very matter-of-
fact.[1] There are no half-way measures, no spiritual overtones.
By such rationalizations all the mysterious intimations of God
are cast out of human nature.

Hobbes uses the disjunctive Ramist method of the Puritans,
to achieve results exactly the opposite of Puritanism. The
Puritans had said, like Hobbes, that there are the elect (Israel)
and the non-elect; they would further agree that only Israel
are ruled by positive divine laws. But they would apply the
promise of the Old Testament Covenant to themselves; the
saints *are* Israel. The rest of mankind may therefore justifiably
be left out of account as reprobated to damnation. Similarly,
they argued that prophets are either possessed, in which case
they bring nothing of their own, nothing that is merely human
to their message; or else they are men speaking as men. Hobbes
takes the second alternative; they take the first. But the same
disjunctive logic is at work in both cases.

Indeed, as far as Scripture is concerned, it may be said that
Hobbes's most astonishingly original achievement was, that in
using the same intellectual instrument as Puritanism, he provided a complete working alternative to Puritanism. They
dismember the Old Testament so as to provide the Covenant-
idea (derived thence) with an immaterial content and an
unworldly object; he dismembers it so as to furnish forth a
Covenant-ideology based on purely material and worldly
considerations. In both processes the integrated spiritual meaning of the Old Testament as a message of salvation for man,
who 'in his flesh shall see God'—vanishes utterly.

[1] In ch. 36, he subdivides prophets into three types, 'prophets extraordinary' (including Samuel, Elijah, and Ezekiel); 'supreme prophets' (in
particular Moses); and 'subordinate prophets of perpetual calling' who
enjoyed no supernatural gifts but only 'the Mind and Disposition to obey'.

VI

We have said that the principle of an independent, rational interpretation of Scripture is one that Hobbes claims as part of his Protestant inheritance. It is a principle that he holds in common with Milton and the Puritans and indeed with all the theologians and philosophers we have been discussing. But there is one use of his Reason in reference to Scripture wherein Hobbes differs from anyone so far mentioned, and that is, in venturing as he does, upon a critical examination of the authority of Scripture itself. To the men of the Reformation, individual judgement was indeed to be used in weighing up and interpreting the Scripture, but the fact of its being the revealed word of God was evidenced by the 'internal testimony of the spirit'. This was the empirical basis for the Reformation as a whole. The light of Scripture was a vivid spiritual reality, not a hypothesis. To understand the nature of one's duty from this blinding revelation was the task of exegesis—and there men might employ their reason and other talents, but the reality itself was no more to be questioned than the light of the Sun to one not born blind.

Hobbes brings the rational spirit to bear upon the authority and authorship of Scripture: Moses could not have written the five Books which bear his name (ch. 33) and, indeed, the greater part of the Hebrew Bible must have been compiled and edited after the Captivity. In fact, Hobbes anticipates the Higher Criticism of the nineteenth century and, together with Spinoza, opens up the way for such writers as Richard Simon with his *Critical History of the Old Testament* (1678). The implication of such an approach (which Hobbes himself does not press however) is to cast doubt upon the complete reliability of Scripture, as a literal record of the events with which it purports to deal. We may ask (adapting some words of Epictetus) 'why do you toil for us, mustering such a heavy weight of Scripture, if only with the object of questioning the authority of Scripture itself?' Here once again, Hobbes is balancing on the brink of absurdity. His own reliance upon Scriptural proof in support of his secular, and materialist world-view, and even more, his use of the Scriptural categories of Covenant and moral obligation, bespeak the powerful effect on him of the *experience* afforded by the reading of Scripture. His rationalizing away of the authority upon which that experience is founded, reveals once again a misapplication of scientific categories to experiential realities. (The Higher Critics of the nineteenth century in Germany likewise spent their lives in a devoted study of the Bible—simply with a view to analysing away its unity!)

It is, as we have said, the Protestant principle of free, individual interpretation on which Hobbes implicitly relies for his critical approach to Scripture; but here we encounter a further paradox, for Hobbes succeeds by some fantastic transvaluation of values in making the sovereign the final judge of Scriptural authority and the truth of miracles! Scripture is implicitly to be believed when it coincides with the laws of nature; but on other matters of doctrine or fact, the sovereign's ruling must be accepted. Thus starting with the Protestant affirmation of the right of individual judgement (whereby he justifies his raising of the question of Scriptural authority and literal credence), he proceeds to solve the problem by surrendering the right of individual judgement to the absolute authority of the State! Mr. Zagorin similarly draws attention to the contradiction implied by the rational decisions which, for Hobbes, bring the State into existence, and the irrational dependence on authority once it is there![1]

We are constantly returning to this central tangle of paradoxes which lies at the heart of Hobbes's system whether considered as anthropology, political science, or Biblical exegesis. To state this inner contradiction in its simplest terms it is the clash between a group of vital compulsions on the one hand and a deadening and stultifying principle of authority on the other. The former is nourished by the vital stimulus of Renaissance Humanism and of Reformation Biblicism, together with the sense of expansion and power afforded by the New Philosophy; the latter is summed up by the term, *Leviathan*, symbolizing the need to govern and control these vital forces in the interest of human civilization and survival, and, in particular, in the interest of social stability and order. The point of intersection between these two psychological forces is provided by the notion of Covenant; by virtue of this Covenant

[1] P. Zagorin, *A History of Political Thought in the English Revolution* (London, 1954), p. 183.

man's rights and his freedoms are invested in the new structure of external authority.

Hebraism, also in its Covenant doctrine, offered to the men of the Renaissance a principle of order and authority, and a possibility of progress; it confronted the New Philosophy with a unique term—Creation; it confronted Divinity with a second unique term—Revelation; and it confronted Man in his political relations with a third unique term—Salvation. These terms were not exactly new to the Christian tradition of the West, but what was of immense and revolutionary significance was the Hebraic way of seeing all these three terms as constituting one unbroken process. The Creator God is at the same time the God who reveals His will to Man and who points the road to Salvation. And the comprehensive word of power by which these three terms are constituted into one process is the term 'Covenant'—for it is the Covenant which at once constitutes and ratifies the existence of the Creature as an independent unit, which confronts the Creature with the challenge of the Divine law, and which points out to the Creature its purposive end in the plan of Providence. The consummation of the Covenant is intimated in such words as peace, salvation, and the 'knowledge' of God. It is essentially a doctrine of Hope based upon an interpretation of History as sustained, or rather summoned into motion, by a Divine promise and a Divine purpose, for mankind at large.

Now when we turn to Hobbes, we note immediately the absence of any wider liberating hope to raise and rejoice the spirit of Man; and this lack follows from the essential nature of the Covenant as Hobbes understood it. To Hobbes, Man is created evil; by means of a political formula which his reason inspires him to construct, he makes his life worth living. He is saved by the Social Contract. But only just. There is, in the strict terms of the Covenant, no hope and no promise—only the possibility of a more complete realization of the political order. Why should this be? Why should the term Covenant be a word of power and promise in Hebraism, but a stultifying and deadening word in Hobbism, a mere counsel of despair. The reason is that in the Old Testament formula, it is a Covenant with the Lord of life; for Hobbes, it is in the most literal sense, a Covenant with death. It is the fear of death, according to Hobbes, which inspires men to leap out of the 'meer state of nature' and commit their fortunes to the demands of the moral law. It is the fear of death, not the hope of a more abundant life, which awakens Man from his egotistic dreams and vanities[1] and urges him to the exercise of his reason. Reason is our highest attribute (here Hobbes is at one with Milton and the Platonists) but it is not that faculty whereby Man is granted the knowledge of God; it is, stated in its highest terms, the faculty whereby we guard ourselves from the danger of a violent death.[2]

Here we must locate the central absurdity of Hobbes's secular philosophy. He cannot escape from the vicious circle of Man's own existence. The object of human existence is simply human existence. Our reason ultimately is not there to save us—in the sense of carrying us forward—but to keep us alive. But this on the other hand immediately takes away the sanction from that important historical emphasis which we have noted in Hobbes. For him, achievement, progress, and continuous effort are, as in the Hebraic view, paramount values. It is because of its lack of historical dimension primarily that he had departed from Aristotelianism. Indeed, we may say, that his Hebraic zeal for this world as the arena of creative effort will not permit him to remain satisfied with mere existence. *Leviathan*, whilst logically securing mere existence, illogically comes to imply progress and salvation; it becomes a sort of inverted Messianism.[3] Already in the *De Cive*, the accent of Messianism

[1] Strauss, *op. cit.*, pp. 18-19.

[2] *Ibid.*, p. 17.

[3] Hobbes's significance as the forerunner of those movements in the eighteenth and nineteenth century which J. L. Talmon has characterized as 'Totalitarian Democracy' (see *The Origins of Totalitarian Democracy*, London, 1952) deserves to be emphasized. The characteristic of that movement was a kind of secularized messianism, a mystique of progress (leading to a classless society, absolute justice, or absolute human perfection, etc.). Talmon does not overlook Hobbes's position at the historical beginning of this movement (*ibid.*, pp. 263-5) but unfortunately underestimates his significance and regards his system as essentially static rather than dynamic. A deeper study of Hobbes from the point of view of Talmon's thesis would probably lead to some interesting conclusions, not the least amongst which might be the discovery that Hobbes provides the essential link between the Biblical messianic ideal and its secularized Jacobin form; indeed, this present Chapter aims to portray Hobbes's political ideology as a kind of bastard Hebraism in this sense.

can be heard as an undertone of his political science. If the rules of human nature were as distinctly known as geometry, he tells us there in a significant phrase, 'mankind should enjoy such an immortal peace, that . . . there would hardly be left any pretence for war'. This is perhaps the main difference between Hobbes and the philosopher whom he most resembles in other respects, viz., Epicurus. Both propound a philosophy which leaves no room for any divine agency;[1] but lurking behind Hobbes's system is the driving force of a religion of Creation, Revelation, and Salvation.

Reason for Hobbes, is, by definition, inescapably human in origin and character; in fact its function is to guarantee human existence and nothing more. Nevertheless, owing to the pressure of Messianism which operates (one should perhaps say, sub-consciously) upon Hobbes, Reason in spite of its *necessarily* human character, must be given Divine powers and honours. With it, through Science, Man comes to achieve control over the physical universe, and with it, through politics, he comes to achieve control over his own nature, and may entertain the hope of ultimate complete salvation. The boundless arrogance of this view (together with its boundless absurdity) is the distinctive feature of Hobbes's rationalism:

> Let your reason move upon the deep of your own cogitations and experience; those things that lie in confusion must be set asunder, distinguished, and every one stamped with its own name set in order; that is to say, your method must resemble that of the creation.[2]

Professor D. G. James, commenting on this passage, remarks 'And when we consider his philosophy, do we not see him near to ascribing to the mind the actual creation of the universe?'[3] This is the utmost limit of human pride; it is a prodigious blasphemy, ruinous and insane. But it is a blasphemy impossible to a mere Pagan whose universe is static and non-created; it is

[1] Cf. C. T. Harrison, 'Bacon, Hobbes, Boyle and the Ancient Atomists', *Harvard Studies and Notes in Philology and Literature*, XV (1933), 206.

[2] From the Epistle, *To the Reader*, prefixed to *Elements of Philosophy*, in *Works*, ed. Molesworth, I, xiii.

[3] D. G. James, *The Life of Reason* (London, 1949), p. 20.

only possible to one who inhabits a divinely created universe, the norm of which is dynamic change, and whose predetermined end, Salvation. In short, such a blasphemy is only possible to the Pagan who has entered the Sanctuary and there laid his hand upon the Ark of the Covenant.

XV

THE PROMISED LAND

Bacon, like *Moses*, led us forth at last,
The barren Wilderness he past,
Did on the very Border stand
Of the blest promis'd Land . . .
                    A. Cowley, *Ode to the Royal Society.*

I

IN THE YEARS after the Restoration of King Charles II,
Hobbes and Hobbism had become a palace-joke, but the returning royalists had brought back with them the brilliant and
apparently invincible ethical geometry of Descartes. And, as
John Ray later remarked, the Cartesians had in some ways outstripped the 'atomick Atheists' themselves. The positivism of
Hobbes remained as an essential ingredient in the whole
Augustan position. His view of the insignificance of the Fancy
and of the necessity of separating it from Judgement in all
serious discourse, is one of the bases of the post-Restoration
theory of communication as later expressed by Locke.[1] His
disenchanted view of human nature and his conception of the
Covenant as the only desperate cure for the malady is echoed
in unexpected ways. In the Restoration Comedy of Congreve
and Wycherley, we see Man through the eyes of a mid-century
Hobbesian materialist. We see love reduced to lust, the hero
replaced by the gentil-homme. The world in which Dorimant
and Mirabell unscrupulously hunt their satisfactions is at once
a reflection of contemporary court-society (exaggerated a little

---

[1] I have in mind the long section in Book III of his *Essay Concerning Human
Understanding* (1690) devoted to the problems of verbal communication.
In it he makes the same fallacious parallel with mathematics that Bacon
and Hobbes had made before him. He also has some interesting general
comment on verbal ambiguities. These are essentially an abuse of the
nature of language. It is, he tells us, a 'plain cheat and abuse' when words
sometimes stand for one thing, and sometimes for another. How would he
have reacted, one wonders, to Mr. Empson's 'Seven Types of Ambiguity'?

here and there for dramatic purposes) and of Hobbes's State of Nature. We may even discern something like Hobbes's Social Contract in the way in which the State of War is suspended, namely by a treaty of marriage. Confronted by a Harriet or a Millamant, the hero cannot achieve his object except by coming to terms, terms which, like Hobbes's Articles of Peace, limit the power but guarantee the interests of either party. Locke's version of the Social Contract is, of course, significantly different from that of Hobbes. Civil Government is based on contract, but natural law has a prior existence. It is, as for the Stoics, a datum of human nature. Locke is thus a liberal; he believes in a native human goodness.

Locke with his easier more tolerant attitudes represents, we may say, the Whig reaction against the absolutism and dogmatism of Hobbes; in this he is typical of the climate of ideas in the later seventeenth century. That was an age altogether more tranquil and less problematical in its characteristic statements and attitudes than the mid-seventeenth century. Dogmatism and enthusiasm were frowned upon, whether it was the 'epicurean' dogmatism of Hobbes or the theological dogmatism of the Puritans. The Restoration of Charles II was greeted both in the ecclesiastical and political spheres as an opportunity to achieve a region of calm weather after the upheavals of the Commonwealth. A less obsessive concern with the soul and with man's immortal destiny was the appropriate corollary of a political order which had eschewed all messianic aims and ambitions. In these circumstances we would be right in supposing also that Hebraism with its doctrine of Creation, Revelation, and Salvation would only faintly be echoed. In the sermons of John Tillotson, a typical divine of the new age, we may take the spiritual temperature of the post-Restoration age with fair accuracy:

> This question, whether the world was created and had a beginning, or not? is a question concerning an ancient matter of fact, which can only be decided these two ways; by testimony, and by probabilities of reason. Testimony, is the principal argument in a matter of this nature, and if fair probabilities of reason concur with it this argument hath all the strength it can have: now both these are clearly on the affirmative side of the question, viz., that the world was created, and had a beginning.

1. Testimony; of which there be two kinds, divine and human etc.[1]

We note here the Ramist dichotomies, the methodical progress of the idea, and the lack of imaginative vibration typical of the prose of the Puritan logic-choppers earlier on. But Tillotson is no Puritan; the question of whether the world was or was not created is a question that a sensible man may settle for himself without worrying too much about it; God and the Devil are not wrestling for his soul and pulling opposite ways at some text of Scripture as in the nightmare visions of Bunyan. Bunyan wrote his Autobiography after the Restoration; nevertheless, he is spiritually akin to the men of the mid-century, whilst Tillotson is, like Dryden and the men of the Royal Society, spiritually of the post-Restoration. Man was saved by good sense and reasonableness rather than by special Grace operating according to the arbitrary decree of Predestination. Tillotson's theology is that of the successful bourgeois who has been bitten once by Puritanism and does not intend to be bitten a second time:

> In a word, our main interest is to be as happy as we can, and as long as it is possible. . . . This is the wisdom of religion, that upon consideration of the whole, and casting up all things together, it does advise and lead us to our best interest.[2]

It is clear also that Tillotson has no time for the wingy mysteries of Thomas Browne[3] or the moral passions of Milton. The tone is one of cultured detachment combined with practical common sense. Blake would have said that here is the spectral decline of the Four Zoas, 'Entering into the Reasoning Power, forsaking Imagination.' It is the fulfilment of that process whereby Albion becomes increasingly separated from Jerusalem, 'For now the Starry Heavens are fled from the mighty limbs of Albion.'[4]

The prose-style of Tillotson is non-poetical; in this he represents a general trend towards transparency, austerity, and

---

[1] *Works* (London, 1742), I, 17.
[2] Cited by Louis G. Locke, *Tillotson, A Study in Seventeenth Century Literature*, Anglistica Series, No. 4 (Copenhagen, 1954), pp. 66-7.
[3] Cf. *Ibid.*, p. 105.
[4] *Jerusalem*, 74, 75.

rational self-possession. Dryden, whose own prose gives us the new ideal in its most artistically refined and attractive form, acknowledged a debt to Tillotson as a model for prose-writing. Both Tillotson and Dryden were connected with the Royal Society—of which indeed one of the moving spirits was Tillotson's step-father-in-law, Bishop Wilkins[1]—and there can be no doubt that they were both in sympathy with the linguistic aims of the Royal Society as expressed by Bishop Thomas Sprat in his *The History of the Royal Society* (1667).[2] The Society aimed at simplifying (and one may add, sterilizing) the oratorical style of its members, so as to render their statements and reports more plain, functional, and unpoetic, all of which shows us the coming-of-age of the scientific-Baconian demand for plain prose and the final banishment of the Idols of the Market-Place from the affairs of men. In Locke's *Essay Concerning Human Understanding*, at the end of the century, the new ideal of unambiguous verbal communication achieves its final philosophical endorsement and authority. In these respects, we may say that the Restoration world portrays the negative results of the ferment created by Hobbes, by the Puritans, and the Baconian scientists. Their moral intensities, their sense of a religious or pseudo-religious driving force are left tactfully behind, whilst their positivism, their tendency to expel the spiritual and imaginative factors from the business of this world are grasped as a satisfactory solution for many difficulties.

II

Perhaps no one reveals the new sense of values better than Dryden. His religious outlook whether in the *Religio Laici* or later in his 'Catholic' *The Hind and the Panther*, is marked by an unwillingness to raise fundamental issues of belief. He wishes

---

[1] On Wilkins's interest in plain prose, and for some valuable comments on the history of 'scientific prose' in the seventeenth century, see D. Bush, *English Literature in the Earlier Seventeenth Century*, pp. 270-1.

[2] One of the chief aims of the Society, according to Sprat, was 'to separate the knowledge of Nature, from the colours of rhetoric, the devices of Fancy, or the delightful deceit of Fables'. The bourgeois impulse is made clear when he speaks of their preference for 'the Language of Artizans, Countrymen, and Merchants, before that of Wits, or Scholars'. Cf. ch. 2, above, p. 27.

to be undisturbed and to lean comfortably upon the tradition of the Anglican Church compromise (*Religio Laici*) or upon the even less exacting traditions of Catholicism (*The Hind and the Panther*). All reformatory zeal is quenched. The whole religious temperature of the age has fallen. Moreover, as an indication of this, there is less of a literary and imaginative debt to the Bible even in Dryden's religious writings. Dryden is near enough to the Biblical religion of the Reformation to feel that some kind of Biblical doctrine is necessary to salvation, but he shows the reaction against the unhealthy Biblicism of the Puritans (with their concentration upon Scripture's literal and unfailing application to themselves) by urging that an agreed interpretation by the Church and State should take the place of the soul searchings and polemics of the past. England had had an excess of light and an excess of depth and what was now called for was a spirituality somewhat shallower and somewhat less brilliantly illuminated. Dryden's verses with their neatness and urbanity struck exactly the required note.

In his witty and satirical, *Absalom and Achitophel* (1681), Dryden did not merely produce a parody of such majestic epic poems as those of Milton, but he also produced a parody of the whole tradition of the Scriptural analogy, whereby pamphleteers and pulpit orators since the days of the Armada and before[1] had compared political events in England with the various episodes in the Biblical chronicles. The England-Israel analogy goes back at least to Foxe's *Martyrs* and it receives a special urgency (as we have said earlier) in the writings of Milton. Dryden, in his ingenious, but essentially witty and non-serious way of relating the palace-intrigue of Shaftesbury and Monmouth to the revolt of Absalom against David, is turning this tradition up on its head. As in so many of the sermons of an earlier day, London is compared to Jerusalem, but this time the reference to the city of Jebusites is intended to amuse; nevertheless, the use of this careful system of equivalences (Charles—David; Shaftesbury—Achitophel; etc.) is dependent for its full significance on the pre-existence of the analogy at a more serious level. In the *Eikon Basilike*, Charles I had been *seriously* compared to David, but Dryden's poem is a poem of

[1] For parallels in earlier Puritan pamphlet-literature, see R. F. Jones, 'The Originality of *Absalom and Achitophel*', *M.L.N.*, XLVI (1931), 211.

Biblical analogies to end all Biblical analogies. It is intended to *explode* the tradition; the men of the new age are made conscious of the fact that the values they respect and desire are essentially the non-heroic and non-spiritual values of a people unburdened with a religious mission.[1] Like the Philistines in the Book of *Samuel* they are anxious to get rid of the Ark of the Covenant.

Another interesting example of the secularized, non-spiritual use of Biblical material is provided in some of Cowley's poems. In *Davideis* (1656), we have a Biblical poem in which the poet's relation to his Biblical theme clearly lacks any existential content. It is clear from his *Preface* that he finds the Biblical episodes lively and dramatic; but they do not call for any gifts of sensibility other than those demanded for the treatment of themes from Pagan antiquity. Wit and elegance are appropriate in both cases. We cannot take very seriously Cowley's opening Invocation to the Holy Spirit,

> Ev'n *Thou* my breast with such blest rage inspire,
> As mov'd the tuneful strings of *Davids Lyre*.

By comparison with the thrilling earnestness of Milton, this is mere bombast. But of course Cowley does not *intend* the same kind of seriousness. His use of the Bible as the subject of his poem is essentially an exercise in virtuosity comparable with his handling of Pindar's ode-form, and his address to the Holy Spirit is merely a witty translation, into Biblical terms, of the conventional invocation to the Muse. It is not intended as a call from the soul's depths, because such depths are not particularly relevant to the kind of poetry Cowley wanted to write. Spiritual compulsion was very well but it was more important to be 'in good humor'.[2]

---

[1] Dryden's tone is perhaps not that of pure parody. To his conception of royalty (especially in the final lines celebrating the glories of the Stuart dynasty) there does cling something of the idea of Divine Right, and the Biblical analogy of David comes to reinforce Dryden's basically Tory conception of royalty and royal privilege. Disraeli in a later age was to take up this Tory strain and convert it into a political ideology based on a pseudo-Hebraic notion of election and mission.

[2] Cf. Cowley's Preface of 1656. (See *Poems*, ed. Waller, Cambridge, 1905, p. 8.)

Cowley was, in 1656, amazingly prophetic of the new order of things after the Restoration. His 'modernity' is well exemplified in this same poem by his account of the college of prophets at Rama. This becomes very much a School of Natural Philosophy, where, in the late-seventeenth-century manner, the prophets show their skill as naturalists and geometers.

> *Mahol* th'inferior worlds fantastick face,
> Through all the turns of *Matters Maze* did trace,
> Great *Natures* well-set *Clock* in pieces took;
> On all the *Springs* and smallest wheels did look
> Of *Life* and *Motion*; and with equal art
> Made up again the *Whole* of ev'ry *Part*.
> The *Prophet Gad* in *learned Dust* designes
> Th'immortal solid rules of fanci'ed *Lines*.
> Of *Numbers* too th'*unnumbred Wealth* he showse,
> And with them far their *endless journey* goes.

Again, this is only half serious. It is the fashionable poet showing how he can be wittily trivial where the theologians had made such heavy going. On the other hand, Cowley here shares something of that rationalization of Scripture which we noted in the Cambridge Platonists. They too, as we saw in connexion with John Smith's Discourse 'Of Prophecy', looked upon the prophets as philosophers, men of reason—this was part of their reaction against Puritanism with its radical division of natural from supernatural gifts. Cowley shared this normalization of Scripture, and he shared with the Platonists their reaction against Puritanism, but he did not share the non-rational elements in their outlook. We remember Smith's recognition of the place of imagination and intuition in the prophetic experience; with this kind of enthusiasm Cowley will have nothing to do—his rationalization of Scripture is more radical in the manner of Hobbes for whom inspiration was a word of no meaning and for whom possession of the Holy Spirit meant simply an inclination to obedience.

The poem of Cowley's which provides, I think, the most remarkable example of his secularization of Biblical images, and his secularization in particular of the Old Testament theology of Covenant, is his *Ode to the Royal Society*, from which we might consider the two following extracts. The first celebrates the Baconian revolt against scholastic authority:

> From these and all long Errors of the way,
> In which our wandring Praedecessors went,
> And like th'old *Hebrews* many years did stray
> In Desarts but of small extent,
> *Bacon*, like *Moses*, led us forth at last,
> The barren Wilderness he past,
> Did on the very Border stand
> Of the blest promis'd Land,
> And from the Mountains Top of his Exalted Wit,
> Saw it himself, and shew'd us it.

In the next stanza he apostrophizes the *virtuosi* of the Royal Society in hyperbolical terms:—

> Methinks, like *Gideon's* little Bank,
> God with Design has pickt out you,
> To do these noble Wonders by a Few:
> When the whole Host he saw, They are (said he)
> Too many to O'rcome for Me;
> And now he chuses out his Men,
> Much in the way that he did then:
> Not those many whom he found
> Idely extended on the ground,
> To drink with their dejected head
> The Stream just so as by their Mouths it fled:
> No, but those Few who took the waters up,
> And made of their laborious Hands the Cup.

The comparison of Bacon to Moses of course begins as a witty analogy in which the elegant appositeness of the allusions (the wilderness, the promised land, *Pisgah*) strikes the fancy. It is essentially, as with Dryden's *Absalom and Achitophel*, a fustian use of Biblical material, and, as with Dryden, the audacity of the comparison between the (comparatively) trivial and the sacred, is intended as a means of discountenancing the serious application of Biblical imagery to contemporary affairs. From this point of view, it becomes impossible to think of Englishmen as being chosen and led into the Promised Land in the way that the ancient Israelites were led by Moses. In the second extract, however, we may note a certain ambiguity in the use of the analogy. The imagery of election, privilege, and historical effort towards a destined consummation is, from one angle, mere fancy; but from another angle, it is a judicious comment on the Royal Society. We smile at 'Gideon's little band' if we respond correctly to the poem, but we do not smile, or at any rate, not in quite the same way, at the 'noble wonders' to be achieved by the *virtuosi*. A good poem (according to Hobbes) must have both 'Fancy' and 'Judgement' and here, in Cowley's concept of the mission of the Royal Society, the kernel of 'Judgement' in this particular poem, is to be found. The phrase 'God with Design has pickt out you' is not without its undertone of genuine conviction; it carries with it the idea—faintly entertained it is true—of the scientists being elected, being the chosen race in fact. Gideon's men lifting the water up in their hands is a stroke of Fancy quickly forgotten as the poem proceeds; the 'laborious hands' of the experimental scientists are not— they belong to the basic theme.

Cowley has in this poem, betrayed something of the basic faith of the Baconian scientific movement. It is a movement of the spirit; a pseudo-messianic enterprise. It gains its inspiration from the Hebraic notion of election but stripped of its religious connotations and only retaining its Biblical vocabulary by a fanciful association of ideas. The driving-force behind it is nevertheless the millennial hope of a world gloriously transformed through the efforts of those called to the great undertaking. All this is not unlike the Puritan sense of election finding expression in a more worldly form and with a greater stress upon practical achievement. Both ideologies are at a great distance from genuine Hebraism, but in one important respect the post-Baconian formula of Cowley is more radically separated from Hebraism than that of the Puritans or indeed of Bacon himself; for with Cowley the serious attachment to the word of Scripture as the life-giving word has gone. The transvaluation of values is complete. For all its distortion of Hebraism, Puritanism was a Biblical Faith; but in the reaction against Puritanism which we have seen exemplified in the extracts quoted above, the secular mind of the century lays hold of the zeal and energy of the Puritans, but abandons their piety and their faith. They dip their laborious hands into the river, but the river is no longer, as in Milton's poem 'Siloa's brook that flow'd Fast by the Oracle of God.'

III

The utilization of the energies of Hebraism or of pseudo-Hebraism without its terminology and reference is the fruit of that ultimate synthesis achieved at the end of the seventeenth century. Here is the motive power of a Biblical religion without the Bible, the final face of Albion when stripped of his poetry and his starry robe. Newton in the General Scholium which concludes the third Book of his *Principia* expresses many of the same attitudes and beliefs that we found in Boyle and the pious naturalists of the previous generation. He too stands in veneration before the divine mysteries which the reason of the philosopher cannot wholly penetrate. Like Cudworth and Boyle he states his belief in the absolute relevance to Physics of Final Causes, for by them we come to apprehend the divine Wisdom as expressed in the universe. He adheres still, though not with quite the same conviction as his predecessors, to the Hebraic notion of the Temple of Nature. But the imaginative colouring, the personal act of devotion, the warmth and eloquence of the Cambridge Platonists are lacking. A more austere and impersonal statement of faith than the General Scholium can hardly be conceived. The scientific and the devotional functions of the mind have been separated; heart and brain no longer beat as one after the manner of Thomas Browne; there is no chance of poetry suddenly peeping through in the act of meditation, as the imagination takes fire from some observed phenomenon or some sudden mathematical insight.

But the most characteristic exponent of Albion in his final incarnation is not Newton, but John Locke. There are many affinities between Locke and Milton. His liberal 'Arminian' outlook in politics has, as Basil Willey points out, a Miltonic colouring.[1] His belief in human goodness and reasonableness echoes the Hebraic optimism of Milton in his account of human nature. He echoes the Cambridge Platonists (and of course *Proverbs* xx, 27) when he speaks of Reason as 'the candle of the Lord set up by himself in men's minds'. But such Biblical touches are rare. In the main Locke achieves the manner and

---

[1] It is not necessary to agree with Willey who goes so far as to treat Locke as a sort of late seventeenth-century Milton 'without the garland and the singing robes'. *The Seventeenth Century Background*, p. 267.

tone of Biblical humanism without the Bible and without any conscious or explicit reference to Hebraism.

We spoke of the pseudo-Hebraism of Hobbes as an example of the extreme image of Albion fallen away from Jerusalem and yet clearly revealing his kinship with her. In a way Locke is less extreme in that he retains the liberal kindly humanism, the ethical optimism of Hooker and Milton. Like his contemporaries, Bishop Lucy, Filmer, and Eachard, he re-asserts in contradistinction to Hobbes something of the Hebraic principle of man's congenital goodness as a creature fashioned in the Divine Image.[1] But in another sense, Locke gives us a more extreme image of Albion than Hobbes, for he carries over many of the basic presuppositions of Hobbism without the Biblical colour and imaginative reference; he no longer reveals the kinship. His association with Hobbes's materialism is so close that there is even a suggestion at one point (*Essay*, Book IV, ch. 3) that he is prepared to accept the Hobbesian notion of a material soul. In his search for 'clear and distinct' ideas, he reduces all our knowledge to Sensation and Reflection, that is to say, to the evidence provided by our senses and our reasoning faculties. He shores up the traditional piety which he has inherited by an appeal to 'assent founded on the highest Reason', but having denied that we have in us any innate or organic spiritual knowledge and having dismissed the evidence of the Imagination, he is left without any possibility of defining this 'highest Reason'. The phrase is thus no more than a pious gesture; and in consequence, Sensation and Reflection are left as the final arbiters not only in matters of scientific fact but also in the region of Faith and Revelation (*Essay*, Book IV, ch. 18, 19). This is clearly in the line of descent from Hobbes and as clearly leads us forward to Hume's *Essay on Miracles*. But Hobbes had been closely enough bound to the Biblicism of his epoch to be able to devote himself heart and soul to the exegetical task of sifting and analysing Biblical texts, if only with the object of casting doubt on their authority! Locke has not quite this same interest, and the result is that his reliance on Scripture is tenuous in the extreme. He shows how Arminianism when

[1] Cf. J. Bowle, *Hobbes and his Critics* (London, 1951), pp. 100, 102, 112. For a treatment of Locke's Arminian connexions, see M. Cranston, 'John Locke: the Exile' *The Listener*, LII (London, 1954), 759-60.

allied to the secularism of Hobbes finally defeats itself and produces a system which is not recognizably Scriptural at all.

Finally, we may isolate a Baconian strain in Locke. He has something of the Baconian 'energy of action' which is lacking in more contemplative philosophers, something of that practical, progressive Puritanical spirit which we have witnessed in Bacon. (It is in this indirect way that the influence of Puritanism makes itself felt in Locke.)

> Apart from the next world, we need trouble our heads with nothing but the history of nature and an inquiry into the quality of things in the mansion of the universe and being well skilled in the knowledge of material causes and effects of things in our power, directing our thoughts to the improvement of such arts and inventions, engines and utensils as might best contribute to our conveniency and delight.

In spite of his liking for Boyle and Pococke, Hales and Chillingworth, Locke's writings everywhere reveal the fundamentally Baconian drift of his Philosophy. God is admitted to the world as a designer or architect but the work that we are to do in the world is not primarily His work. It is not to be supposed that 'the Earth is the Lord's and the fulness thereof'. We are the practical masters; the ends to which the whole Creation moves are our ends.

Locke does not arrogantly assert the Faustian dream of Baconian science; from Boyle, he has learned philosophical modesty, and from Whichcot and Cudworth, that our naturalism is not to be too rudely separated from our theology. But in his unobtrusive (and perhaps for that reason, supremely effective) way he completes Bacon's work. In his 'Epistle' prefixed to the *Essay*, he exclaims:—

> In an age that produces such masters as the great Huygenius and the incomparable Mr. Newton, with some others of that strain, it is ambition enough to be employed as an under-labourer in clearing the ground a little, and removing some of the rubbish that lies in the way to knowledge.

To which world then, does Locke belong? He is not citizen of Athens. It is true that he stresses liberty, wisdom, magnanimity, and the culture of reason, but at the same time, he abandons the wider aims of *philosophia*, as a wisdom beyond and above the mere visible phenomena and mere practical work, and instead as an under-labourer submits philosophy to the narrow ends of natural science, cutting away from it its ideal purposes and its wider horizons. Nor is Locke a citizen of Jerusalem. He has a driving purpose, indeed, and a power of narrowing all ends to one, but that one end is not the consuming moral purpose of Hebraism, with its concentrated intensity and its deliberate subordination of all particular ends to the will of God. Nor is it even buttressed as with Bacon by the tropological use of Hebrew phrase and image. The temple of philosophy is not Solomon's House any longer, but some perfectly neat and well-swept Queen Anne mansion, built in the neo-classical style. There are no Gothic traceries on the ceiling, no Biblical legends on the walls, and no stained-glass windows with pre-figurative Biblical illustrations. All is well-lit, regular, and unadorned.

Locke in short is neither of Athens nor Jerusalem. He belongs to that *tertium quid*, Albion. Here, as in Blake's mythology, Albion having forsaken the beauty, the imagery, and the idealism of Jerusalem, weds himself instead to Vala, symbol of natural morality, natural religion, and the rejection of vision.[1] To adapt a phrase of Hobbes, Locke is the ghost of seventeenth-century Hebraism, sitting crowned upon the ruins thereof.

[1] These phrases are culled from D. J. Sloss and J. P. R. Wallis, *The Prophetic Writings of William Blake* (Oxford, 1926), II, 245 f. (s.v. *Vala*).

EPILOGUE

I

TO USE the fine distinctions of literary criticism to deal with a matter so manifest as the influence of Hebraism on Western culture, and then to confine the inquiry to one century, namely the seventeenth, must seem like using a candle to seek a pebble on the shore: the means employed is over-delicate and the object of the search insufficiently rare and unexpected. However, if we consider with Blake that there may be a world in a grain of sand, it may be worth while picking up the pebble and looking at it in a new way and by a new light, and as for the special interest of the seventeenth century, perhaps the foregoing chapters have sufficed to show that the challenge of Hebraism was, in that century, peculiarly concentrated and many-sided. It came from the direction of Theology, as well as from Anthropology and Natural Science. Likewise the response to the challenge was of unusual interest, for defence-mechanisms were invented in that century which were intended to secure for their inventors the maximum benefits of Hebraism, in particular the driving zeal, the concept of work, and the image of a world full of creative power and energy, whilst releasing them from the moral obligations affirmed by Hebraism, from its more disturbing and humbling implications. One of these defence mechanisms was a mode of discourse, coupled with a new theory of communication, which were intended to eliminate from serious discussion of Man, God, and Nature, the mystery, the grandeur, and the beauty of a universe which might be felt to be the Kingdom of God. This is a literary factor, and it is for this reason that the method of literary analysis and evaluation has been stressed. But the implication of the argument has been that the literary situation was the index to deeper movements of the spirit that were then taking place. 'The eye altering alters all.'

The impoverishment of vision, the separation of Reason and Imagination, of Prose and Poetry, is at bottom a process of spiritual disunification, a deviation from an integrated picture of the universe. This has been the argument of this book, but the present study has not been based on the theory of the neo-scholastic critics, that spiritual unity and integration belong to the pattern of thought inherited from the Christian Middle Ages; on the contrary, if the Christian Middle Ages had been our theme, we would have been bound to point out, along with glimpses of unity and wholeness, the many extraordinary dualisms of thought and feeling characteristic of that epoch, the separation of worldly from other-worldly concerns, the unnatural and (I fear) ungodly asceticism of many of its forms of piety, and the growth in that era of theories of double-truth. The investigation of such phenomena would surely have resulted in the recognition of a 'dissociation of sensibility' as radical as that which is said to have occurred in the seventeenth century. No, if the seventeenth-century writers discussed here, such as Herbert, Jeremy Taylor, Milton, Henry More, and Thomas Browne were capable of a certain spiritual integration, it was because in that century the sense of expansion and hope which we associate with the Renaissance and the new Science, the new intoxicating belief in the value of our earthly existence, which these encouraged, fused temporarily with the realism of Hebrew truth as newly recovered and brought forward in the Reformation.

We are thus not here concerned with the waning light of the Middle Ages, but with a light which smoulders only dimly in the centuries before the Reformation and then bursts into a bright but brief incandescence in the seventeenth century. True it is that then it was partially extinguished, but it has flared up again from time to time since, and is no doubt capable of doing so in the future. However much men may strive to disrupt and divide their inner vision, traces of an integrated and wholesome world will remain. In the centuries following the period under review, such a vision was attested intermittently by poets such as Blake and Whitman, and prose writers such as Ruskin and Matthew Arnold. Of course, all the negative trends of the seventeenth century were also continued. In our own day, the materialism of Hobbes is echoed in the Marxist ideology, in Freudian psychology, and in modern logical positivism. Such avenues have not been explored in these pages, nor can more be done in these concluding paragraphs than to indicate the lines which lead out from the seventeenth century towards our own time.

II

To begin with the moral philosophers. Voltaire and the French rationalists of the eighteenth century took their stand upon the same ground as Locke and Bacon and indeed looked back to them for inspiration. There was (in England and elsewhere) eighteenth-century liberalism with its roots in the work of Locke and the Deists and their idea of a static natural order of goodness. This reveals itself in the Whig tradition (in England), and the Liberal, *laissez-faire* inheritance in general. The shallow optimism of Pangloss is reflected (with a more subtle shading) in the writings of Shaftesbury, for whom Man is a naturally friendly animal and 'society is the true state of Nature'. Shaftesbury has his links with the Cambridge Platonists,[1] but like Locke, he is no true inhabitant of Jerusalem. He represents indeed the more humane side of the eighteenth-century temperament, but basically he carries forward from the Stoics the ideal of human self-sufficiency expressed in the old Roman motto, *nec te quaeseveris extra*. His spiritual ancestors are Seneca and Polonius.

Eighteenth-century liberalism suggests to us the non-dynamic ideal of a society hypnotized by the idea of reason, order, and liberty. But we should not be deceived by this Augustan exterior—the revolutionary ferment was active beneath. As far as the Lockian-liberalist school was concerned, it expressed itself in an insatiable zeal for economic, commercial, and scientific progress which was eventually (in the Industrial Revolution) to transform the face of England and the world. That was the fruit of a secularized Hebraism at one level. Then there was Hobbism.

The inspiration of Hobbes (direct or indirect) is undeniably present in the eighteenth century. Among the utilitarians such as, Helvetius, Bentham, and Paley, Man was regarded as a machine whose actions were determined by the relative pro-

---

[1] Cf. Cassirer, *Platonic Renaissance in England*, ed. cit., pp. 161-93.

portions of Pain and Pleasure involved. He had no innate idealism and no mystery. Poetry was a misrepresentation and had better be avoided (Locke would have agreed here of course as well). As Bentham put it with his inimitable bluntness, 'quantity of pleasure being equal, push-pin is as good as poetry'. The Hobbesian ideal of an artificial society, a Leviathan, made to measure according to the rules of Reason, also bears fruit in the eighteenth century. The whole revolutionary trend culminating in the French Revolution bears witness to it.[1]

We saw that it was the Puritans (basing themselves on the Pauline epistles) who first detached the Covenant-theology from its proper ethical setting, and that it was Hobbes who took it up under the aegis of unbridled materialism and gave to it its peculiar secular and political character. The Covenant-idea, as such, evaporated during the eighteenth century after masquerading for a time as the Social Contract, but what remained was the sense of imperative obligation and purposeful freedom that went with it, together with the idea of the infinite enrichment which would come as the reward of earnest devotion and loyalty. In Judaism, this latter is the messianic hope— the hope of a world renewed and at peace and filled with the knowledge of God as the waters cover the sea. For the modern secular visionaries, the divine glory is missing and is replaced by the arrogant assertion of man's self-sufficiency as the author of his own destiny, with his good as the final good to which the whole Creation moves.

[1] J. L. Talmon (*The Origins of Totalitarian Democracy*, pp. 10 f.) has recently produced illuminating evidence about the 'messianic' character of the expectations connected with eighteenth-century revolutionary theory and practice. 'The point of reference of modern Messianism,' he writes, 'is man's reason and will, and its aim happiness on earth, achieved by a social transformation. The point of reference is temporal but the claims are absolute.' Dr. Talmon has no hesitation in relating this pseudo-messianic driving force to the spirit of the Old Testament (pp. 23-4). Nor were all the revolutionaries atheists. Rousseau still felt the nation to be a sort of holy community guided by a kind of Providence. The psychological background of this is akin to Hebraic prophetism. When, in the nineteenth century, the torch was passed from the bourgeoisie to the proletariat, the messianic aim and colouring are no less decisive, but in the dream of a classless society brought about through rigid dialectical processes, all theological sanctions have been abandoned.

As for the scientists, Boyle's physico-theology did not survive the eighteenth century. Deism gives way to atheism, and 'the argument for God drawn from the phenomena of things' goes the way of lost causes, leaving the men of the eighteenth century on the cold hill's side far from the Kingdom of God and the Temple of Nature. Later, in the nineteenth century we see where natural philosophy has tended in the work of a representative spokesman such as T. H. Huxley. In him, we find a defiant materialism which has all the boldness of Hobbes without his sophistry. He holds that only two beliefs are necessary to facilitate human progress—

> the first, that the order of Nature is ascertainable by our faculties to an extent which is practically unlimited; the second, that our volition counts for something as a condition of the course of events.[1]

That is Baconianism in a nutshell. Huxley, however, having followed the scepticism of Hume through to its final limit, is less dogmatic than either Bacon, Hobbes, or Locke. His materialism is pragmatic rather than speculative. He is unconcerned with the nature of ultimate reality and perhaps that is an indication of how narrow the philosophical range has become. Truth is not merely unattainable; it is unimportant:

> In itself it is of little moment whether we express the phenomena of matter in terms of spirit, or the phenomena of spirit in terms of matter: matter may be regarded as a form of thought, thought may be regarded as a property of matter—each statement has a certain relative truth. But with a view to the progress of science, the materialistic terminology is in every way to be preferred. For it connects thought with the other phenomena of the universe, and suggests inquiry into the nature of those physical conditions, or concomitants of thought, which are more or less accessible to us, and a knowledge of which may, in future, help us to exercise the same kind of control over the world of thought as we already possess in respect of the material world; whereas the alternative, or spiritualistic, terminology is utterly barren, and leads to nothing but obscurity and confusion of ideas.[2]

We should notice here the stress upon the necessity for functional clarity of language and the contemptuous dismissal of

---

[1] 'On the Physical Basis of Life', 1868.   [2] *Ibid.*

the language of spiritual or imaginative apprehension—an echo of Hobbes's treatment of metaphors and theological terms in the *Leviathan*, and also an anticipation of the linguistic policy of the logical positivists in our own century.

This matter-of-fact ideal of language was with Hobbes linked to that form of positivism which sees no mysterious components either in the World or in Man. For Hobbes, Man was brute matter whose actions (mental as well as physical) were ordered by the laws of pressure and recoil. With Huxley there is this difference: Man is not now a machine, but an organism. For him, 'protoplasm' is the comprehensive substance of man common to him and all organic matter—'thus it becomes clear that all living powers are cognate, and that all living forms are fundamentally of one character',[1] he writes. There is a change here from mechanical Physics to Biology. It was not exactly new to state that all flesh is grass, but Isaiah had recognized this Truth as a mystery. He knew well that Man was both grass and more than grass, and when saying, Man is grass, he was stating simply one side of a paradox: in a later verse he stated the other side, 'they that wait upon the Lord shall renew their strength'. For Huxley such a paradox is unrecognized. Instead we have inconsistency. On the one hand, he states that man is a mere organism perishing like the flowers of the field; on the other hand, he declares that 'our volition counts for something as a condition of the course of events'. We may well ask, If Man is merely protoplasm, whence comes this power in us to control events and whence comes the peculiar urgency which makes it necessary for us to do so, which makes the human will something other than the mere will to survive and produce its kind? We may (in the fashion of Epictetus) turn the argument upon Huxley himself and ask him, What is the driving-force, the spiritual motive behind his own system; what makes it so urgently necessary for him to propagate his philosophy of materialism and make it prevail?

If we were to press that question, we should discover I think that the driving-force behind Huxley's philosophy was the intangible dream of power (not exhaled surely by the protoplasm as such) which we have traced back to Bacon. Huxley's

[1] *Ibid.*

style and manner owe their buoyancy to this irrational, pseudo-messianic dream of Man's complete power over nature. There was indeed at the time that Huxley wrote, a millenarian spirit abroad as keen as that of some of the Puritan sects of the seventeenth century. Soon, it was felt, the world would be conquered to man's use. We were on the eve of a scientific Utopia. How sadly have we now been disillusioned! Indeed some of the disillusionment has been expressed by a later scion of the same family, Aldous Huxley, in two gruesome and terrifying novels. The hopeful Utopian fantasies of the nineteenth century have turned to terrible nightmares, in which Man's distinctive freedom is lost, and he becomes a mere shred of germ-plasm in a vast and dismal laboratory.

III

What happened to Puritanism after the Age of Faith? In eighteenth-century Methodism we may undoubtedly discern a partial revival of Puritan spirituality. Mr. W. J. Ong has produced evidence to show that the term 'methodism' originally signified the Ramist methods of logical demonstration used by Wesley and his followers in their tracts and sermons.[1] These men were in fact discovering, as the Puritans of an earlier generation had discovered, the special advantages of a combination of Faith and Intellect with the Imagination largely excluded.

As a parallel development, we find in this century a strongly practical moral divinity—the Arminian inheritance fortified by Deism and Spinoza's *Ethics*. But there is clearly a qualitative difference between the religion of Works in this century and that of Milton or the Caroline Divines such as Jeremy Taylor. In Kant, for instance, the imaginative colouring is absent, as is also the dramatic tension which results from setting before our moral choice the behest of a personal God. The same would apply to Samuel Clarke and Joseph Butler.

But the Imagination has a way of coming back to revenge itself. Side by side with the religion of Works and the equally limited religion of Faith to be found in William Law and the Methodists, we may also note among the theosophists a reaction

[1] 'Peter Ramus and the Naming of Methodism', *J.H.I.*, XIV (1953), 237 f.

in favour of a religion of the Imagination. And this, like the other two, is marked by an unbounded stress on one part of our sensibility. For students of literature, the chief exponent of this eighteenth-century reaction against rationalism is William Blake; with him we have a spirituality characterized by unusual imaginative intensity but lacking in rational control and order. 'Imagination,' says Blake, is 'the real & eternal World of which this Vegetable Universe is but a faint shadow.'[1] On the one hand, this could be interpreted merely as the traumatic reaction against the suppression of Imagination and Enthusiasm in the Age of Gibbon, Hume, and Voltaire; but on the other hand, it may be viewed as a recovery of something of the health and wholeness of the seventeenth-century world of Imagination as represented by such Hebraic writers as Thomas Browne and Traherne. For them, poetry and in particular the poetry of the Bible, gives a clearer view of reality than does mathematical demonstration.

One of the things we noted in the seventeenth century as characteristic of enlightened Hebraism was an appreciation of the literary beauty of the Bible. The tendency of Puritanism was to obstruct this by reading it as mere trope, or by a barren literalism; its appeal to the Imagination and the insistence upon its use as a model for literary composition was the theme rather of the Hebraic reaction against Puritan narrowness— the theme of Milton and of Robert Boyle in his Essay on the Style of the Scriptures. We saw also that in such a writer as Traherne, the Imagination takes flight from the poetic suggestions of the Book of *Psalms*. Blake, has in this respect (as in so many others) much in common with Traherne. His imaginative world is centred on (and in some sense circumscribed by) the poetry of the Hebrew Bible. 'The Stolen and Perverted Writings of Homer & Ovid,' Blake notes, 'which all men ought to contemn, are set up by artifice against the Sublime of the Bible.'[2] There can be little doubt of the direct influence of Hebrew poetry with its free system of versification on the so-called 'Prophetic Books' of Blake. He evidently felt (like Whitman later on) that his energies could be most adequately

---

[1] Letter 'To the Christians' prefixed to *Jerusalem*, Bk. IV. *Poetry and Prose of William Blake*, ed. G. Keynes (London, 1948), p. 535.
[2] Preface to *Milton, ibid.*, p. 375.

released within a loose framework of vehement and freely
flowing parallelistic members:

> But Albion is cast forth to the Potter, his Children to the Builders,
> To build Babylon because they have forsaken Jerusalem.
> The Walls of Babylon are Souls of Men, her Gates the Groans
> Of Nations, her Towers are the Miseries of once happy Families,
> Her streets are paved with Destruction, her Houses built with
>   Death,
> Her Palaces with Hell & the Grave, her Synagogues with
>   Torments
> Of ever-hardening Despair, squar'd & polish'd with cruel skill.
> Yet thou wast lovely as the summer cloud upon my hills
> When Jerusalem was thy heart's desire, in times of youth &
>   love.[1]

Nor does Blake use his Biblical imagery (after the Puritan
fashion) as mere trope. Blake's *Be'ulah*—the state of fulfilled
desire—is taken from *Isaiah* lxii, 4, where it denotes a relation
with God which, like marriage itself involves both body and
soul. It carries a sexual overtone of meaning which is certainly
retained in Blake. In 'soft Be'ulah's night' gentle souls come to
rest under love's wings, or else 'they guide the great Wine-press
of Love'. By contrast, the same term used by Bunyan in *Pilgrim's
Progress* had been handled in a purely allegorical fashion.
In the Land of Be'ulah, 'the contract between the bride and
bridegroom was renewed'. But there is not the faintest sensual
echo: that materialization of spiritual things which belongs to
the imagery of the Hebrew Bible is really alien to Bunyan. In
Blake, however, a full-bodied Hebraism is achieved both in the
style and versification, and also in this positive appreciation
of the body and the senses and in the pervasive use of the
imagery of marriage and betrothal.

The romantic poets and some of the pre-romantic poets were
indeed more than hospitable to the poetic riches of the Old
Testament. That Scripture, primitive, vigorous, and earthy
could provide a valuable refuge from the frigid elegances of
neo-classicism. Wordsworth's *Michael* is Biblical in a more
particular and comprehensive way even than Milton's *Samson
Agonistes*. Blake, in his attachment to the imagery and rhythms

[1] *Jerusalem*, 24. (*Ed. cit.*, p. 461).

Epilogue

of *The Song of Songs* is merely the most crucial example of this phase; there was no *Song of Songs* in the New Testament, and to that extent, Blake's imagination is Hebraic rather than Christian. But here we become immediately aware of the enormous difference between the traumatic Hebraism of Blake, and the more thoughtful and balanced intuitions of the seventeenth-century Hebraic poets. The romantic poet seizes on the richness of Old Testament poetry and narrative, a literature of men speaking to men and speaking of the earth on which men live, but he turns his back very often on the doctrine and discipline of righteousness. Milton could strive for freedom to divorce pointing out the world of difference between freedom secured by law, and vagabond licence 'without pale or partition'. But Blake strives for free love and aims the arrows of desire against the whole Hebraic code of conduct. In this he has Shelley and Byron with him. It seems that in the reaction against the eighteenth-century religion of works and against the residue of Puritanism (termed by Blake 'Tirzah'), all moral restraints have been repudiated. It is a case of the baby being discharged with the bath-water.

The most alarming contradictions in Blake's theological system may be explained as a consequence of this juxtaposition of the extremes of his judaism and his anti-judaism. Everything that God has made is good—this is sound Hebrew doctrine—and consequently the Law that limits sexual freedom is bad. This is perhaps emotionally valid, but theologically it is a *non sequitur*. For Blake, as for Shelley, the Ten Commandments are the work of some Demiurge, some Satanic agency. In 'The Everlasting Gospel,' he pictures Jesus coming to destroy the Mosaic Law for ever, with all its curses and restraints:

> He laid His hand on Moses' Law:
> The Ancient Heavens, in Silent Awe
> Writ with Curses from Pole to Pole,
> All away began to roll.[1]

This, of course, is not orthodox Christianity, though it finds support in some texts from the New Testament. Basically, it is part of the Gnostic heresy to which undoubtedly Blake sub-

[1] *Ibid.*, p. 139.

Epilogue

scribed.[1] Good and Evil are false categories created by a male-volent deity. In the State of Innocence, all things are good; they only become bad through Experience, through the righteous-ness of the Pharisees, through the Hebrew Law against adultery, and through the false doctrine of the Puritans. There is, we note, once more a theological zeugma, a false identification of Heb-raism with Puritanism, which it is a main aim of this study to try and dispel. Unfortunately, this is a deep-seated popular error, one of those 'Idols of the Tribe' (as Bacon termed them) which occur constantly along the path of the student of Euro-pean ideas. It occurs in Voltaire, in Blake, in Matthew Arnold, and down to our own day in a hundred uncritical remarks of scholars who have not the slightest knowledge of the original sources of Hebraism, and very little of Puritanism either for that matter. It is surely easy enough to see that the emetic which caused the Romantic poets (and later Whitman) to discharge from their systems the entire Law of Works was not the Hebrew Law against adultery, but the evangelical, Pauline hatred of sex as such, the doctrine which says, in contradiction to Hebraism, 'if ye live after the flesh ye shall die: but if ye through the Spirit do mortify the deeds of the body, ye shall live'. It was not the discipline of divorce to which they inwardly objected, but the Christian ban on divorce; not marriage, but the Pauline view that marriage itself is a mere concession to our evil concupiscence—'It is better to marry than to burn.' It is really against St. Paul and not Moses that the campaign is waged, against the Greek, Platonic ethic which divides the 'fallen' world of Matter and Flesh from the 'ideal' world of Spirit. Such divisions are unknown to Hebraism.

How did the confusion arise? How did Blake with his deep instinct for the imaginative and emotional values of Hebraism come to identify the Puritan doctrine of Original Sin, Predes-tination, and the eternal perdition of the reprobate majority—doctrines which have not the slightest foundation in Judaism—with the laws of Moses and the Synagogue, which, says Blake, 'worship Satan under the Unutterable Name'? Here we are in the region not of some form of lunacy peculiar to Blake but of a

[1] Cf. D. Saurat, *Blake and Modern Thought* (London, 1929), pp. 1-10, and S. F. Damon, *William Blake, His Philosophy and Symbols* (Gloucester, Mass., 1958), p. 116.

277

widespread, indeed a collective mania. If I am not mistaken, we are here somewhere very close to the psychological and theological springs of anti-semitism. And the word anti-semitism is meant here in its widest application, for the same confusion enters into the Jewish Literature of the so-called *Haskalah*, or Enlightenment, in the latter half of the nineteenth century to produce amongst Jews a parallel revolt against forms of Jewish piety which for these writers lose their warmth and humanism and take on a grim Puritan countenance. The joyful Jewish Sabbath begins to look like the sombre and joyless Puritan Sunday. It may be ventured that we are faced here with a form of psychological substitution.[1] The Jew and his God become the scapegoat for sins against the Spirit of which Western Man, and in particular the Puritans, have been guilty.

One could put it in a different way: the Jewish God and his Law certainly stand for duty, obligation, responsibility. But there is at work in us also the urge to avoid responsibility, to be carried along and lulled in a kind of pre-natal universe of Pagan forms and rhythms. The 'tents of Be'ulah' in Blake's system, certainly carry a Pagan overtone. They represent a sort of return to womb; and that, as we are nowadays well-aware, is very close to the death-wish. It is Tiamat, the Abyss, the warm and enclosing, unutterably peaceful order of pre-organic, or non-organic existence. The love of Nature in this sense (which is certainly a theme in Romanticism) is something against which Western Man has struggled and from which he has fought free. Hebraism is the Law of Life, but it is in a way so much easier to slip back into Nature and Death. The stupor of drunkenness, the abandonments of fornication, the loss of identity (and hence of responsibility) in some pantheistic communion with Nature, all these are part of that deep regressive instinct, that *Baal*-worship, against which the prophets bid us guard ourselves. And of course we do guard ourselves; the price of regression is much too high. To slip back into the abyss of Nature is to forsake all the profits of culture and civilization: it is the way of death. It is in Blake's system 'Rahab', just as the

[1] I have pursued this idea in relation to the portrait of the Jew in English Literature from Chaucer to the present day in a brief study entitled, *The Dual Image* (London, 1959).

violent Puritanical recoil from the Abyss is 'Tirzah'.[1] Blake with astonishing insight recognized that the two were sisters—the Pagan abandonment of responsibility and the intolerable ethic of Puritanism. Both are products of that failure to respond to the challenge of a Covenant with the Lord of Life. One is a spiritual, the other, a physical, castration.

And who is to be blamed for this? Paradoxically, Hebraism itself and the Hebrew God are blamed. Nothing is easier than Father-hatred. If we find growing up difficult, we turn our resentment against the Father; were it not for him we would not have had to grow up at all. If we find learning difficult, we blame our teachers; but for them, we could enjoy the long summer's day of ignorance. Thus Puritanism which is a religion of castration becomes confounded with Hebraism which is a religion of circumcision. And so, for Voltaire and Blake, the Old Testament God is the enemy. In this way, Blake may be said to have missed the wholeness and balance necessary for a true marriage of Albion and Jerusalem.

His *Milton* is a polemic against Puritanism, and indeed his conception of the portentous significance of Puritanism—'a black cloud redounding spread over Europe'—is exactly conformable to the point of view taken in this study, but he shows supreme lack of critical discrimination in making Milton, the poet who had most successfully combated the moral narrowness of Puritanism, into the chief exponent of the Puritan spirit. Before Milton can enter into Blake, he must be cured of that Puritan proclivity. This is the main theme of Blake's poem. What is this but the false identification of Puritanism and Hebraism? It is an error indeed which more logical minds than Blake are guilty of, but it is nonetheless a cardinal and disastrous error. For Milton was the apostle not of Puritanism but of Hebraism. He had found, intermittently and unsteadily it is true, the connexion between Liberty and Law, between the imaginative components of Hebraism and its code of righteousness. By doing so, Milton had offered a remedy for the evils of Puritan dissociationism. Blake, however, repudiates this combination. He embraces the sensuous and imaginative components of Hebraism, regarding himself from this point of

---

[1] Cf. Damon, *op. cit.*, p. 385. 'Tirzah is the prude, Rahab is the harlot.'

view as the reincarnation of Milton, but he condemns the code
of righteousness, as the false path of Puritanism which Milton
in his folly had chosen to take:

> . . . his body was the Rock Sinai, that body
> Which was on earth born to corruption . . .

In rejecting the Law of Works (just as the Puritans themselves
had done) Blake is thus himself guilty of dissociation. And this
is in fact the root dissociation in romanticism—the splitting-off
of Law from Liberty, Reason from Imagination, and Faith
from Works. These forces, integrated in Milton at his best,
divide and fall apart in Blake and the writings of his contemporaries. Innocence and Experience become two utterly
incompatible orders of existence. All human institutions,
Churches, and establishments, all rational accommodations
and legal forms become inherently evil and corrupt by a con-
demnation as total as the Puritan decree of Original Sin. Only
the free Spirit of man—the Divine Humanity—winging like a
lark (the bird-imagery of the romantic poets is in this regard
highly significant) and totally free either of moral restraints or
the necessity to adapt itself to the conditions of earthly existence,
is to be reckoned with as pure and good.

IV

The unitive powers of Reason, Faith, and Imagination indeed
deteriorated in the eighteenth century and they functioned
instead in isolation from one another.[1] Unity is recovered to
some extent later on in the writings of Coleridge. From his
standpoint of moderation, he is able to accord to the seventeenth
century divines, such as Henry More and Jeremy Taylor, a
much truer and more enthusiastic appreciation than had been
possible in the eighteenth century. He also appreciated and
shared their enlightened rationalism—a use of Reason enriched
by Imagination and other forms of intuitive knowledge.[2] This
kind of *recta ratio* was, from his point of view, a surer way to
knowledge than the way of *mere* rational understanding as
employed by the scientists.

[1] Cf. S. L. Bethell, *The Cultural Revolution of the Seventeenth Century* (London,
1951), p. 66.
[2] Cf. B. Willey, *Nineteenth Century Studies* (London, 1949), pp. 33-4.

Fortified by this approach, Coleridge, brought to the discussion of poetry an interpretative power which had been denied to the critics of the eighteenth century such as Dr. Johnson, and in this way, as is well known, he revolutionized criticism. With him, criticism was a positive thing, a matter of reconstructing the original experience of the poet. It was constructive rather than destructive, synthetic rather than analytical.

He approached the poetry of the Bible in the same spirit,[1] believing that the Scriptures ought to be expounded not by discursive Reason primarily but by the spiritual Imagination. What struck him most was the imaginative potency of the text; its authenticity was a fact which could be empirically tested by every reader who approached it in the right spirit. The aim of the reader must be not to break the text down by analysis on pseudo-scientific grounds as the new school of Bible Critics was doing on the Continent, especially in Germany, but to try to grasp the total meaning synthetically. Coleridge's lesson has certainly been understood in the field of secular literature, but it is doubtful whether it has yet been heeded in Biblical studies. At the same time, he criticised the overliteralness of Protestant dogmatic exegesis. To claim for the whole of Scripture an unvarying level of literal and logical consistency is to take away from it its human texture and depth and also its literary variety; it becomes an oracular statement not a living literature, and as such makes no appeal to the heart or the imagination. 'The Doctrine in question', he declares, 'petrifies at once the whole body of Holy Writ with all its harmonies and symmetrical gradations.'[2] We note how similar is Coleridge's approach to that of John Smith in the seventeenth century with his idea of prophetic grades, of the human element in prophecy, or to Boyle's Essay on the *Style of the Holy Scriptures* with its insistence that David's Psalms were the work of a traveller, a courtier, and a poet. Once the doctrine of rigid, literal consistency is abandoned, and the living tissue of Scripture is restored, the significance of the destructive Higher Criticism also vanishes—for all that it tells us is that Scripture is subject to the accidents of

[1] Cf. his *Confessions of an Inquiring Spirit*, Letter III, where he refers to his approach to Shakespeare in *Lectures on Dramatic Poetry* as a useful model for Biblical criticism.

[2] *Ibid.*

literary transmission in general; it does not and cannot take
away its spiritual effect, which is vouched for not by legalistic
or 'scientific' reasons of the type to which such critics appeal
but rather by the response of our moral being to the living
word of power that Scripture addresses to us.

A positive literary evaluation of the Bible inspired partly by
Coleridge and partly by Spinoza, is found later in the nineteenth
century in the writings of Matthew Arnold; he finds in the Old
Testament a pervasive unity of spirit, the keynote of which is
righteousness:

> The real germ of religious consciousness, therefore, out of which
> sprang Israel's name for God, to which the records of his history
> adapted themselves, and which came to be clothed upon, in time,
> with a mighty growth of poetry and tradition, was a consciousness
> of the *not ourselves which makes for righteousness*.[1]

To Arnold, the answer to dogmatism is literature. The Bible is
not a 'system of theological notions about personality, essence,
existence, consubstantiality'; it consists not of theological
formulae but of vivid experiences of God's action in human life.
The Bible speaks in metaphor not syllogisms: its language 'is
literary not scientific language', and because that is so, it is best
understood by the reader whose literary sensibilities are awakened—and who is not hidebound by dogmatic prejudices. In
short, literary culture must invade the province of theology;
otherwise, theology is barren.

Like Coleridge, Arnold deals summarily with the Higher
Critics. He points out that among the members of the Tübingen
school, it is apparently sufficient to break down the text into its
parts (or its imagined parts); its underlying unity escapes them;
he accused them of prejudice against the Old Testament and of
a mechanical, rigid approach which stultified any imaginative
approach to the text, a mode of interpretation which we recognize as an echo of the Ramist-Puritan methods of exegesis in
the seventeenth century:

> Among the German critics of the Bible, a sort of criticism which
> we may best, perhaps, describe as a *mechanical* criticism is very
> rife. . . . Things like persons, must be rigidly consistent, must show
> no conflicting aspects, must have no flux or reflux, must not
> follow a slow, hesitating, often obscure line of growth. No, the

[1] *Literature and Dogma* (1873), ch. i, sect. v.

character which we assign to them they must have always, altogether, and unalterably, or it is not theirs.[1]

All this is astonishingly true and astonishingly ahead of its time.
In fact, Arnold's strictures might still be pressed against much
that passes for literary criticism of the Bible today. But Arnold's
rebuke was directed against dogmatism at large—the dogmatism of the Higher Critics was merely the obverse side of the
dogmatism of Protestant theology in its approach to Scripture.
For him such dogmatism concealed or obscured the grand
simple practical truth which Scripture taught throughout with
ceaseless iteration, the one saving truth more important than
the fat of lambs, or creeds and catechisms, viz., that 'righteousness tendeth to life'. To him, this concept of righteousness is
the core of Israel's religion, the living message of the Hebrew
Bible so that 'as long as the world lasts all who want to make
progress in righteousness will come to Israel for inspiration,
as to the people who have had the sense for righteousness most
glowing and strongest'.[2] Righteousness is religion applied to
conduct, he tells us, and conduct is three-fourths of life. This
very briefly is Arnold's moral teaching, the teaching which he
usually terms 'Hebraism'.

Arnold was, perhaps, the last great Englishman to conceive
the ideal of a truly national culture based upon religious
sanctions and to preach it with passion and confidence. In this,
we may say that he was following in the traditions of the finer
spirits of the seventeenth century. In particular, by his combination of Hebraism and Hellenism, we are reminded of
Milton, and the Cambridge Platonists.[3]

In his eloquent Conclusion to *Literature and Dogma*, Arnold,
with a fine insight, declares that Science, Culture and Morality
are required for the total man and that they must be developed
harmoniously together, if we are to fulfil the laws of our being.
Culture—in the form of a literary sensibility, was an almost
indispensable medium through which to view the Scriptures,
and, on the other hand, it was Religion which gave meaning to
both Science and Culture. It was the combination of the three,
therefore, that Arnold taught and that, as an educationalist,

[1] *God and the Bible* (1875), ch. 3, sect. i.
[2] *Literature and Dogma*, ch. 1, sect. v.
[3] Cf. Willey, *Nineteenth Century Studies*, pp. 266-8.

he sought to propagate throughout the land. The similarity of this to the system outlined by Milton in his *Letter to Hartlib*, is most evident. In education Arnold tried to make a humane ideal prevail, and perhaps the survival of the humanities as a central feature of our present-day secondary education is due in some measure to his zealous advocacy.

The mention of Arnold's active work as an educationalist suggests a further dimension of his Hebraism, for with the Hebraic ideal of 'strenuous virtue' goes the historical effort to transform society, or, in Arnold's words, 'to make reason and the will of God prevail'. When Arnold is writing in such moods there is more than a suggestion of revolutionary messianic ardour. He is in this much like Milton. He fiercely attacks monopolies, even questions the idea of private property, proclaims human equality, and in a true radical spirit, condemns the *laissez-faire* system for having produced an industrial population consisting of 'vast, miserable, unmanageable masses of sunken people'.[1] He does not try to give his various revolutionary suggestions a coherent shape, first because he was not in complete possession of the revolutionary idea and, second, because he was no political philosopher. But we can if we wish try to reconstruct a philosophy from the various mottos and axioms with which he generously besprinkles his writings. Thus, in his stress on the 'national best-self' as the source of dynamic improvement he has evidently in mind something like the imperative 'General Will' of Rousseau which is both immanent in, and yet, in a way, beyond Society, and which commands mankind forward on its path of achievement. Who will deny that here we have also something of that Hebraic demand for the Kingdom of God on earth (and not merely a vision of God in the soul) which man is imperatively summoned to foster through his own efforts? Finally, is not Arnold speaking the authentic language of Hebraism when he insists that such efforts must be related to the whole tendency of the national life and not merely to a sect or Church? His final criticism of non-conformity is not directed at its Puritan ethic but at its alien, provincial spirit.

When all this has been said, however, it must be confessed that Arnold did not always succeed in harmonizing the virtues

[1] Cf. Lionel Trilling, *Matthew Arnold* (New York, ed., of 1949), p. 289.

of Hebraism with the other parts of his inheritance. In *Literature and Dogma*, he is emphatic that conduct is three-fourths of life and that conduct is to be guided by the Hebrew doctrine of righteousness; a little earlier on, however, in *Culture and Anarchy*. whilst recognizing the importance, if not the primacy, of conduct in certain spheres, he had urged the Hellenic virtues of 'beauty and a human nature perfect on all its sides' as the final virtues at which a man should aim. The 'devout energy' of Hebraism must be made secondary to that.[1] The ideal is (as with Humboldt) the contemplation of a perfected selfhood. This suspicion of moral energy was borne in on Arnold partly as a result of his classical upbringing with its stress on 'Sweetness and Light' and partly as a reaction against Puritanism, and what went with it, the furious spirit of middle-class enterprise. Here we may locate a central error in Arnold's thought. Like Blake and so many others, he fails to see that Puritanism is not quite co-extensive with Hebraism. Indeed, the main ideological criticism that one would wish to make against *Culture and Anarchy*, is that it falsely identifies the two. Arnold condemns 'English Philistinism' as the characteristic of the 'Puritan and Hebraising middle-class', and he complains that its Hebraising tendency was responsible for keeping it from 'culture and totality'. Recognizing (rightly) in the zeal of the Puritans the energy of Hebraism, he goes on (wrongly) to assume that the Puritan sense of Original Sin, the Puritan pessimism, the Puritan narrowness, and the joyless Puritan Sabbath are also marks of Hebraism.

In his reaction against the dissidence of Dissent and his consequent stress upon the more inactive aesthetic virtues, Arnold was not unlike the Cambridge Platonists in the seventeenth century. They too were in revolt against the intensities of Puritanism, and were consequently thrown back upon a cloistered virtue. Arnold similarly appears to us often as something of an 'ineffectual angel beating his luminous wings in vain'. He criticized Ruskin and Carlyle for soiling their hands with public affairs and wrote in one of his earlier essays,

. . . the critic must keep out of the region of immediate practice in the political, social, humanitarian sphere, if he wants to make

---

[1] Cf. ch. 4, entitled, 'Hebraism and Hellenism'.

a beginning for that more free speculative treatment of things, which may perhaps one day make its benefits felt even in this sphere, but in a natural and thence irresistible manner.[1]

His ideal as reflected in such passages was that of a spontaneous reform of society through the gentle influence of culture and beauty. It was not without justification that Arnold was attacked by the liberals for being an ineffectual aesthete;[2] indeed, there was a certain highbrow aloofness about him which linked him with Newman, that other apostle of culture, on the one hand, and the aestheticism of Pater on the other hand. It is this aestheticism of Arnold which, in the last analysis, and in spite of his occasional Rousseauesque sallies of radicalism, marks him off from the progressive forces of the century, not only from the middle-class entrepreneurs, but also from the Christian socialists and other moral reformers. Arnold, in short, inconsistently tried to worship at one and the same time, the Olympian Jove, distant and immobile, and the God of Israel, active, creative, and zealous to save.

V

Arnold was struggling for wholeness, for integration, but the forces of disintegration were often too strong for him: the symptoms of disintegration, as we have just seen, are even to be found in his own work and in his own literary personality. We may consider the distintegrative tendencies of the nineteenth century as a continuation of that process which we witnessed in the seventeenth century, the process which has been called, 'the Counter-Renaissance'. Now—in the nineteenth century—it takes the form of a preference to divide culture, ethics, politics, religion, etc., into autonomous strands, a tendency which has been, in the twentieth century, very much intensified—to our cost and danger. If we are to sketch in the various historical factors at work here, we shall note that this process has been assisted to a remarkable degree by the German philosophers, notably by Kant, by Schleiermacher, and by Nietzsche. Culture (in Nietzsche) becomes an absolute

[1] 'The Function of Criticism at the Present Time', 1864.
[2] Cf. Frederic Harrison's satire, 'Culture: A Dialogue', quoted by Trilling, *op. cit.*, p. 275.

in its own sphere, free of moral restraints or controls; Religion (in Schleiermacher) becomes separated from the totality of thought and science; whilst in Kant, the separation of Science from Aesthetics, and of both from Ethics, achieves the status of a philosophical dogma. The results of such splitting-up and division of spheres have not been hopeful, and the signs of it are with us in the West and most particularly in Germany itself. One wonders what advantage there has been to the human family in discovering a means of producing a race of men capable of being at one and the same time mass-murderers and kind and indulgent husbands. The fragments of the divided mind and soul have a habit of becoming extraordinarily uncontrollable, even demonic.

Since this study has been concerned with poetry and the signs of disintegration afforded by poetry, it may be worth pointing out that in our own time (a time which of course began in the nineteenth century) poetry has often frustrated the hopes of those who look to it for comfort and guidance by forming itself too into an autonomous strand. This doctrine, clear already in the writings of Baudelaire, and Mallarmé, is one which denies any aim or ideal for poetry outside of poetry itself. It is one which effectively divorces poetry both from morals and from public affairs. There is a hint of this already in Keats's Pagan worship of Beauty: it gathers momentum in the work of Swinburne and Pater (who introduces a new religion of art), and is propagated at a somewhat cruder level by Oscar Wilde. For the English-speaking world, it receives its final and most sinister expression in the work of Yeats and Ezra Pound in our own century. This is not to say that these were not men of rare genius; nonetheless the religion of Beauty, in spite of the imaginative gifts brought to its propagation, is in the last analysis, destructive of human values. In Yeats's two Byzantium poems, the imperial city becomes the symbol of a purely aesthetic Paradise from which all human values are banished.[1]

Naturally, there have been attempts to combat this trend. The twentieth-century English poet-critic who seems implicitly

---

[1] Speaking of the images in *Sailing to Byzantium*, Mr. J. Heath-Stubbs remarks, that 'they evoke the static beauty of a world of perfected art'. He adds that the ideal of Yeats 'implies a deliberate and heartless régime in the cause of beauty'. (*The Darkling Plain*, London, 1950, pp. 208-9.)

by his writings to invite a comparison between himself and Matthew Arnold is Mr. T. S. Eliot. His work has the same ambitious range; he maintains the same interest in theology and wider problems of education and culture. But his work, when compared with that of Arnold, will show us that there is here less in the way of genuine integration; there is a greater gap between religion and everyday concern, between poetry and ordinary human hopes and fears, or, to use Arnold's terminology, between Sweetness and Light on the one hand, and Righteousness which tendeth to life, on the other. Eliot's tract, *The Idea of a Christian Society* (1939), exhibits certain points in common with several writings of Arnold. There is a common dislike of liberalism as a policy of chaos; a common attachment to the idea of an established church which shall guide the life of the nation.[1] In Eliot's poem *Little Gidding*, there is also to be found this sense of a religious culture based on geography and tradition. Such sentiments do not, however, carry Eliot's main emphasis. We note in Eliot's writing a stress on the position of the elect whom he calls the Community of Christians in contradistinction to the general mass (whom he calls the Christian Community)—who would be attached merely by social habit to the religious life. The Community of Christians, 'would contain both clergy and laity of superior intellectual and/or spiritual gifts'.[2]

Eliot's idea of an intellectual or spiritual côterie raised by Special Grace above the common herd reminds us not a little of the Puritan belief in the special calling of the Saints, with also a suggestion of a kind of monastic ideal (we learn that celibacy will be encouraged). This is sufficiently unlike Arnold. But even more decidedly unlike anything to be found in Arnold, is Eliot's stress on the necessity of dogma. The Church must be on its guard to preserve such dogmas as those relating to the Trinity. 'It is not enthusiasm, but dogma, that differentiates a Christian from a pagan society.'[3]

Eliot mentions in passing the importance of solving economic problems, but quickly passes on to other matters. We noted in Arnold also a certain aloofness very often in regard to economic

[1] *The Idea of a Christian Society* (London, 1939), p. 51.
[2] *Ibid.*, p. 37.
[3] *Ibid.*, p. 59.

or political controversy. But with Arnold such aloofness was dictated by the thought that the critic could do more by irony and suggestion than by a frontal assault. With Eliot, however, one has the feeling that the critic has more completely abdicated from the task of exploring the profit motive or the pattern of government in present-day society, because he holds on principle that salvation is not to be sought along those lines:

> We must remember that whatever reform or revolution we carry out, the result will always be a sordid travesty of what human society should be—though the world is never left wholly without glory.[1]

This is quintessential Calvinism with its stress on the Pauline text which says that flesh and blood cannot inherit the Kingdom of Heaven.

Eliot's later treatise, *Notes Towards a Definition of Culture* (1948), carries the same general message. It was evidently intended by the author to be compared with Arnold's *Culture and Anarchy* (1869) and no doubt Eliot believed that he had produced a more satisfactory definition than his nineteenth-century forbear. What strikes one in the main, however, when the two books are set side by side is that whereas Arnold conceives in his Hebraic fashion a religious culture to be that which permeates the life of the nation as a whole and gives meaning to it, Eliot apparently feels that religion and culture are things separate from the economic, social, and political life of the nation. This is what is meant by saying that for him religion has become an autonomous strand. Eliot lacks any fundamental social concern. His plays insist likewise on a radical separation of Nature and Grace.[2] His religion does not lead in the Hebraic manner to positive action for the betterment of the human species. It moves towards a passive stage of contemplation, rather in the manner of the Puritan search for the Inner Light, and salvation comes to the elect with the achievement of the 'timeless moment', whilst the uninitiated masses sink in the deep Serbonian bog of Original Sin. The best that can be said of such a religious outlook is that it lacks any

---

[1] *The Idea of a Christian Society* (London, 1939), p. 59.
[2] Cf. W. Stein, 'After the Cocktails', in *Essays in Criticism*, III (Oxford, 1953), 85-104.

fundamental helpfulness in the complex crisis of the twentieth century.

VI

If any more helpful solutions are possible at the present time of day, it must be clear I think that these will not be dogmatic solutions. There is no road back from modern depth-psychology to a medieval notion of Man as a rational animal, subject to a natural moral law; there is no road back from modern nuclear Physics to Newton or Aristotle; there is no return from our modern experience of the World and Man to a simple nineteenth-century belief in inevitable progress. Nor is it any use in a world which is capable at any moment of destroying itself utterly, to murmur piously, 'Believe on me and you shall be saved.' The appalling truth is that mere belief, unallied to action, to practical righteousness, will not save us, if salvation in this world is what we seek.

Indeed, if we seek salvation in dogma, we must eventually despair, for what dogma is there, what intellectual scheme, which can piece together the shards, the broken fragments of our culture and produce another medieval synthesis? When the world was circumscribed in its nine concentric spheres, it was possible to hold it together in a unified mental picture. Now, there is hardly a single department or subdepartment of Science which it is possible to confine in this way. No chemist can now comprehend even the whole of Chemistry, no physicist, the whole of Physics. If we look to philosophy or dogma, we shall therefore have to conclude that that way is barren, that the intellect cannot comprehend in one synthetic image the multiform realities of God, Man, and Nature. But that is only when we seek wisdom by means of the *logos*, by means of intellectual concepts and schemes. It does not follow that the knowledge of God who is at once, Creator, Redeemer, and Revealer is completely denied to us. There is a fable of Kafka about a dog who tries as a result of intellectual speculation to convince himself that his master does not exist and who thus comes to repress in himself the instinct which makes him paw the ground and look up for food. The dog naturally pines away. We are much in that position. The way of the mind is indeed only one way to God.

In the Book of *Proverbs*, which I suppose is still as wise a book as one may find in a week's search through the Library of the British Museum, we are advised, 'Be not wise in thine own eyes: fear the Lord, and depart from evil. It shall be health to thy navel, and marrow to thy bones.' The organic nature of the knowledge of God is well revealed in the corporeal imagery which the wise King here employs—bones and navel. The child in its mother's womb is not perhaps intellectually aware of its mother's existence, still less of the father who begot him. The truth on these matters is a truth *of relation*, but nevertheless as certain and as real a truth as the navel-cord which attaches it to its origins. In much the same way, we are (to change the metaphor slightly) always in the hands of God; for that reason the fear of God is health to the navel and marrow to the bones. To renew the Covenant-dialogue with God, is therefore, in one sense, an extraordinarily simple matter;

It is not in heaven, that thou shouldest say, Who shall go up for us to heaven, and bring it unto us, that we may hear it and do it?

Neither is it beyond the sea, that thou shouldest say, Who shall go over the sea for us, and bring it unto us, that we may hear it and do it.

For the word is very nigh unto thee, in thy mouth, and in thy heart, that thou mayest do it.

(*Deut.* xxx, 12-14)

Of course in another sense it is an extraordinarily difficult matter. It is so much more difficult to abandon Pride when we are at the top of a skyscraper; it is so much more difficult to agree that the fear of God is the beginning of wisdom when we have achieved such outstanding technical advances without it. It is the same with relations between human groups. In one way, it seems that nothing could be easier than for the representatives of the Great Powers to unite in brotherhood, on the basis of a recognition of their common mortal and creaturely status; in another way, nothing could be more difficult, for to do this would mean abandoning Pride and abandoning the dream of Empire in which fallible man and fallible human aims are thought to be sovereign. And yet not to abandon this folly is the way of death and disaster.

The dilemma before us is thus inconceivably sharp and challenging. Never before was universal destruction so real a possibility, but likewise the possibility of accomplishing all the dreams of the human race was never more tantalizingly within our reach. We should have a false sense of values if we under-rated the blessings which new science and new knowledge have brought to us in every sphere, in economics, in medicine, in communications, and all things needful for an abundant life. But if the dilemma is today so much more existential and the alternatives of blessing and curse so terrifyingly real to everyone, we should not make the mistake of thinking that this situation is new. The issues have been implicit from the beginning; they were defined in all their simplicity and urgency by the Hebrew lawgiver a great while ago, when he said, 'See I have set before thee this day life and good, death and evil.' Such alternatives belong to the structure of Covenant-history. We may either conform to our Covenant-bonds, in which case we are united to the Lord of Life, or we may attempt to revoke them, in which case we face the danger of death and destruction. The bonds are there all the time, and we are free to take which course we please. Such is the dialectic of History conceived as Covenant-history. Hebraism does not regard history as inevit-able progress; nor in the most tragic phases of history, does it regard Man as unredeemable.[1] There is always a divine challenge and a human response. The difference between the present age and what has gone before is that the challenge is now so much more acute, and the response demanded of us, so much the more universally momentous.

We shall obviously need help to enable us to make the right choice. The doctrine of righteousness is 'in our mouth and in our heart that we may do it'. Yet, as has been argued in these pages, it is no automatic property of human nature. It is a command, not a datum; a task laid upon us, which we are at liberty to refuse. 'Is there any cause in nature', asks King Lear, 'that makes these hard hearts?' The answer is that it is not Nature that makes people wicked, nor Nature that makes people good. For goodness, for 'righteousness which tendeth to life', we need a point of reference beyond Nature. Paradoxically, we need Divine help to carry out the tasks which God lays upon us. Can it be that Hebraism can yet mediate that help? This

[1] Cf. Emil L. Fackenheim, 'Judaism and the Idea of Progress', *Judaism*, IV (New York, 1955), 127-8.

study has sought to indicate from an examination of literary and philosophical documents gathered over a chosen field, that the law of righteousness and the doctrine of salvation are not only offered in Hebraism—but that the offer has in some sense been taken up by Western Man to form a part, and perhaps a central part, of his inheritance. If it has also appeared that these gifts have been abused and their nature frequently perverted, we are surely not to suppose that the true laws of life are to be permanently obscured. To suppose that would indeed be to succumb to an ungodly despair and to deny the meaning of our strife and freedom.

INDEX

Abbot, George (Archbishop), 118
Abrahams, I., 15n
Adams, Thomas, 42
Aeschylus, 140
Agreements of the People, *see* Levellers
Albo, Joseph, 191
Alchemists, 3, 113, **201-205**, 206, **218-219**
    Hebraic tendencies of, 204-205
Allen, D. C., 28n
Altmann, A., 190
Ames, William, 6, 106
Andrew of St. Victor, 192
Anti-Ciceronian Movement, 27-29, 65
Anti-semitism, 278
Aquinas, Thomas, 39, 68, 73, 75, 78, 107, 150, 182, 183, 237
Aristotle, 19, 68, 69, 71, 72, 75, 79, 104, 114, 137, 198, 202, 206, 226, 240, 290
Arminianism, 6, 53, 97, 174, 177, 187-188, 263, 273
Arnobius, 73
Arnold, E. V., 29n
Arnold, Matthew, **9-11**, 95, 120, 268, 277, **282-286**, 288, 289
Ascham, Roger, 19-20
Ashmole, Elias, 205, 206, 218
Auerbach, E., 15n
Augustine, 82, 155, 230n
Aurelius, Marcus, 88, 136-7
Avicebron, *see* Gabirol, Solomon Ibn

Bacon, Francis, 8, 9n, 11, 15n, 39, 44, 57, 69, 74, **78-92**, 93, 112, 195, 202, 207, 208, 211, 216n, 218, 229, 239, 261, 262, 265, 266, 271
    his theory of Rhetoric, **24-30**
    his *Essays*, 28-29
    link with Puritanism, 81-82, 90-92, 112-113
    a magician, 83-86
    link with the alchemists, 83-84
    link with Hebraism, 89-92
    Biblical quotations in, 91
Bacon Roger, 208n

Bailey, J., 138n
Bar-Cochba, 166
Barker, A. E., 118
Barker, E., 235n, 236n
Bastwick, John, 35
Bateson, F. W., 1n
Battenhouse, R. W., 103n
Baxter, Richard, 6, 31, 33, 34, 39, 102
Bellarmin, Robert, 49, 51
Bennett, Joan, 9n
Bentham Jeremy, 269, 270
Berkeley, George, 73
Bethell, S. L., 1n, 2, 9n, 280n
Beulah, 12, 275
Blake, William, 1, 13, **11-15**, 94, 114, 124, 133n, 167, 216, 256, 266, 268, **274-280**, 285
    and the *Kabbalah*, 12n
    his view of Milton, 12, 279-280
    his use of parallelism, 55
    his Biblical imagery, 275
    'Gnostic' heresy in, 276-277
    and the Mosaic law, 276-280
Blau, J. L., 15n, 72
Boas, Marie, 211n
'Book of Nature', 67, 216, 216n-217n
Bowle, J., 264n
Boyle, Robert, 3, 8, 67, 113, 174, 206, **210-218**, 220, 221, 263, 265, 271, 274
    his literary appreciation of the Bible, 7, 215, 213-214
    as writer of Meditations, 50, 213-214
    his interest in Jews and Judaism, 210, 210n
    a Baconian, 211
Bradley, F. H., 1n
Bridges, Robert, 141n
Birth, *see* Covenant
Brooks, Cleanth, 1n
Brown, W. A., 104n
Browne, Sir Thomas, 8, 50, 67, 113, 126, 152, 198n, 201, 203n, **206-210**, 212, 213, 215, 216n, 217, 218, 220, 229, 256, 263, 268, 274
    his prose style, 19, 38, **46-48**, 93

U

295

Index

Index

Index

Plain prose, in the seventeenth century, 9-10, 9n, 27-31, 36, 65, 256-257
Plato and Platonism, 21, 69-71, 114, 158, 194-195, 206, 216n; *see also* Cambridge Platonists
Plutarch, 28n
Pococke, Edward, 15n, 265
Pope, Alexander, 9, 73, 199n
Pope, E. M., 153n
Port-Royal, 26n
Potter, G. R., 43n
Powys, J. C., 36
Priest and Prophet, in Hebraism, 165-167
Prince, F. T., 141n
Prophecy, theories of, 191, 246-247
Prynne, William, 117
Puritanism, *passim, but see*: Covenant, Doctrinal Puritans, Election, Calvin, Grace, Scotland

Quintilian, 21
Quakers, 117

Raine, Kathleen, 133n
Rainolde, Richard, 21, 22
Rajan, B., 131n, 136n, 162n
Ralegh, Sir Walter, 80, 128, 203n
  his Biblical style, 45
Ramus, Petrus (Pierre de la Ramée), 26, 31-34, 256, 273n
  Bacon's debt to, 26n
  and Hobbes, 245-247
Rankin, O. S., 181n
Ray, John, 254
Remonstrants, *see* Arminianism
Reuchlin, Johann, 72, 151n
Rhetoric,
  seventeenth century theories of, 19-21, 24-27
  ecclesiastical, 43
  of Scriptures, 43, 49, 51, 54, 56, 57
  see also, Bacon, Cicero, Hooker, Ramus, Seneca
Robinson, H. W., 150n
Rochester, John Wilmot, 177
Rosenroth, Knorr von, 12n
Rosenzweig, Franz, 111-112
Roth, C., 15n, 187n
Roth, L., 15n
Royal Society, 8, 27, 257
  Cowley's Ode to, 260-262
Rousseau, 236, 237, 270n, 285

Rowley, H. H., 165n
Ruskin, John, 268, 285
Rust, E. C., 112n
Rutherford, Samuel, 35, 234n

Sainte-Beuve, C. A., 26n
Sales, François de, 49n
Saurat, D., 12n, 14n, 150, 151n, 277n
Schleiermacher, Friedrich E. D., 286-287
Scholem, G., 12n
Scotland, Puritanism in, 105
Scott, N. A., 140n
Scott-Craig, T. S. K., 140n
Scottish Covenanters, 3
Selden, John, 15n, 184, 190
Seneca, 87, 88, 103, 213,
  the Senecan style, **27-29**, 44, 47, 48
Servetus, Michael, 153
'Seven Commandments of the Sons of Noah', *see* Noahide Covenant
Sewell, A., 152, 153
Shaftesbury, (third Earl), 269
Shakespeare, William, 20, 28, 68, 74, 80, 89, 120, 199n, 229, 281n
  Hamlet, 76, 77-78, 80-81, 88
  Troilus and Cressida, 76
Shelley, Percy Bysshe, 25, 82, 119, 276
Sherburn G., 199n
Sidney, Sir Philip, 22, 24
Simon, Richard, 248
Simpson, Evelyn M., 43n
Sloss, D. J., 266n
Smalley, Beryl, 71n, 192n
Smith, John (Platonist), 190, 191, 193, 197n, 200, 246, 260, 281
Snaith, N., 98n
Social Contract, 227, 233, 237, 241, 250, 255, 270, *and see* Covenant
Solemn League and Covenant, 236
Sophocles, 140, 155
Spenser, Edmund, 21, 22, 68, 75, 128-130, 132, 133, 156
Spinoza, Benedict, 273, 282
Sprat, Thomas (Bishop), 27, 257
Starkey, George, 212
Stein, W., 289n
Sternhold and Hopkins (version of the *Psalms*), 215
Stoicism, 77, 103, 137, 146, 220, 230n
  the stoic style, 29, 44, 229

300

Index